The Creek Rats of Mission San Jose

Bay Area Boy 1961-1979

By Jens Moyer

Table of Contents

Introduction

In Sweden, middle names are optional.

My name is Jens Moyer. My last name is my father's, an eighth generation Pennsylvanian. Pappa liked the name Michael, however, my mother, a Swede, whose ancestry dates to the Vikings, chose my name. I first saw the light of day at Kaiser Hospital in San Francisco, I was born there.

This is my story.

My mother, Inger Marianne Bergstrom, was born and raised in Stockholm, Sweden. While working as a clerk in a Paris wine shop, Inger is introduced to a 32 year-old American and World War II Veteran, John Wesley Moyer. They fall in love, Jack proposes and Inger says, "ya."

At 28, Inger decides to leave everything familiar; family, friends, home, church and country, never to return.

Swedish Inger pins her hopes on Yankee Jack. Arm in arm, they steam across the Atlantic Ocean to The United States of America, to start their new life together.

Shortly after the honeymoon on Martha's Vineyard, Jack and Inger move west. Their first stop is Columbus, Ohio. As an Assistant Professor, Jack teaches art at The Ohio State University and my sister Hannah is born.

Opportunity knocks; the young family pull up stakes, load the Pontiac, point west again and drive to the Golden Gate; San Francisco, California. Jack starts his new Assistant Professor job, at San Francisco State University, teaching art.

On August 17th, 1961, Norman and Tessa Moyer's only child's only son, was born at the advent of the 60s - *warning: random music news alert:* As a name for his older brother Brian's new band, Dennis suggests, "The Beach Boys." A surfing theme because, "all the kids are into it." - and two blocks from Golden Gate Park.

John Wesley Moyer is the nice man my three sisters and I call Pappa, and everybody else calls Jack. Pappa's first American ancestor, Solomon Jennings, was a pioneer and woodsman, farming the Pennsylvanian Western frontier in 1722, and a part of local history; the "Walking Purchase." I'll save you time; it was a crooked land grab from the Delaware Indians by William Penn's two sons, and a catalyst that started the Colonial War.

Later Captain Solomon served in that same Colonial French-Indian War.

Solomon's son and grandson, Isaiah and John, both served in the American Revolutionary War.

Solomon fathered Isaiah, Isaiah fathered John, John fathered John Junior, John Junior fathered Daniel, Daniel fathered Charlotte, Charlotte begat Tessa, Tessa begat John (Jackie) and John fathered Jens (me).

After the United States enters WWII, 17 year old Jack wants to kill Germans. Underage, Jack's Mother signs the necessary waiver, and he enlists. However, due to a rare bone disease, rather than board the next ship to Europe and charge to the front, Pappa serves as a Dental Assistant in the Caribbean, aboard the Battleship USS North Carolina. "Yaa monn."

I count myself fortunate to have been raised by a WWII Veteran. As a father, Pappa is strict, but fair and funny.

Pappa tells me frequently, "Jens, you're spoiled, living here in California" plus the classic cliche; "I walked to school in the snow."

As toddlers in Stockholm, my mother and her older sister, Chersti, often played barefoot in the snow. Not for the want of shoes, grandfather made a good living as an engineer at Ericsson rather, 45 degrees outside and bare feet in snow is common for children of the North. Like many North European children, Inger can ski before she can walk.

When I consider where I grew up, the San Francisco Bay Area, and compare it to Pappa's home state or mother's home country, and that only four regions in the world boast a Mediterranean climate, the Bay Area being one of them, I count myself lucky to be from here; California Viking! The four-season world is beautiful of course, attractive and fresh; fall colors, people who like people, icicles on the porch, hot cocoa etc. etc. etc. but ultimately, Pappa is right, as a Bay Area native, I am spoiled rotten from the abundant golden sunshine and clear blue sky, but I do fight climate complacency.

In the future, I hope to travel the USA, outside my "comfort zone." Take in the sights and smells, the history, the nice people, their flora and fauna, their hostile weather; the scirocco-scorched valleys, blizzards, tornados and charming accents.

Why print this account of myself? Who wants to read about the average Joe? I don't know. Then why bother? If inconsequential, why set it to type? Because I want to, want to try. Because this stuff happened to me.

I don't want to fade away, or worse, be misunderstood.

By taking a small peek at this BABAR (Bay Area born and raised), newcomers may find common ground, improve harmony?

Here, where cultural diversity flowers; distrust and division rule the day, bridges must be built.

Let's fight ethnic alienation, break through the prejudicial inertia that keeps us apart and the daily news that nurses distrust. Let's breach those tall walls that separate us, for peace. Not just the young, but the gray heads too, mutual respect for others and our differences, *understand one another.*

We *have* to work *together.*

I appreciate histories besides my own, their struggles and contributions, it's important. It increases respect and admiration for other people. Immigrants, welcome! Here's a cheap seat to yesterday's Bay Area culture, a baby boomer's life, good and bad.

Hey, don't judge me because I still use a checkbook. I know they have an APP for that. Remember, you're next on society's Out-of-Touch list. Sooner than you think.

Rather than avoid and look away, let's smile and say hello, with sincerity of heart, and yes insist on kindness in return. I remember a friendlier Bay Area, and you miss home. Let's get to know each other. Why not? These are not empty words or superficial platitudes. As a BABAR, I don't just appreciate diversity. I require it.

Quick story: There's a very popular hike at Zion National Park in Utah. It's magnificent. You hike through a narrow, picturesque canyon (20' wide in some places) through an inch of cool clear water. On either side are tall, sheer cliffs as high as the Empire State Building. A wonderful, inspiring place. Utah's population is predominantly Mormon. Mormons are predominantly white. I'm white (not Mormon). I trek past many hikers going the opposite direction, and *every* person is white. After 100 parties file past, frankly, it gets weird, creepy even. Instinctively, I squint in the distance, looking for a color beside white. Brown, yellow, black, red, anything but white. I've never experienced a feeling like that before or since, a real eye opener, all to say, I'm from the Bay Area, I love the Bay Area and as I go, I'm still learning why. The palette of color here is beautiful, believe me.

Though many friends leave the Golden State, I desire to stay (more so after writing this). This is my California experience, good and bad. This is me: a Pennsylvania Dutch Viking in San Francisco. So breathe, relax, *brace yourself* and enjoy the voyage.

San Francisco

My memory is not great (more on that later), yet my scattered childhood memories are precious to me. I was born August 17th, 1961, driven home from Kaiser Hospital, wrapped and laid in a crib at 1861 Judah Street on 19th Avenue, in the Sunset neighborhood of San Francisco. Before I know left from right, Inger, my kind mother with a pleasant accent, walks me daily in the cool fresh coastal air, strolling me up and down the streets of San Francisco, with sister Hannah walking happily alongside. The daily strolls always include Golden Gate Park, two blocks away.

My sister Hannah, is 17 months older than I. She's smart, dedicated and no-nonsense, perhaps due to the climate and culture of her home state, Ohio. Hannah's claim to fame is being our family's only Ohioan. Hey, don't knock it, the midwest heritage has tons of upside: homespun family values, friendliness, etc. etc. etc. Hannah tends to dress in layers. Does the fact she's not a Bay Area Native bother her? I doubt it. But, I've never asked her. If it does, I get that. Hannah's been good to me and understanding too, but she is tough, like a second mother, not letting me get away with much.

Jack and Inger forge lasting friendships in the City. One of these LF's are the Hatfields. Howard and Louise Hatfield are Vermontian transplants. Inger met Louise strollering through Golden Gate Park. Me in my stroller, and Bruce Hatfield in his. Bruce is the fourth out of their five children, starting with the oldest; Vicky, Steve, Lisa, Bruce, and Brian.

Our family's growth gains momentum. The Moyers move from Judah Street to Chenery Street in Glen Park, and here on November 18th, 1963, my sister Marja is born.

To this point, I'm unaware of the hubbub, except for one pleasant repetitive memory; once a week Mom ties a scarf to her chin and covers her wavy strawberry blonde hair. We walk east on Chenery Street to the corner grocery store. Inger pulls behind a rolling metal wire-basket, the lightweight type that collapses flat for storage. We walk past several homes, to a mom and pop market; the old-fashioned type. Outside on the sidewalk, a colorful display of produce is stored in waist high bins, shaded by a green canvas awning with the store's name in big white letters. I remember Mom discussing with another grown-up, Pappa perhaps, that the family grocery might have to close, due to competition from the big grocery stores. I was only three, but remember clearly hearing this bad news. Prior to this revelation, neither bad news nor money existed.

An early affliction may be partly to blame for my rusty memory. Years later, Mom said to me, "Jens, you had Scarlatina when you were three." Scarlatina is another name for Scarlet Fever. I don't like the sound of that. Scarlet sounds scary.

On Judah Street, we lived two blocks from Golden Gate Park. On Chenery Street, we live two blocks from Glen Park. Both locations are centrally located and public transportation allows Jack and Inger to enjoy the city easily.

About this time, Jack leaves his teaching job at San Francisco State University, to work for the United States Postal Service, delivering mail. More hours, better pay and benefits for his young family.

Mom likes the Glen Park neighborhood very much. For Inger, a city girl, Glen Park is San Francisco all the way. Mom loves it here. My parents attempt to purchase a home in Glen Park. A financial shortfall of $5,000 is the deal breaker. Inger begs Jack to ask his parents in Pennsylvania to borrow the money; Jack says, "no." Decades later I learned Mom never forgave Pappa for this. The Pennsylvania Dutch can be as stubborn as the Swede.

Two years later we move again, to Shakespeare Street, located on San Francisco's southern border.

Here, I awake to the world and all its glory!

Jack and Inger's Parents

Let's continue my folk's story a bit, since our stories are intertwined.

My father was born in Sayre, Pennsylvania, a railroad town near the New York - Pennsylvania Stateline. The mighty Susquehanna River flows southward defining the east side of town.

Norman John Moyer is the American grandfather I never met. Later, during a rare but serious scolding in our mid-teens, Pappa told Hannah, Marja and me, about *his* father and mother. First, Pappa points out to us our worst character flaw, then in stark contrast, Pappa spells out our heritage, "My father was the toughest man in town, and he married the prettiest girl in town."

This is what I know about my American grandparents. After serving in the United States Army in WW1, Norman John Moyer was an engineer on the Lehigh Valley Railroad. There are some great railroad pictures of him, a black and white shows Norman's head poking out the small window of the engine car, donning a classic blue and white striped engineer hat, and a beaming smile (Hannah has the hat). A later color photo shows Norman proudly driving a brand new diesel-powered locomotive, same pose.

Norman Moyer was a devout Catholic and a proud member of the Knights of Columbus. My grandmother descends from an equally zealous, long line of Protestants.

Uh Oh.

Norman passed away at age 67, when I was two. No matter, he is my grandfather in name and blood and I'm certain we'd have hit it off, and I look forward to meeting him some day. Our deceased ancestors are equally important to those living. If family doesn't matter once they die, neither do we as we breathe.

My American grandmother, Tessa Pauline Moyer (Vanness), lived a long, socially active life, and a glorious musical life. She united with her Lord in 1983. I recall one visit, when I was twelve. We're 3,000 miles apart, money's tight on both ends. Back then, folks didn't ping pong around the globe like today.

Tessa's a musician, a wonderful pianist and organist. She was the Minister of Music at the Church of Christ in Sayre, Pennsylvania for decades. Grandmother, also the Choir Director, leads the congregation in worship every week. Every Sunday, with Tessa at the helm of the pipe organ, the church's thick stone walls reverberate a block in every direction with traditional hymns and worship music. During her visit in 1973, we all piled into Pappa's Ford station wagon; and drove to the local shopping center. As we window-shop our way through the outside mall, we arrive at Allegro Music, featuring many fine, expensive instruments. Back then, music stores like Allegro frequently rolled an organ outside and a clerk played toe-tapping tunes to lure business. Before I know what's happening, Grandmother is performing a live concert!

Tessa dismisses the clerk, sits down, and gives the organ its best life. A complex instrument, three rows of keys and a myriad of knobs and levers envelop her small, tough, Dutch frame. Her hands, fingers, arms, legs, and feet, all work feverishly together. Grandmother set a precedent for Elton John at Dodger's Stadium two years later. Her repertoire shocks me. A seamless melody of jazzy stuff, honkytonk, a terrific arrangement of How Great Thou Art; Tea for Two is her closer. Her torso arches back, head erect. She's really, *really* good, a wonderful pianist.

At age 11, musically speaking, I'm slow. I don't appreciate what I heard that day. Was Grandmother showing off? No. She's being who she is, introducing herself to her grandchildren.

Hi guys, You don't know me, but I love you, and this is me, your Grandmother speaking to you the best way I know. Since that day at Allegro, for me, life is a symphony.

I recorded "Grandma LIVE" on a small cassette recorder. The recording exists today.

Back to the Uh Oh. Norman John Moyer and Tessa Pauline Vanness were married in 1923. My Father was born in 1925. John Wesley Moyer was an only child. Only-children get it all; all the love, and all the heat. When Jackie is old enough, Norman prepares to take his son to his first Mass. Tessa asks, "where are you two going?" Norman responds, "I'm taking Jack to Mass." Tessa declares, "no son of mine is going to be raised a Catholic." Norman scoffs, "Then you raise him."

No comment. I wasn't there. There must be more to that story. From then on, mother and son dutifully attend the Church of Christ, on Lincoln Street, popular for its excellent music.

Mom told me about her first meeting with her new father-in-law. "He was stern and I don't think he liked me." In 1958, Mom was brand new to the United States, fresh off the boat. She's nervous, eager to make a good impression. Inger speaks perfect English with a thick Swedish accent that must have been exotic to the blue-blooded, seventh generation Pennsylvanians. Father-in-law, mother-in-law, daughter-in-law; these relationships take time to build and grow. Fondness, appreciation and love, take a minute, not overnight. It's an acquired taste. You have to get through a Christmas or two, a few birthdays, a trial, a cry, hugs. In-law relationships strengthen, problems are dealt with or tolerated. Recipes are passed down, cars get fixed, furniture gets moved. Neither Inger or her in-laws had that luxury. My parents were married right away, and very soon moved to Ohio, then California. Mom left Pennsylvania with only that *first* impression. Norman and Tessa are left with an empty, quiet house and two separate lives; knights, trains and coal & choirs, keyboards and hymns.

I am far, far away from my parents' birthplaces. I live in a wild coastal city, severed from family roots. Would life be different, living nearer to grandparents? Listening to stories from grandfather's railroad days; gritty rail tales, nuggets of wisdom learned the hard way. Stuff that can make a big difference to a boy. How and why did Tessa Vanness learn to play the keyboards so well, so inspired? Who were her influences, her heroes? How long have you played Bridge, Grandma? What did your parents say about their life in the 1800's? You saw who? They met who?!? World War 1? Civil War? No way! Wouldn't life have been better, knowing my grandparents? A shot of old fashion? A hearty yes. And what about the seventh generation Pennsylvanians with an only child, and a daughter-in-law, and four grandchildren? Not watching them grow and learn? No hello? No hugs, no tears; contact too rare to be warm. Affection contrived? No acknowledgement from their only grandson? Piano lessons upon piano lessons. Tessa taught over a thousand students in her lifetime. The importance of a relationship with surviving grandmothers is lost on me. How do I reconcile that?

Let's shake off the Pennsylvania coal dust, and switch to the pristine air, and endless emerald green forests of my mother's homeland, Sweden. Inger Marianne Bergstrom was born in 1930. She had one sister Chersti, two years older. Her father was an engineer for Ericsson, the huge IT company in Stockholm, where the family lives. My Swedish Grandfather died young at 52, so we never met. Grandmother Daga I did meet once. Her summer visit to the Bay Area coincided with my 14th birthday, and to my surprise my towering, smoking, Swedish grandmother, in very cool fashion, presented me with the Led Zeppelin album: Physical Graffiti. Perfect! How in the wide North American world, did she know I was a big Zepp fan?

Daga is an exotic mystery. I know she likes tobacco, and she knows I like Led Zeppelin. That's not much to build on. Tall and imposing: think Xena Warrior Princess 78 years old. I'm 6' 2", not short, but Daga still looks tall. She grew up in a rough neighborhood. As a Stockholm highschooler, Daga, while getting a drink from the school's drinking fountain - you know these school drinking fountains, white porcelain covered steel troughs with three chrome spickets spaced evenly across - some boys snuck up behind Daga and hit her on top of the head, causing her to break teeth against the metal water spicket. For this vicious act of cruelty, the boys paid dearly. She really let them have it, a beating. Viking Shield Maiden! Don't mess with Daga!

Mr. & Mrs. Bergstrom raised Chersti and Inger in Stockholm. The sisters were teenagers during WWII. Mother told me that during the war, certain food items were rationed, including butter. There's an extremely popular flat cracker made in Sweden, then called Rye King, now called WASA. I still eat it. The cracker comes in a variety of grain flavors, but all are the same shape and thickness; 4 ¾" long, 2 ½" wide, ¼" thick; about 20 pieces to a pack. My Swedish grandparents were raised on it, my mother was raised on it, and my sisters and I were raised on it. We've eaten WASA our entire lives, a Viking staple. You find it today on the cracker aisle in supermarkets, on the bottom shelf. Sourdough is the best in my opinion. The cracker surface is heavily dimpled on one side, and relatively smooth on the other. Everyone spreads the butter on the dimpled side, not the flat side, for more taste. However, during WWII, because of the butter ration, Chersti, Inger, and Daga spread butter on the flat side of WASA crackers, so the butter lasts longer. My Swedish grandfather was an exception to this. He applied butter on the dimpled side, to maintain his strength for work.

Regarding the spiritual aspect of their lives, Inger and Chersti were confirmed in the State Lutheran Church near their home in Stockholm at the prescribed age.

Pappa's Parents, Mr. and Mrs. Norman and Tessa Moyer

Mother's Parents, Mr. and Mrs. Hjalmar and Daga Bergstrom

Jack and Inger

How did Jack and Inger meet? How on earth did a 32 year old, eighth generation Pennsylvanian, small-town USA, WWII Veteran; meet, fall in love, and marry a 27 year old Swedish lass, working in Paris?

Between WWII and their marriage in 1958, Jack while working as a butcher, trained in various art disciplines. I've listed a few of Jack's art-education highlights:

- Liberal Arts at Temple University in Philadelphia, Pennsylvania.

- A graduate of the Philadelphia Museum College of Art in Industrial Design.

- One year at the Royal Academy of Fine Arts in Kobenhavn, Denmark, where Jack studies sculpture under Professor Mogens Boggild.

- And five months at the Berlitz School of Language, Helsinki, Finland, where he studied Swedish.

Inger rooms with a girlfriend and clerks @ a Paris boutique wine shop. I have a great picture of her, working behind the counter, young and Euro, Nor-Euro.

Inger's roommate introduces them. The courtship and engagement are short and at times long distance, corresponding by letters. Jack cast an American marriage proposal, and reeled in a Scandinavian "ja." The plan is to marry and raise a family in the United States. They board a steamer, and after a five-day voyage across the tempestuous Atlantic, disembark in New York. Inger processes through the US. Customs, then on to Sayre, Pennsylvania to meet the parents. Jack and Inger Moyer were married February 27th, 1958, in the Park Avenue Church in New York City.

After the wedding, Jack and Inger honeymoon on Martha's Vineyard for a month. There's a great picture of the two of them grinning, basking on the sand, in the throes of love. Jack is already bald and has been since he was 24! His Father Norman became bald at 18!! My Swedish grandfather had an impressive shock of brown hair until the end of his short life. I suppose I'm lucky, a wisp of white at 62.

After the honeymoon, Jack and Inger move to Columbus, Ohio. As an Associate Professor, Jack teaches his first art class at The Ohio State University. A Buckeye.

Newlyweds for nearly two years to the day, on February 25th, 1960, Hannah was born. A sweet photograph survives of Inger, and Jack's mother, Tessa, holding baby Hannah. So a visit occurred either in Ohio or Pennsylvania. A 460 mile trip, seven hours one way by car.

Soon after Hannah came along, Jack was offered an Associate Professor job at San Francisco State University's Fine Arts Department. A Gator!

For Inger - a city girl - moving to San Francisco is her American dream come true.

For an eighth generation Pennsylvanian, trading in his small-town east coast roots for the wild wild west, may have required soul searching, but since age 17, Jack has been on the move, sailing the seas, traveling the world, attending various art schools on the east coast and in Europe; so pulling up stakes might be second nature by now.

Mom

Pappa

Baby Hannah

Daly City

The year is 1965, the place, Shakespeare Street, San Francisco. I'm four, a year before kindergarten and it's here, spotty recollections cease and the headwaters of steady consciousness gush forth.

I live in a small room, in a small house, on a high hill. When morning comes and light is outside, I wake up in my small bed, hungry. The feeling in my stomach pushes me out of bed and I walk through the door of my little room, toward Mom's room. I climb up to where Mom is and lie down next to her. She doesn't move, she's sleeping. The house is quiet, Mother is quiet, so I am quiet.

Soon Mom starts to tickle me. I like this. Not the kind of tickle where you start laughing and have to get away, but a gentle kind, my Mom's finger slowly runs up and down my forearm, just brushing the skin. Soon I scratch my arm because it tickles. I say, "Mom do that again" and she does. Then we get up and I eat breakfast.

The rest of my life has been spent in pursuit of that tickle-sensation.

Breakfast consists of a bowl, a spoon, cereal and milk. The cereal is stored in a box, the cardboard box is covered with brightly-colored, fun cartoons. The cold milk is in a pitcher, stored in a white refrigerator with rounded edges. The joy of eating the milk and cereal is enhanced by the artwork on the outside of the cereal box. The box-art review concludes with the last spoonful of cereal. The milk is homemade, Mom makes the milk herself. From an orange and white colored box, Mom pours white powder into the pitcher. Next she adds water from the metal pipe above the sink into the pitcher. Mom vigorously whips the ingredients into gleaming white milk. The procedure is noisy and fun, and I like to watch.

The hungry feeling is gone and I go back to my little room to play. In the little room, on a wall, is a little window. When the sun tells the dark to go away, I see many different things happening on the other side of the window. Nearby I see other little houses, like ours. Farther away, I see many tiny houses.

Through the window, I see far, past the houses to a big flat gray cloud. My little window is higher than the gray cloud. I look down at the cloud, and the cloud goes far that way, and far that way. After I see everything there is to see through the window, I play with toys in my room.

A little later I look through the magic window again and everything looks different. There is more detail and more color on the houses below. The long gray cloud is still there, but something pokes through the top of the cloud. Two red things poke through the cloud, each red thing has a little light on top. One red thing is closer to me and the other red thing is farther.

I leave the window again, and play with toys again. I wonder if the other side of the little window is the same, or different? I look out the window again, it is different! The two red things with a light on top, are taller, much taller and have red ropes going closer and farther away. They are not houses and they are not boats, buses or planes. They are something else. I leave the window again, but this time I plan to return and look for change.

Later I look through the window in my room and everything is different outside. The cloud went away. Blue water! This way and that way, blue water. I know it is water because I see boats on the water. Large flat boats and many tiny boats with white sails.

Occasionally I hear a loud repeating boom sound. UHHHHHHHH!! . . . UUHHHHHHH!! The sound comes from the water. Over the water the red things make sense to me because the cloud is gone. Red ropes and a red road connect the two red tall things. The tall red things go into the water, the red road is above the water. I know it is a road, because I see tiny cars moving along the road, over the water. Some cars move closer and others move farther away.

All these things are very good; I am a four year-old boy and happy. Waking up hungry is good, Mom tickling my arm is good, eating cereal from the colorful box and milk from the pitcher is good. Watching the red road with tiny cars moving on it, appearing slowly from under the gray cloud, over the water with little boats, is very good.

The gray cloud over the water stays away until the next morning. Each new day, I look through my little window, and the gray cloud comes back!

When Pappa comes home from work, we eat dinner. Mom makes dinner. The family eats dinner together: me, my little sister Marja, my older sister Hannah, Mom and Pappa. We are all very hungry. The five of us sit around one table, and each of us sits in our own chair. Dinner is very good for us.

After dinner, it is dark outside. Mom reads to all three children. She reads different stories, from the beginning to the end. I like the different pictures on each page. Hannah, Marja and I take turns turning the pages. After the story, Mom says, "bedtime kiddos."

Bedtime is a little sad because I want to stay up. Mother is there, so I slide into bed under the covers. Sometimes I slide under the covers by myself, and Mom comes into my room after. I wait for her. Then Mom comes into my room, sits down on the edge of my bed and gently strokes my hair with the palm of her hand, again and again. Starting on my forehead, Mom strokes my hair back gently, toward my neck. I think, don't stop Mom, the tingling on my head feels good. But my serious side knows this will not last, so I enjoy it even more. When Mom stops stroking my hair, she says in a whisper, "Jens, stretch your legs straight, don't curl them up, and you'll grow tall and strong." So I do.

Memories before kindergarten are simple and few; a preschool hallway, a dance class studio, funny costumes. That's it, not much. I do remember the first day of kindergarten.

Holding Mom's hand, we walk onto the campus of Longfellow Elementary School. Mom shows my sisters and I how to cross the busy street, "Jens, hold my hand, look both ways, if no cars are coming, then we cross the street." "Okay." Mom is serious because crossing a busy city street is dangerous, so I pay attention to her and look both ways, before I cross streets.

On Longfellow's blacktop, we join other mothers and their children. It is cold. We all stand in a circle and the teacher speaks to us with words of comfort. Kindergarten is like home, but with a different mother and more sisters and brothers. I learn a new word, "friend."

There is one boy, tall like me and similar in appearance. His name is David and he smiles a lot. He is nice, so we play together. Kindergarten has wood ABC blocks, windows, green carpet, and a nice teacher.

Every morning from my little bedroom window, I watch the little red road, over the big blue water, push away the big gray clouds. Windows are very good.

During kindergarten I learned how to ride a city bus. The training from Mom on how to safely cross the street is now very important. Hannah and I walk to the bus-stop by ourselves. With Hannah's help, we cross a street and wait at the bus stop. Me and Hannah bahnahna wait for the bus, get on and ride it to school. With Hannah's help, I attend kindergarten and learn four things: wood block building, recess, snacktime and naptime.

Kindergarten is over. I say goodbye to my teacher and to David and the other children, and we part ways for summer. I am very happy at home, and happy at school. The only difference between the two, was my Mom wasn't at the school, and my teacher and friends weren't at home. There is enough time in a day for both. This is good.

I passed kindergarten, feel good and look forward to the first grade. With Hannah leading the way, directing me on and off city buses to and from school, I am ready for the next step. Hannah is a very good sister.

On the first day of first grade, Mom and I go to school together. We walk past the new kindergartners and they look little. I am more grown-up. I see a familiar face, David from last year! He recognizes me and smiles his big grin. I stop and wave and say "hi David" and David says, "hi" back. After we pass each other, I ask Mom, why is David with the kindergarten class and not going to the first grade with us? Mom explains to me; David has trouble with his thinking and has to repeat kindergarten. This is sad, but David looks happy.

I remember the first time I got scared. It is nighttime; outside the house, raindrops are falling and the wind is howling. I am inside the house, in the kitchen with Mom, Marja and Hannah. Then we hear the loudest noises; boom, boom . . . BOOM!! The loud noises rattle the kitchen windows! Marja, Hannah and I hug Mom tight and we begin to cry. We ask, what's that loud noise Mom?!? What's that very loud noise"?!? Boom . . . BOOM!! Ahhh! In a calm voice, Mom says, don't be afraid, it's thunder you hear. Sometimes during a storm, lightning bolts and loud thunder claps occur. The thunder and lightning will stop soon, don't be frightened. After Mom explains this to us, I stop crying and when the thunder stops, I am not scared anymore.

Shortly after our arrival to San Francisco, Pappa takes a job with the United States Postal Service. It is during these five years working at the Post Office, he makes lifelong friends. One of them is Robert (Bob) Boni. Bob and Jack share a mutual passion: love of and commitment to art. Bob Boni is a very fun person, his wife and mother are wonderful also. Robert and Cachi Boni have three beautiful daughters; Bombe, Susan and Robin. Bombe is four years older than me, Susan is Hannah's age and Robin is Marja's age.

On a winter day, halfway through the first grade, Pappa comes home from work. Mom is in the kitchen preparing dinner and I am nearby when Pappa strides into the kitchen smiling. Pappa picks Mom up and hugs her. Pappa whirls Mom around three times! "I got the job, I got the job!" Hugs and kisses follow the whirling. Pappa's new job is at Cal State Hayward College, in the Fine Art Department.

Art has always been Pappa's first love, at least since the War. From 1946 to 1958, he trained for it, then taught University level art and sculpture classes in the late 50's and early 60's. Art is Jack's everything.

Part of Pappa's new job is managing the Tool-Room in the Fine Arts Building. To keep everything sharp and functioning and keep track of all the tools the art students use and need. Like a tool library for the Cal-State Hayward Art students. Jack is an art-tool librarian and is surrounded by art majors and art professors. This suits him perfectly. Now Jack has access to workshops, and every tool he needs. There is only one thing left to do; move closer to the new job.

My best friend is David Williams. David is black. David and I deliver a local weekly newspaper together: The San Francisco Progress. Our deliveries are close to home. David comes from a large family, including several man-size, older brothers. One day while playing with David, his older brothers lock me in a closet in their house. With all my might, I try to get out. I cannot get out, I hear them laugh and it is dark, so I cry. Eventually they let me out.

The layout of Shakespeare Street is different from a typical street. To adapt to the hilliness of the area, instead of another row of small houses across the street at the same level, another street is 12' above our street. Both upper and lower roads are considered Shakespeare Street. So the view across the street from our house is a 15' high concrete retaining wall. A friend and I display our bravery to the world, hanging from the top of the wall, by our fingertips.

The wall runs along the street a short ways and ends abruptly. At the end of the wall, a concrete pedestrian stairway connects the two street levels. Just beyond the stairway, a wild hillside takes over. The grassy hill is a popular slide spot. A hotspot for older local kids, it tends to get crowded. A big piece of cardboard is all you need. Sliders use the concrete stairs to get up the hill, then slide down. Sit on the cardboard and slide fast on the grass, again and again. The kids are older than me, and I only slide there once. I walk up the stairs and out onto the wild hill where the big kids go. My descent starts slow but quickly I reach high speed. I slide so fast, I slide too far! I lodge deep under a thorny scrub bush lining the lower street. The bush saves me from the hard street ahead, but at a high cost; embarrassment, bloody scratches and covered in . . . dog poop.

There are two sisters who live on upper Shakespeare Street. The older sister's name is Stinky. Everyone calls her Stinky. The sisters are acquaintances of mine, not friends. One day Stinky invites me to her house. Her parents are not there and she makes a strange move on me. I am clueless. I got out of there confused, but happy to say, fully dressed. Stinky is my first encounter, with an aggressive member of the opposite sex. I do not like when Stinky tries to tell me what to do, especially when the activity makes no sense. I get out of there and make a solemn vow, never to return.

Pappa suffers from severe arthritis in his hips. It prevents him from many activities most take for granted, such as straddling a motorcycle for example. However, Pappa is able to sit on a motor-scooter and owns a Lambretta.

Before moving away from San Francisco, I rode with Pappa once or twice on scary scooter rides. I clutch his thick black leather jacket as tight as when I hang from the top of the Shakespeare Street wall. Up and down the city hills; vroom straight up and vroom straight down. Up is definitely worse, I really have to hold on. Going down is much better, I just lean against Pappa, and loosen my grip. Up is scary, down is fun.

Life on Shakespeare Street ends on a high note: On October 10th,1967 my youngest sister Tessa was born.

I beam with pride for Mom, and my new baby sister. I ask Mom, "may I bring a friend in the house and show Tessa to him?" Mom says, "yes, but go quietly, Tessa is sleeping." David Williams and I stand next to the crib and stare down at her. We are very quiet, like in a library. We whisper only. Tessa is wrapped up tight in her blanket, like a cocoon, and asleep. We smile at Tessa, then at each other, then at Tessa again. Baby Tessa is two weeks old and sleeping, so we smile quietly.

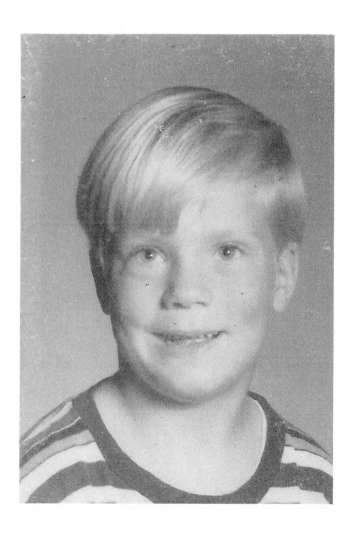

Golden Gate Park

Palma Ceia

In November of 1967, right after Tessa was born and before Marja's fourth birthday, the six of us: Jack, Inger, Hannah, Marja, Tessa and I leave Shakespeare Street, the wind, and my little window.

Twelve eyes peer from the station wagon as we head east on the bridge across the bay.

Twelve eyes see their new destination: the Palma Ceia neighborhood and the mean streets of Hayward. We move here to be closer to Pappa's new job at Cal State Hayward College.

The small blue and white flat-top house located on Mantilla Avenue in the town of Hayward has small white rocks on the roof and a tall palm tree in the front yard. I still have my own room.

Cal-State Hayward College is located on top of a row of hills that run along the edge of town. Wherever you are, you can see the college on the hill. Pappa says, "the hills are pretty to look at." I like them too and their two different colors, green in winter, brown in summer.

The back fence is a concrete wall that backs up to busy Tennyson Road, which is convenient for us. Mom often says, "Jens, here's fifty cents, be a gem and go to the Quick Stop Market and buy a loaf of bread; here's the kind I want you to get," and shows me the old bread wrapper. I scramble over the backyard block wall and I'm standing on the Tennyson Road sidewalk at the Patrick Avenue intersection. I push the button and wait for the green light, look both ways, cross four lanes of traffic and wala, QuickStop. Three minutes each way, tops.

Many years later, Oscar Grant lived in Palma Ceia. I learned this from the movie; Fruitvale Station. The movie highlights Oscar's story and the senseless tragedy that ends his young life. This tragedy and similar injustices create a tidal wave of racial unrest throughout the United States and around the world. Twice in the movie, Oscar reveals a large tattoo on his back; in two inch tall, old-fashioned letters, two words from shoulder to shoulder: **Palma Ceia**. During the movie you see the street sign; Calaroga Street, at Tennyson Road. That's on the west side of the Nimitz Freeway. Though still Palma Ceia, the west side is the best side, close to Kaiser Hospital, nicer shopping, better school. The west side homes are bigger, two car garages, and cost more. The east side homes are smaller, less expensive, one-car garages and more fist fights.

In Hayward, I learn about money. Mom and Pappa give Hannah and I a specific amount of money each week, the amount is based on age, it's called an allowance. Our allowance remains the same for a year. On birthdays our allowances double. Hannah receives a dime, and I a nickel. In 1967 a nickel purchases a full-sized candy bar, a dime will buy two. My seventh birthday finally arrives, my allowance increases 100%, to a dime. The increase keeps pace with inflation and will still buy a full-size candy bar. Payday is my favorite. I like the combination of sweet caramel and salty peanuts. When I finish the Payday, I savor the few loose peanuts left in the wrapper.

Easter break is over and it's time to attend my new school, Ruus Elementary. To show off, I say to Mom, "I can walk to school by myself. You don't need to take me." Mom's hands are full, pushing Tessa in the stroller while walking Marja to her new classroom. Besides, back in San Francisco, I rode a bus to school by myself almost (with Hannah's help). How hard can it be to find a new school 15 minutes away?

Once our house is out of sight, I am lost: once I know I am lost, I am in tears. Lost and crying. A small bald man with glasses driving a car stops and says, "My name is Mr. Howe. I'm the principal of Ruus Elementary. Are you walking to Ruus?" I say, "yes." "Is your name Jens?" "Yes." "Are you lost?" "Yes." "Do you want a ride to school?" "Yes."

Graffiti near the schoolyard says, "Principal Howe is a big fat Cow." Students and friends say Principal Howe is mean, and if you are sent to his office for misconduct, he will hit you. My first grade teacher's name is Miss Barksdale. She is tall, brown and beautiful, with long soft wavy brown hair. On my first day Miss Barksdale, uses a big chart to test my knowledge of the ABC's. She is tall next to the ABC Chart. She points at each letter with her wooden pointer and asks me to identify out loud, each letter and its associated sound. Miss Barksdale and I get along fine and first grade finishes well.

Our family activities beyond school and work are: visiting friends in San Francisco (the Boni's, the Wakefields, The Hatfields and the Waltons), or picnics in Golden Gate Park.

Pappa drives us to Ocean Beach to look at the Sunset.

Pappa's other good friend is David Wakefield. The Wakefields live in Colma. Big Dave Wakefield is the head mechanic for Harley Davidson of Oakland. His son, Little Dave, is twice my age. At the Wakefield home I learn a valuable, life-long skill: riding on two wheels.

Pappa suffers from arthritic hips and knees. The classic Pappa runs alongside child, while child learns to balance a bike experience, is not going to happen. Plus I don't have a bike. So at 7 years old, I can't ride a bike.

During a visit to Colma, I'm in Big Dave's garage with Little Dave. Inside the large garage, in every direction, polished paint and buffed chrome dazzle the eyes; two-wheelers of every description, pedal and petrol powered; full-dressed Harley Davidson motorcycles stand side by side with red and blue Schwinn Stingrays with matching color handlebar grips and tassels, chrome spoked wheels with white-wall slicks. Little Dave can ride them all.

The Wakefield and Moyer kids, oblivious to their parents' whereabouts, are consumed with fun, and adventure. The sun retreats and the moon, planets, and stars turn on, the streetlights turn on too.

The long driveway descends from the large garage, crosses the sidewalk, and enters the street. It's much wider and longer than our driveway in Hayward. The driveway's pitch is perfect, not too flat, not too steep. Perfect for what?

Under the moonlight I face a critical crossroad: to continue to walk and run on two feet, or ride on two wheels. I see the bike, I see the long, gentle down-slope driveway and I see the quiet, lit street to roll onto. The unknown is scary, I need a little courage. Little Dave looks at me quizzically. His countenance brightens and he says, "you can do it." Pappa told me recently, Big Dave offered Little Dave $5 dollars if he could ride a wheelie on his bicycle for a ¼ mile. Little Dave did it! Little Dave is the authority on anything with two wheels and I trust him.

Okay, I'll try.

I focus on the red Schwinn stingray, leaning on its chrome kickstand. I approach and throw my right leg over the white, glittered, curvy banana seat, long enough for two riders, but it's just me. My left and right toe tips touch the ground. I familiarize myself with the coaster brake. Little Dave takes hold of the sissy bar at the back of the seat. "One, two, three!" Little Dave shoves me out of the safe, lit garage, into the dark.

Slight left right wobble, then balance. I roll down the long driveway gaining speed. With increased speed came improved stability. I glance left, right. The street entry is smooth and there's a cool breeze on my face. Now is the time for action. I grip the red handles tight and push the pedals round and round. Not only do I stay upright and roll, I continue to the end of the street!

Modulating the coaster brake I do a U-turn and pedal back to the Wakefield driveway, grinning ear to ear. I repeat the maneuver again and again, until we leave Colma, and return across the black bay to Palma Ceia.

I crossed an invisible line that night under the streetlight, from little kid, to big kid. In Hayward, I have no bike to ride. Technically that's untrue. Pappa has an ancient black, adult-sized bike; huge wheels, huge frame, and tiny seat. Maybe he got the bike before the War, when he was a kid. Maybe it belonged to his father, nobody knows. Pappa's bike is too big for me and not remotely cool. Arthritis prevents Pappa from riding it anymore. Mom rides it occasionally.

Mom does not drive a car, she has no license. She walks, rides the bus, and occasionally for fun, rides Pappa's old black bike. For my sisters and I, we walk, ride the bus (with Mom) and now, I ride Pappa's bike sort of.

When I mount the old bike, my toes don't reach the ground, so any attempt to ride it includes the risk of a high fall. Failure to maintain balance ensures a mighty crash. And forget about a helmet, in 1968, helmets were for football and Vietnam, not riding a bike. Occasionally, I throw caution to the wind and ride the junker around the neighborhood. Fortunately for the Moyer kids, something very big is heading our way; a gift Pappa receives from a co-worker. A gift good enough to forget all about Pappa's bike, two sizes too tall.

Pappa sets up the 3-1/2 foot deep, Doughboy swimming pool. It is used but in good shape. A thin piece of dark blue sheet metal forms the outside, the inside is one very large sheet of light blue plastic, with only a few repair patches. It's magic.

By late Saturday afternoon, the water hose is draped over the pool wall and the spicket is open full blast. The water runs all day and night and by the next day the pool is half full. It's summertime and we're out of school. The sun is hot and we hold our breath until the pool is full. We are very excited. During the summers of 69, 70 and 71, Hannah, Marja and I splash with friends in the noisy pool. We have a great time, every time - except once; I went under water and became disoriented and choked a little water - Each summer day we're allowed to invite one friend to swim. The Moyer's Palma Ceia popularity grows in leaps and bounds.

Mom is so cool, everyday she makes frozen juice pops for her little splashers. She walks through the screen-door, into the sunny backyard holding a tray full of brightly colored frozen popsicles. The pops are perfect while splashing on a hot day. We never know which color they'll be: orange, red or purple. The orange pops are made from orange juice, the red ones from Hawaiian Tropical Fruit Punch and the purple ones from grape juice. Tessa is two or three then, too little to swim. I don't remember Tessa during the Doughboy summers. A lot happens during those years at Palma Ceia.

Mom takes us children to swim lessons. We ride to swim lessons on the public bus. We are each responsible for our own swimsuit and towel. We roll up the swimsuit inside our towel and hold it on our laps.

My parents own one car, a 1960 Pontiac station wagon. Pappa drives the Pontiac to work, up the steep hill to the college. The hill is a strain on the engine, but the car makes it up. In Hayward as in San Francisco, Mom and us kids use the public transportation system to get places. Because of Mom's unique bus driver-communication system, getting around town by bus is a snap. To eliminate lengthy wait times at the bus-stop, Mom lights a cigarette, and sends smoke signals to signal the bus driver. Mom's Smoke Signal System MSSS, alerts the bus driver, and lets him or her know, we're waiting at the bus stop, and to get a move on. It works every time. After Mom sends smoke signals skyward, within three minutes, I spot the front grill and headlights of the bus, heading straight for us. A beautiful sight.

Second grade comes and goes; I grow taller. Mom makes small pencil marks on the wall to monitor our growth. I grow faster than my sisters and catch up to Hannah. At night when Mom tucks me in, she recites a prayer: "Now I lay me down to sleep, I pray to God my soul to keep. If I die before I wake, I pray to God my soul to take." This prayer scares me a little at first, because of the reference to dying. Then Mom strokes my hair for a few minutes which I love. I already mentioned my little Viking secret for growing tall. Mom says, "Jens, when you sleep, stretch your legs out straight, not curled up, but straight. You'll grow tall and strong." "Okay." "Good night Jensie." "Goodnight Mommy."

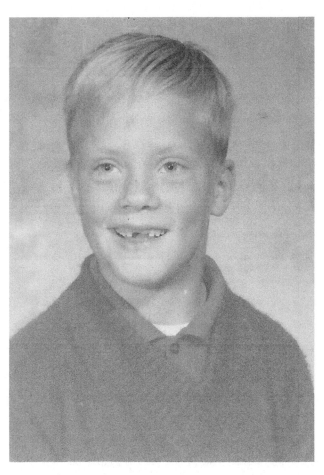

Seven years old

Music

Jens' third grade highlights? Learning to read quietly to myself, (hearing the words in my brain, without my lips moving) reading out-loud in class, recess, learning to throw a football and music. Not the old music Mom used to play on her little record player, the 45s and 78s, but the new music on the radio and big vinyl albums, the 33s from the 60's and some 50's. Prior to this time, I did love mom's 78s and 45s. There was a magical period consisting of Peter Rabbit etc. etc. etc.

What I did *not like* in the 2nd, 3rd, 4th and 5th grades at Palma Ceia, Hayward, were the fist-fights after school. Everyday after school, regardless of which route I take, fifteen to twenty kids form a tight, loud, jeering circle on the sidewalk or a front lawn. In the center of that mob, two kids fight . . . fist . . . fight. The reasons vary: someone misspoke, made a careless or careful insult. Slights are not tolerated, there's no delay of justice. Infractions are settled, same-day. The fights are fair, no weapons are ever used. Just fisticuffs, kicks, hair yanks, scratches, gouges, screams, blood and tears. Fights are fought standing, or ground level. Fights are 80% boys and 20% girls. The girls did 99% of the hair pulling. Participation is high, almost everyone feels the sting of battle. If you don't fight, the other kids say, "what's wrong with you?? " or he or she, "is a chicken" etc. etc. etc. Girl fights put pressure on the boys, not to be outdone, to show up. Fights create lifelong memories, and strengthen the participants.

After the final bell of an average Palma Ceia school day, my friend Chuck and I walk home amongst a large mixed group of classmates. Large group because a fight just concluded nearby. Bloodlust hangs in the air.

Chuck and I stall as long as possible. We both know how pacifists are treated here. In Palma Ceia, kindness *is* mistaken for weakness. Kids who don't put up their dukes are verbally and physically harassed continually. No, to keep the peace, it's necessary to convincingly pound each other sooner than later, and be done with it. Chuck and I look at one another and silently agree to give it a go. We shrug, raise our eyebrows . . . bristle. One of us initiates a strong shove, the other reciprocates full strength. The circle is formed, and tightens (we're not going anywhere until this is over) and we commence to drop atom bombs on each other. Dust in the air, clothes and hair disheveled, pain and tears. It climaxes in a ground scramble of blood and dirt. The mob gets their money's worth and Chuck and I call it a day. The brawl is a sound investment; within the violent neighborhood, it buys peace and respect for two years. Good pop for our punch.

Chuck and I met in the third grade. One day after school, he invites me to his house to listen to a couple of new 45 records. They blew me away. The first is an Osmonds song: One Bad Apple. The label is blue with a lion on it and says MGM. I love this song! What a fun and exciting song. We listen to One Bad Apple a couple more times, then Chuck plays the other 45 hot off the press, Suspicious Minds by Elvis Presley. Wow, how can anyone sound this good? Elvis' record label is black with a sitting white dog looking into the speaker of an old fashioned turntable. These two songs kick me musically and I recall that day so sharply, very moving. It's funny, as memorable as One Bad Apple, Suspicious Minds and our fight was, after that, I don't remember Chuck at all.

Let me introduce you to my Palma Ceia Posse: David, Roy and Robert. David and Robert are Mexican and Roy is Black. We all play together, and meet one another's families. We have dinner at each other's homes and attend one another's birthday parties. During the summer Roy invites me to attend Vacation Bible School with him and his little brother.

Vacation Bible School went five days a week, for two weeks. On the last day the Pastor sat with me on the front steps of the church, next door to the Jack in the Box and asked me, "would I like to accept Jesus as my personal Savior?" The Pastor also says, "Jens, if you believe in Jesus, he will live inside of you and dwell in your heart." I didn't understand the part about Jesus living inside of me. I pictured a miniature Jesus living in my stomach. I figured if Jesus is approximately ¼" tall, the plan *could* work. The Pastor is nice and Jesus is very nice, so I reply, " I believe in Jesus."

Roy's father is a police officer and one time while having dinner over Roy's house, I accidentally went into their bathroom while Roy's dad was taking a bath! I forgot to knock and am very embarrassed. Fortunately the bubbles secure his privacy.

I ate my first homemade tortilla at David's house, made by his very nice mother. Her tortillas are delicious and in a category by themselves.

The first song I remember singing out loud is Raindrops Keep Falling on my Head. I am walking to school with a classmate and neighbor, Troy and start singing, "raindrops keep fallin on my head, but that doesn't mean my eyes will soon be turning red, crying's not for me, cause, I'm never gonna' stop the rain by complaining" . . . etc. etc. etc. And Troy says, "that sounds good." I stop singing and we go to school. BJ Thomas is an excellent singer.

Often, our family picnics at Golden Gate Park. Mom packs sandwiches, Pappa spreads out a large blanket on the grass and we join many other people doing the same. During one picnic in the park, while enjoying my sandwich, from out of nowhere a football emerges. A full-sized leather football, with raised white leather laces and official insignias burned into the leather.

Sensing my interest, Pappa and another younger man taught me how to throw. How to grip the laces correctly, how to release the throw, roll the ball off my fingers, create a spiral; where on the person to target my throw. And most important for pass power, the wind-up; coil the ankles, legs, hips, upper and lower body like a spring, use my entire body to support the throw. Others join in the throw-around. At first my throws are flimsy, then more deliberate, then accurate, then spirals. Next, Pappa shows me how to pass to receivers on the run, hitting your receiver in full stride. "Lead your throw to the running receiver. Estimate his speed, and pass the ball so the receiver doesn't have to slow down to catch the ball." Pappa's running is better described as hurried walking due to his arthritis. Passing on the run is fun. In 1969 the people I met were friendly, smart and generous, especially at Golden Gate Park.

The remainder of third grade goes well. I enjoy sports, reading aloud and to myself. The teacher made a note on my end-of-year report card: "*While in class, Jens has a tendency to stare out the window and daydream.*"

The Birthday

Another splashy-fun summer in high gear! My ninth birthday has almost arrived, my height increases and riding Pappa's ol' black bike is a tad easier, though still embarrassing and scary (walk a tightrope without a net). Birthdays are still a big deal. Mom creates very nice birthday parties for each of us, with a homemade cake and lit candles to wish upon. A few friends are invited and fun homemade games are played, gifts are received enthusiastically. Birthdays and Christmas are important days in our house. The best days. My birthday is different in 1970. I don't recall a party. There is a cake but no party. Instead the family takes a ferry trip to Sausalito. I am allowed to invite one friend. A picture survives of Pappa, my sisters, Eddie and me on the San Francisco Bay Ferry. In that picture I'm wearing the style pants I dislike, brightly colored, loudly patterned and sharply creased flares.

I'm not sure why Mom dresses me funny. I know the Moyer budget is tight, but Mom's fashion sense is unique, perfectly suited for Northern Europe, but every time I get dressed and leave the house, a culture clash is loosed on Palma Ceia! Especially those flares, geez. Loud color patterns, thick synthetic material, a permanent inseam crease and a too wide cuff at the bottom. In San Francisco flares fit in, but not here in gritty Palma Ceia. Flares are either 15 years ahead or 15 years behind the times. But in Palma Ceia NOBODY wears them. Brother from another planet. *Uncool, uncool!*

In the U.S. my name is most unusual. I'm told Jens is a common name in Germany, Denmark, Sweden, Norway, Iceland and cold places like that.

A Swiss Olympic ski-jumper on TV was named Jens, that's it. Not until the mid-80's do I even meet another Jens, and he doesn't pronounce his name correctly. I correct every new teacher from kindergarten through 12th Grade, "Jenz Moyer?" 'Yence . . . here." Flare pants makes popularity hard to manage. Too young to be different, nowhere to hide! In Palma Ceia, negative peer pressure equates to persecution or black eyes.

The day after the ferry ride to Sausalito with Eddie, I receive birthday gifts. My anticipation is large, but the gifts are small. Though disturbed by gift size, hope never waivers. The first gift: a bike bell, you know the type, round chrome metal, thumb-lever on the side, clamps to the handlebar, an American flag decal on top. My disappointment veiled, I move forward. The next gift: a chrome side mirror, you know the type, clamp to the handlebar, left or right side mount depending on rider preference. My heart rate slows, my fake gift-joy becomes difficult to maintain, cheeks begin to cramp. The final gift: a pair of hand grips, you know the type, brightly colored plastic with tassels hanging from the ends. Confused, my countenance darkens.

Mom and Pappa make the big announcement: the old black bike is mine! And the new chrome accessories are to jazz it up.

No.

I have an internal crisis and build an emotional wall of granite. After all, they did give me a bike of my own, with chrome accessories. And I am four inches taller than that night in Colma. "Thank you Mom, thank you Pappa."

Strange name, strange clothes, now strange bike. How will I manage the fourth grade recoils? The stinging barbs from my classmates?!? Every verbal attack will require physical retaliation from me. Great.

After Mom's nice lunch Pappa says, "Jens, let's install the new parts on your bike." "Okay." "We'll need a couple tools, go into the garage and get the crescent wrench and hammer." "Okay." On the garage wall, Pappa installed some pegboard to store hand-tools. I know what the adjustable wrench and hammer look like. From the front yard I walk through the big garage door because it is open. In the middle of the garage, on the floor is a large, clear plastic sheet draped over something. This wasn't here before. I squint at the plastic and strain to identify the opaque shapes underneath. About the size of a . . . *stingray* . . . black *tires, whitewalls, spokes* . . . chrome upright *handlebars*. Quietly my parents circle behind me. My senses intensify, my heart races, I freeze and time stops.

"Happy Birthday Jens! Take off the plastic," my parents exclaim together and it startles me. I remove the plastic sheet. Leaning on its kickstand is a brand new, Royce Union, *5-speed* Stingray!

The stick-shift style gear shifter on top of the frame gives the bike a cool chopper look; a small US flag decal on the seat post. My American dream; gold frame, white sparkly banana seat. Chrome upright handlebars and a chrome gear shift. Mom wipes a tear, Pappa and I install the side-mirror and bell. What became of Pappa's old black bike? I don't know, I never saw it again. August 17th, 1970, a great day.

Best Teacher

Mr. Turentine is tall, thin, and black. He wears a suit and tie and speaks with a friendly deep voice. When he speaks, we listen. A student in Mr. Turentine's class who fails to complete his or her homework assignments, or misbehaves in the classroom, gets spanked on their backside with a wooden yardstick in front of the class. Mr. Turentine is my teacher for the next two years, for the fourth and fifth grade. My grades improve during this time. My fourth grade report card is all S's (satisfactory), my fifth grade report card is all G's (good), improvement in every subject!

In the fourth grade I receive a spanking for missing a homework assignment. "Jens, come to the front" - days before, a classmate was called to the front for missing homework. He held out as long as he could, but cried before the spanking was over - Oh no, I stood up from my desk and walked to the front. Mr. Turentine removes the wooden yardstick from the wall. I receive ten whacks on the bottom; I hold out til #6, but the pain increases with each crack and I cry. After that day there are no more late or missing assignments from me.

After Mr. Turentine's fifth grade class, my scholastic performance declined.

On April 4th, 1971 Ruus School held a student rally to commemorate Doctor Martin Luther King Junior's life. Mr. Turentine asked me to read a section of Mr. King's famous speech; I Have a Dream, in front of the whole school.

Standing alone center stage, behind a microphone on a stand, in front of the entire staff and student body, I read an excerpt from Mr. King's Speech. The reading went smooth, but lacked the

fire and conviction it deserved. I was happy to do it and I hope up in Heaven, Mr. King likes it.
Mom and Pappa admire Martin Luther King Junior very much. A poster of the slain Civil Rights
Leader is tacked to the wall in our home in Palma Ceia.

On the playground we play football everyday. I have a new black friend at Ruus named Reno.
Reno's older brother, Andre, is Hannah's grade.

Andre is a very good softball player, a pitcher. At Weeks Park behind the Quick Stop on Patrick
Avenue, are two beautiful baseball fields, surrounded by shiny metal chain-link fences and
bleachers and dug-outs. Little League baseball games are played there. Sometimes if my friends
and I are bored, we ride over there, get a snow cone and watch a couple innings. Rather than suck
the juice through the straw right away and be stuck with a cone full of juiceless ice, we chomp the
ice directly from the top first, until only icy juice is left. I love snow cones. One time Andre was
pitching there, but instead of playing baseball, it's called softball. A softball is bigger than a
baseball. How Andre pitches the softball, is magic. With theatrical arm wheels, the big softball
shoots out underhand like a cannonball past the batter to the catcher.

Reno and I discover that by combining Reno's sure hands and speed, with my quarterback arm,
we annihilate the opposition. In the huddle using my right forefinger I draw simple pass route
patterns on my left palm or stomach for Reno and the others. "Hut, hut, hike," Reno the rocket
loses the defense and I loft a spiral to his waiting hands. Reno's speed and my passes beat the
5-alligator pass rush, not every time, but almost.

Reno and I hit it off and I went to Reno's house after school one time. He wasn't far, just down
the street and around the corner on Mandarin Avenue. They have a huge open backyard, flat grass
and dirt, perfect for catch. I heard rumors that Reno's dad is mean. In addition to Andre, Reno has

several more brothers, older and younger. That day in the backyard it's just me, Reno and a younger brother. Reno has an extra mitt, so we play three-way catch.

I hear a deep and loud manly sound, coming from within their house. "Reno, Dad's home, hide," his little brother advises. We go on high alert. A giant black man comes slowly through the back screen door, into the backyard. "Squeeeeek." "What are you boys *doin!?* Reno . . . *RENO*!! I thought I told you . . . *what*!?, you better . . . that's *it*, I'm getting my *bat*! I'm gettin' my *BAT* right *NOW*!!" When Reno's giant dad disappears into the house, I fly through the side gate and run home fast and never go to Reno's house again.

You are alert in Palma Ceia. In the blink of an eye, anything can and does happen. One day, I'm standing in our front yard and a muscle car roars down our street, Mantilla Avenue then makes a hard squealing left turn onto the street that T's off Mantilla in front of the house, Pensacola Way. The car jumps the curb at the first house on the right of Pensacola Way, bounces up onto the front lawn and hits the house! Immediately, three police cars roll up fast, lights flashing, sirens blaring. On his loudspeaker a policeman says: "you in there, come out with your hands up!" Mom ushers me inside.

Another time, the same car is driving too fast on the same street, Pensacola Way. I didn't see this but heard about it the next day. Eddie lives on Pensacola Way, farther down near the other end by Sumatra Street. Eddie's little three year old brother was riding his tricycle and that car hit him and killed Eddies's little brother.

Eddie's older brother, George, is very funny, he talks a lot and tells a lot of jokes. Eddie is tall and solemn most of the time. Eddie and I get along well but George is a crack up.

Between 1969 and 72 my musical foundation was laid. After hearing Elvis and Donny Osmond, I dive into my parents' record collection. What do *they have*? Beatle albums: Magical Mystery Tour, Sergeant Pepper's Lonely Hearts Club Band and Revolver get the most play. I play those Beatle Albums over and over. Every song gets heard so many times. I sing along with the lyrics printed on the album's inner sleeve. Hannah received a gift: Hard Day's Night. She lets me listen to it once in a while. Janis Joplin's <u>Pearl</u> album receives full attention, but Beatles' albums are played the most. I love to sing along with John and Paul, George and Ringo to a much lesser degree.

I listen to Elvis Presley's Greatest hits. Elvis sings better than anyone I'd ever heard. Mom explains Elvis is a ladies man, very handsome and talented, an actor too. I ask Mom, do you like Elvis that way? She says, "no, for me, Frank Sinatra is too old and Elvis too young. I'm in the middle, age wise." Pappa leans toward jazz: Miles Davis, Count Bassie, Jack Benny etc. etc. etc. He likes the song, <u>Me and Mrs. Jones</u>. Besides belting the catchy chorus for a laugh, I don't care for it. The song celebrates very hurtful and damaging behavior in a person and mocks the family. I hate that song, but the singer's voice is very smooth and the chorus is very catchy.

Pappa pulls a clarinet out of an old black case a couple times. He learned to play it as a boy for his school band in Pennsylvania. Pappa sounds rusty now. Off-key notes and no fluidity. But he played it well before the War.

At nine years old, my music exposure is solid, but far behind the times. It's funny, I was stuck in a musical time-wharp and didn't know it. I need to catch-up. David's 10th birthday party shoves me forward.

ABC of Cooking

During fourth grade, I'm invited to my friend David's 10th birthday party. Life moves fast in Palma Ceia; in class Lorena lifts up her dress in front of David and I and brings us up to speed. Boys and girls attend David's party. I walk into the house and set down David's gift. Not sure of what to do, I head toward the dark family room; a pool table stands in the center. I survey the dark room before entering. On the left side of the room, the birthday boy kneels next to a fancy phonograph. A nice stereo record player, in a wooden cabinet. On the front are large stereo speakers hidden behind taught sparkly fabric. Colored balloons and streamers hang over the pool table, shiny gold letters read, HAPPY BIRTHDAY!

A blacklight ignites blacklight-art on the walls. Woah!

Unprepared, a new song explodes from the stereo speakers, very loud, I'm startled. Familiar to everyone but me, the song <u>ABC</u> by the Jackson Five, has an exciting lead vocal, vocal harmony and strong bass beat. The song is a thrill. The album cover shows the five Jackson brothers on the front, dressed colorful and cool. Their outfits are a colorful splash like Pappa's paintings, big bell bottom pants. Kids start to dance, both boys and girls dance the Funky Chicken and other hot dances.

The latest sound? These kids are on top of it. Seizing the moment, I thumb through two long rows of 45's on the floor. Temptations; Ball of Confusion, Smokey Robinson; Tears of a Clown, several by Diana Ross and the Supremes. Too many to count and all foreign to me. A lot of Motown labeled records. Roy and Robert are there. I hang out with them. I don't recall kissing any girls.

David's 10th birthday party shifts my orbit. At the party, three mysteries swirl around me like a tornado; (1) girls and their beauty, (2) Michael Jackson and the Motown sound, and (3) how a black light can distort perception.

I don't remember many horrible things in Palma Ceia. There is a creek near my school to play in, older boys play there and misbehave. Knee deep in the creek we catch pollywogs and frogs, put them in a coffee can half-filled with water, poke holes in the plastic lid and bring them home to show family. The amphibians make mom and sisters uneasy.

Sometimes dirty mean white boys visit the creek. One time those boys had firecrackers and put them in the frog's mouths and lit them off! The poor frogs are blown apart! Graffiti is sprayed on the cement walls at the creek. "HOWE IS A BIG COW" is written there. A dirty mean boy beat me up once.

I'm sent to the Principal's office for fighting. I heard Principal Howe is mean and will hit you. The rumor is true! He grabs me by the shoulder and hits me on the arm a couple times with something, then cites my offense. Mr. Howe says, "are you going to do that again?" "No."

Mom's a good cook and she cooks for us everyday. Mom's always banging and clanging in the kitchen, chop chop chop, baking casseroles, washing and drying dishes, setting the table; hot pots and pans on trivets, silverware, "set the table Jens," "you're a gem Jens," yada, yada, yada. Clang bang, water from the faucet sssshhhhh.

Mom bakes a lot too; cakes, pies, lots of delicious and different cookies, *especially* at Christmas. Date bar, bundt cakes, coffee cakes year round. Muffins, biscuits, dumplings. Molasses cookies, jam cookies, pepper cookies cut in various animal shapes with steel cookie cutters. Sugar cookies, chocolate chip cookies. Fudge, frosted cakes, brownies etc. etc. etc. Swedes love sugar!

Mom watches TV at night and keeps a bowl of white sugar on the table next to her. She watches her favorite show, smokes, and every so often licks the tip of her right index finger, touches the sugar bowl and licks her finger.

In the mornings we eat cold cereal in cold milk. If the cereal's #1 ingredient is sugar aka Cap'n' Crunch or Tony the Tiger's Sugar Frosted Flakes or a dozen others, I wake before sunrise, to enjoy a private breakfast with the Captain, in peace and quiet, before it's gone. I eat the stuff until the roof of my mouth hurts. I'm hungry all the time.

Mom's repertoire of repetitive dinners is impressive. Dinners always include vegetables. Eating vegetables is not optional. Both Mom and Pappa are resolute on this; no sour face, sorry excuse or even genuine disgust will work. Gagging, retching or choking though entertaining, is pointless. Plainly put, the law of the land states: thou shall eat thy vegetables, and thus we shall. Eat the evil green veggies first, before the good stuff, that's my strategy. Get the gaggables down quick, like Cool Hand Luke. Don't make the torture any longer than it has to be.

Mom bakes tuna casserole three or four times a month. Baked and served in a glass casserole dish. Hot on the table, set on a trivet. Dinners are served so hot, nine times out of ten, you have to blow on your loaded fork or spoon a bit, before you can stuff your beak.

I will rate Mom's individual meal popularity, (per me) on a scale of one to ten.

Tuna Casserole, 5.

Mom's lasagna (rare), 10.

Steamed hotdogs three times a month, no bun, 6.

Shake N' Bake chicken, four times a month, 9. The *entire* chicken is used; Pappa eats the two breasts, one for dinner, and one for lunch the next day. Mom *always* eats the back and the neck.

Four kids divvy up two thighs, two legs and two wings. In Pappa's defense, he removes the breast skin and offers it to a well-behaved child. Shake N' Bake skin is the best!

Beef stew with dumplings, once a month, 7.

Beef stroganoff over mashed potatoes, once every two months, 10.

Poached eggs on toast, breakfast or lunch, three times a month, 10.

Waffles with hot chicken gravy on top, for a weekend lunch, once a month, 8.

Hamburger no bun, three times a month, 10.

Chef Boyardee Cheese Pizza, once every two months, 10.

Crispy ground beef tacos, once every two months, 10.

Fish sticks twice a month, 7.

Besides corn on the cob, or cauliflower, all vegetables are canned or frozen, all milk non-fat powder mix poured from a pitcher.

Pappa works for the state, Mom stays at home with us. California state employees are paid once a month and Pappa is no exception. Money is tight, but we never miss a meal. I am hungry, but adequately nourished, we all are.

Dinnertime involves the whole family and the seating pattern is rigid. That popular party game, Musical Chairs, is not played at Moyer mealtime. Pappa sits at one end of the large rectangular dinner table, I sit at the other end. Mom always sits to my immediate right, and Tessa next to Mom near Pappa. Hannah sits to my immediate left and Marja next to Hannah, near Pappa.

Viewing me eat straight on, Pappa plays the same broken record; "Jens, what's the rush? 'No one's going to take it from you. 'Where are your manners? 'Take time to breathe. 'Slow down for Christ sake." ''You're not an animal Jens." And most annoying, "Jens, how was your day?"

Talking over one another is not permitted at the dinner table. "Jens, don't butt in," Pappa says. At every dinner, the noise meter slowly rises. When decibels reach the ceiling, Pappa goes through the roof; he slams his large hand on the table, *boom*! And says, "*quiet!*" Pappa gets upset often but doesn't hit us or anything. We just hear it, then respond accordingly. I received a few spankings, not much, and always well deserved. We try not to upset Pappa, but I try least.

Jens n' Friends

The summer of 71 finds us once again in the Doughboy, splashing with friends and sucking juice pops. This is our final Palma Ceia summer. Weekend visits to friends in the city continue. The Boni's, Hatfields, and Becky Walton the most frequent.

The Hatfields have known my parents since my genesis at Judah Street. Louise and Inger gaily stroll with Bruce and I, young mothers born and raised worlds away, explore Golden Gate Park together, compare notes, laugh. Jack met Howard while working at the Post Office. The Hatfield children cover a wide spectrum of ages. Vicky the oldest, Steven, and Lisa are older than I, Vicky and Steve are adults, at least Vicky. Lisa is off doing her own thing but we see her often. Bruce is my age and Brian Marja's age. Bruce, Brian and I always have a blast together, non-stop fun and laughter.

Robert and Chachi Boni are 100% Italian. For Jack and Bob, creating art is their love and bond. Jack and Robert also met while working at the Post Office.

Art is great, sure, very nice, inspiring, dazzling, spiritual. But the three Boni daughters are *my* kind of art.

Raven haired beauties all three. Smart? Yeah. Bombe, the oldest, four years older than me, is a whirlwind like her father. A glimpse into her room is a lot to take in, so much going on. Books, art, music, fashion, music, games. A beautiful environment. Susan, oh boy, Susan is two years older than me, Hannah's age with a great smile so nice and genuine. And Robin, Marja's age, is very nice too, statuesque and quiet, loving and brilliant.

Robert and Chachi Boni are great people, caring, and fun. Their homelife has a taste all its own, extra spicy. Every wall grabs your attention. Stimulating, fun and disturbing, but always engaging, art and life are celebrated in the Boni home. Fine pieces, originals, framed photography (posed and candid, family, friends and strangers) everywhere. Martin Luther King Junior's brave face is there. And inside the bathroom on the door? A cool Bruce Lee poster, complete with cocked Nunchakus. The Boni's living space sizzles with creative fire.

After dinner, adults remain at table and debate current events with conviction you can hear through the wall in the next room.

Robert's mother lives there. A very loving, and spunky woman. Mamma Boni leaves no one unnoticed, a warm embrace for each of us. Mamma Boni, with gusto, brings us up to speed on the latest family news; the ups, the downs, current events, politics, weather, her aches and pains. Mama B, there's just one problem . . . we don't understand Italian! Mamma Boni's will to connect with people she loves is so strong, no language barrier can stand against it! My sisters and I just nod, and agree with her. Our relationship with Mamma Boni is intuitive, body language, head nods and, "uh huhs."

A 12 foot wide, sliding partition door separates the dining room from the living room. The glass is opaque, creating privacy, only people's shadows near the glass can be seen. Friends, diverse and creative, pack the Boni dinner table every Saturday night. When dinner is done, the partitions close and adults and children separate. On one side, mature themes are aired, challenged and defended passionately. In the case where the adult side spills over to our side, the children scream and run for their lives.

On our side, it's TV. Creature Feature is everyone's favorite. While Robert, Cachi, Jack, Inger and friends hoop and holler in the dining room, in the dark living room, TV lights flicker on scared young faces. The beauty surrounding me in the Boni living room, would make King Solomon proud. It's good to be King.

My last birthday in Hayward was good (no bad birthdays) but different. I'm growing up, traditional birthday parties are replaced by a fun destination trip. I'm allowed to invite one friend this year, Robert gets the nod. Robert lives in a house on Dickens Street near Tennyson Road.

We drive the station wagon to Fremont and board a train. We ride the train from Fremont to San Jose. In San Jose, we go to the theme park, Frontier Village. There's a fishing pond where you can catch real fish, cool rides and hokey staged gunfights in the middle of main street, complete with cowboys and Indians in 10 gallon hats and feathered bonnets, yelling at each other and gunning one another down. The guns are very loud, like real guns. The day is a blast, and I'm touched by the extravagance of the gesture. Travel by auto and train, going to a real theme park with rides. Unprecedented, a big deal.

Prior to Frontier Village I'd ridden one amusement park ride; two counting the Zipper ride in the nearby Tennyson strip-mall parking lot with Eddie's funny brother, George. Hannah and I rode the scary ride at the Santa Cruz beach boardwalk. Scary good. Outside under daylight's safety, we sit side by side in a little car on tracks within view of our parents, but quickly we disappear through a door that opens and closes behind us. Hannah and I are captives, subject to terrors of the dark.

My 10th Birthday is the first time the day's activity exceeds the gift itself, which surprisingly, I don't recall, a bolo tie maybe, or a pair of flares.

Later, I say to Mom, "Mom, we did so much today." "Yes, Pappa spent $20 for us to go." I close my eyes and picture a 20 dollar bill as large as my school's flag, flapping high on a pole.

Here comes fifth grade, and I sense significant personal change on the horizon (not a fortune cookie either). It's only fifth grade but changes are happening fast, like Judo lessons and reading complex books. Faster bikes, louder music. Fishing, football, girls.

Pappa develops an original abstract painting technique, using Ditzler Auto Lacquers. He sells his paintings including one to Ben Davidson's wife. Mr. Davidson played for the Oakland Raiders and played very well.

I attend my first NFL football game. Pappa's friend gave him a pair of tickets to see the Oakland Raiders play the Denver Broncos at the Oakland Coliseum. It was okay, too long, too far away. I prefer to play football, not watch.

My quarterbacking gets better, more accurate, tighter spirals, longer passes. I enjoy kicking and punting too. In season, basketball is great too. Baseball gets some attention, but without joining Little League, progress is marginal.

At school, we played an organized game of baseball, two full teams, girls watching. I get a hit and wait at first base. Robert is up next and gets a good hit, a double. Lost in thought, Robert appears suddenly, three steps away and yells, run! I don't remember a more embarrassing moment in elementary school. I still see the indignation on Robert's face as he races to first and I'm standing there on first base. The moment's not a waste, I swear, I'll never do anything *that dumb,* again. Boy was I wrong.

A young man, an art student from Pappa's work, Cal State Hayward, stops at the house a couple times. The art student has a motorcycle and wants to customize the gas-tank. Pappa paints flames on the gas tank with him, and shows him how he does it. I remember the painted tank, very cool. A photo exists of the student picking up the tank at the house, his face turned away. I remember the picture, he had thick, shoulder length, scruffy, dirty blonde hair. I've tried to recover the picture, but no luck yet. I believe that art student may have been Arlen Ness, the famous custom motorcycle designer and manufacturer. Mr. Ness did attend Cal-State Hayward at this time.

Mr. Turentine is back as our fifth grade teacher, all my friends too; Roy, Reno, David and Robert and the pretty girls are even prettier. Reading takes off for me then. I race through books. For kicks I read as fast as I can, trying different speed-reading approaches. I can't see the whole page at once, but almost.

Mom takes us to the library for story hour and to check out books. In the evening Mom read us longer stories, stories not finished in one sitting. Stuart Little is one I remember. At this time Mom hands me a worn science fiction paperback, Ray Bradbury's Short Story Collection, and encourages me to read it. The stories are involved and disturbing. I enjoy them all.

One early morning, Pappa and I go to Cull Canyon Lake in Castro Valley with a small fishing pole, a red and white bobber, hooks and a blue plastic container of red worms wriggling in moist brown dirt.

I pierce a worm's side with the sharp hook.

Pappa connects the bobber a foot or so above the hooked worm and from a small wooden dock, I cast bait and bobber onto the water, ten feet from the dock. The worm sinks and only the bobber is visible, floating on top of the water. I cannot see underneath the water. We wait a short while and . . . the bobber moves sideways, then, kerplunk, disappears! This excitement is new and intense. There is a secret world underwater. After a few more lateral and vertical bobber movements, Pappa says, "lift up the pole, set the hook." The struggle between boy and fish is on. I catch my first fish, a bluegill! The fisherman's triumphant return to Mantilla Avenue includes special guests, the Bonis. The fish and I are honored and congratulated. My first fish kicked off a great day, but I haven't caught fishing fever yet.

Hannah starts sixth grade at a different school, Peixoto (pronounced pishoto). The city of Hayward consists of affluent folks in the hills, and working families in the deteriorating flatlands. Amongst the flatland neighborhoods, Palma Ceia east is the worst. More violence, more drugs and more crime. Among the schools in this area, Peixoto is the worst. Hannah, the most serious of the four Moyer children, grows tougher still, attending Peixoto.

My spare time is filled with reading, all my Mom's science fiction stuff first, then a lot more from the library at Weekes Park. Math is basic and fun. My goal for any math quiz or test, any test, is to finish fast and first. Adding, subtracting, multiplication and dividing stuff is not my first or second or choice, but I do get into it. Sports, reading, music and pretty girls are my top four.

I have a low mechanical aptitude. My bike maintenance skills are lacking. In a year's time, my glorious Royce Union falls into disrepair, unrideable. Flat tires, rusty chain, gears don't shift etc. etc. etc. Eddie has another older brother, Juan. Juan differs from funny George, he's quiet and wears silver wire rimmed glasses and is shorter. Juan is the master of the deal. He notices the disabled Royce Union and with cunning and precise timing, presents his lowball offer. A few bucks sounds good to me, so with Pappa's permission, I sold the one year old wonder bike to Juan for $15 bucks. My disgraceful lack of resourcefulness and appreciation must have disappointed Pappa, the bike being a financial sacrifice only a year ago.

Two days after the sale, Juan rides his like new bicycle slowly past the front of my house, grinning ear to ear. I blew it! I'm standing there, mouth hung open, helplessly watching my gold stick-shift treasure roll past, shiny again. Like when I pulled off the plastic sheet. What a tough lesson to learn; fix it, don't sell it. If you can't do it, find a friend who can help. Elbow grease is the key.

Mount Hamilton, San Jose

The Dive

Judo means the gentle way. Pappa's co-worker's son is a national judo champion. He can bench press 400 lbs. Pappa takes me to a judo dojo in Castro Valley for lessons. The sinsei's name is Mr Ormsby. He has two sons, one my age and one Hannah's age. The dojo has excellent mats, covered in oatmeal colored natural canvas, not vinyl or rubber like a wrestling mat. The dojo is open and roomy, not cramped. Large plate windows run along the entire front and a small, three row bleacher provides a watch & wait area for the parents. The entire large rectangular space is covered in mats except where the bleachers are near the windows and a 3' wide strip around the other three sides. On my first night I got a gi (thick cotton long sleeve jacket) and a white belt. The beginning of every judo lesson begins with a 40 minute warm-up; comprehensive stretching and strengthening calisthenics. Next, different throws and counters are learned and improved, then every lesson concludes with several one-on-one matches. The students sit on the mat cross-legged, forming a circle around these matches. Everyone fights, no exceptions. The warm-ups enable the body to perform the different judo moves and counters, and prevents injury.

Sensei Ormsby pulls me and the beginners to the side and our judo journey begins. "Always keep your toenails and fingernails clean and trimmed. To show respect, bow to your opponent, and bow before entering and leaving the mat." The first technique we learn is how to fall down on the mat. We start from a sitting position, roll backward and slap the mat. Slap the mat with both palms at the same time, and shout, HUH! Or OHH! in sync with the slap.

The shout exhale helps prevent injury to the core area. After learning fall basics from a sitting position, we learn to fall from a standing position. We practice falling straight back, and left and right sides. If falling straight back, we slap both hands at the same time, if falling to the left or right, we slap the mat with the corresponding left or right hand and shout. Training moves fast. As fast as you can grasp a move, on to the next.

Next the forward roll; lean forward, lead with the right or left hand, continue rolling forward, somersault, slap mat with the other hand, and with the momentum, jump up to your feet. The slap-shout helps with the impact and propels you back up to a standing position.

Near the end of the warm-up, students line up single file and do continuous forward rolls around the entire dojo, either left or right shoulder. Then back rolls in single file; from a kneel, roll back, slap both hands and backward somersault onto either the left or right shoulder, back up to kneel, repeat. The class in single file, rolls back, slaps, kneels and repeats, around the dojo perimeter a couple times. Now your body is putty.

After a long list of exercises: sit-ups, push ups, scoop push-ups, leg lifts, ankle stretch, neck stretch, back stretch, hip and leg stretch, shoulder stretch, jumping jacks, leg lifts, forward rolls, back rolls etc. etc. etc. we line up and dive/roll over the back of Sensei Ormsby. This progression of stretching builds on itself to the point of being ready to compete in a judo match, to throw and be thrown.

Judo is a sport of fighting.

Sensei begins in a low position, hands, knees and forehead touch the mat, then each student one after the other, runs to sensei, leads with the left or right hand and dives over sensei's back, rolls slap/shout and jumps back to his or her feet.

You're supposed to clear sensei's back.

Your gi can brush him but don't collide and knock him over. You don't want to hurt sensei in front of the class. After students dive over sensei, it's back in line; sensei gets higher, in a crouch. After students do that jump-dive roll, sensei stands higher, and our stress goes higher. Sensei stands leg straight and leans his torso parallel to the mat. Wow, we made it. Can this get worse? Yes it does! On the final jump, sensei stands fully erect, only his head and neck pitch forward. sensei literally sticks his neck out for us.

Each judo lesson ramps up slowly: stretches, strengthening, rolls, dives, throw drills and mat work. The night concludes with one-on-one matches and hair dripping sweat.

The word judo, means the "gentle way." But advanced students learn, judo is the toughest martial art. Choke until your opponent passes out, arm and leg breaks etc. etc. etc.

Judo competition is international and held at every level; from neighborhood garage dojos, to the Olympics.

Judo gives me a lot; confidence and strength, respect for my contemporaries and instinctive ability to deal with physical confrontation (MOTL). The different belt colors indicate your level of ability, knowledge and experience. Belts are earned not bought. Beginners wear a white belt. After a student can demonstrate a modest list of throws correctly, sensei gives him or her a yellow belt. Then and there the student removes their old belt and ties the new belt on.

The belt is for life.

After the yellow belt learns many more throws, and participates in several tournaments, a green belt is given. Receiving a green belt is a big deal; there's a solemn ceremony in the dojo. With more development and competition, a brown (purple if under age 18) belt is earned, then black a belt. The first black belt is not the pinnacle however. There are ten degrees of black belt. The last few degrees of black belt have thin red lines in them and the 10th degree, the highest level, is entirely red.

There are two other brothers at the Castro Valley dojo, one my age a green belt, and a 20 year old black belt. The older brother is a National Collegiate judo champion. I hate when the younger brother leads warm-ups. He has us do 200 sit-ups and laughs about it. Their father watches over their workouts carefully, and calls out encouragement from the bleacher. Pappa too, but not in an intimidating way.

After the two-hour workout and hard fought matches, I'm beat. On the drive home, we stop at Jack in the Box for a renewing chocolate shake. In the drive-thru, you speak your order to a literal Jack in the Box figure. Jack the jester's large head protrudes from a black box, mounted on a black, stiff metal spring. Jack's mouth is a speaker and his ear a microphone. The worker inside brings Jack to life. One night Jack recites Jack's order back to Jack. As Jack struggles to review Jack's order and complete the elongated sentence, Pappa cuts him off and says, "yes" and proceeds to the pick-up window. I still hear Jack talking as Pappa rolls toward the pick-up window and I laugh so hard. Pappa gets vanilla; he takes the lid off and drinks straight from the cup. I get chocolate, on occasion strawberry, and use a straw.

Fifth grade at Ruus Elementary, under Mr. Turentine's care is my best school year; I feel strong, on track and unlimited; the sky's the limit, the universe, infinity . . .

Mom and Pappa tell me about a special opportunity. Mr. Turentine called them recently to discuss a special program at Ruus Elementary called MGM, Mentally Gifted Minors. I like being considered gifted. Years later I learn we're all gifted. Mr. Turentine recommends two students from his class to participate in MGM, David and myself. If we're interested, testing is required. If I pass the tests, I'm accepted to the program. Once a week we leave our class at Ruus and drive to another location in town, to learn different things from a different teacher. Mom and Pappa ask me if I'd like to test? "Yes." Wow this is great. To have this chance. I'd never heard of it and don't know what we'll do, but I want to pass the test and be set apart.

The day finally comes. Pappa drives me to the test site, but this test is different. No questions on paper, no multiple choice fill-in bubbles, rather a man asks me questions. He says, "answer whatever comes to mind." He is white, wears silver wire rim glasses, and has straight thin short blonde hair. He's dressed simple but sharp: white shirt, blue jacket, a tie and slacks. He looks kind and smart, not angry or intimidating. I am put at ease, and tell him my take on things. No adult asks a fifth grader what they think about this or that, but he did. Words come out easily. "Pappa, did I pass? Am I in the program?" 'Yes, he said you passed." Good!

In elementary school we're taught to follow instructions, and I like that. Understanding instruction and the questions make the correct answers possible to find. I believe to follow wise direction to the best of your ability, is the best chance one has in life.

Annual State testing is for me, the epitome of following directions. When those narrow answer cards with all the answer bubbles are handed out, it is time to do my *absolute best*. Use only a yellow #2 pencil, fill in the answer bubble completely, wait until the teacher says, "start now." I want every answer to be right. No mistakes if possible, and it *is* possible, and be the first student done too, that's the goal. Every quiz, every test, I approach this way. I make mistakes, but not always.

Whether State test scores are used to place MGM kids, or solely at the teacher's discretion, I don't know. None of the MGM qualifications are ever explained. Mystery shrouds the selection process and the program. I like the tension. I'm happy to get in, but now what? I don't know. What does it mean in the big picture, this mystery? David and I are friends and doing MGM together; the two Ruus knights will slay the MGM dragon together!

The big day finally arrives. David and I are driven to an undisclosed location in Hayward. There are five other children already there, three boys and two girls, co-ed. The teacher is a short, average build, white lady, older than Mom. She's very nice, enthusiastic and energetic. She introduces us to a man, maybe 34 years old. He has a dark blonde mustache, short beard and is slightly bald. He's thin, tall and muscular. In a thick Slavic accent he speaks little, only when giving us direction. Mrs. So and So explains to us that Mr. So and So is a dancer from the Soviet Union and will teach us how to dance Russian. How funny and unexpected, learning Russian dance from a communist defector. Why not?

Within a month he whips us into shape. There's a boy in our dance troop, a year younger than David and I, who has a knack for the tough dance move, Prisyadka. From a squat position, arms folded, alternate right and left kicks. I can do the move in practice, but not reliably, wearing the correct leather bottom shoes helps a lot, because they slip more. Authentic satin Russian dance costumes are produced and five performance dates are booked. Wow, here we go!

Our troop is decked out in matching costumes: for the boys, green satin shirts, black pants, a wide black cumberbund, black knee high socks and black leather shoes; for the girls, the same but purple satin shirts.

Music, lights, let the show begin! The troop enters stage-left doing the "Duck." Waddling single file, in squat position, arms folded, we circle the entire stage twice.

So far so good.

In a single line across the front of the stage, in unison, we spring upright and face our audience. To rowdy Russian dance music, the troop in unison drops to a squat, immediately leaps up to stand, with arms crossed, right leg kick out, right foot plant on stage, back to squat, leap up, left leg kick out, left foot plant. Up, down, right, left, up, down, right, left, repeat to the beat!

This move repeats four times, then David and I step forward, away from the troop line, closer to our audience, the troop line continues arm-crossed, squat-leap-kick repeat behind us. David and I also continue the squat-leap-kick repeat (SLKR) in time musically with the troop behind, after two more SLKRs, David and I both squat down, palms on the ground and from a squat extend our right legs out, remain in a squat, sweep our straightened right legs in a circle counterclockwise, dragging our right toe on the ground toward our left legs, step over circular sweep motion of right leg with the left leg, then swing right leg in a complete circle right toe dragging. After 10 revolutions, David and I leap up, two more SLKR moves then back up into the troop line, the complete line continues SLKRs in tight musical unison.

Mr. show-stopper steps forward . . . the troop's youngest dancer, a fourth grader alone, in front of Tennyson High School, and performs Prisyadka. Step forward, two SLKRs then squat down, stay down, arms folded, kick out right leg, left leg, right, left, right, left, continue . . . yeaaah! Applause volume increases to crescendo! Yeah, yeah, yeah! Prisyadka brings down the house!

I dance my way through the fifth grade.

One Saturday afternoon, as a merit award, Mr. Turentine drives three of us, a skinny white classmate, Ray, myself and Roy to a weekend matinee performance of Circus Vargas. We drove there in Mr. Turentine's cream puff classic, a white Ford Falcon. He buys us popcorn and the circus is fun.

April 11th is my last day at Ruus Elementary and Palma Ceia. The Moyers are moving to Fremont, California, to Jackson Street. The fifth grade is over in eight weeks. Mr. Turentine threw a party for me; complete with cake and a gift, a cool hot-rod model called <u>Rommel's Rod.</u> Driven by a uniformed skeleton Nazi officer in the front seat (bony hand on the wheel) and the famous Nazi General, Rommel, the Desert Fox (also a skeleton) in the backseat. Rommel wears his Nazi General's cap.

Robert, Roy, David and Lorena are there. I have not seen them since. They were my good friends and Mr. Turentine was the best teacher. ABC, 123.

June 1971

Jackson Street

Our new Fremont house is beyond words, but I'll try. Spacious, *four* bedrooms and *two* bathrooms! I have my own room, the first one off the hallway, the window faces the front porch, lawn and street.

The backyard is large and very deep, descending southward in three level tiers. There's a roofed, red-concrete patio, walled on three sides and accessible from the family room sliding door and a man-door from our parents room. The first tier, the largest, drops abruptly four feet from red concrete patio (don't fall), the second tier drops five feet from the first (tapered with steps) and is half as deep as the first tier; the third final tier drops five feet lower than the second (tapered with steps) and is half as deep as the second tier. Then the back fence. The backyard is peppered with a half-dozen mature fruit trees. The property continues another 50' beyond the back fence, bounded by a small creek and freeway off-ramp.

The large front yard has a single, tall palm tree in its center, the kind that occasionally drops large dead fronds, with large thorns, like shark teeth. Back in Palma Ceia every front yard has a palm tree like this one. At least six of those palm trees in Palma Ceia have carved out niches in the trunk, four feet off the ground, to house a Polynesian idol.

Pappa trades in his 1968 yellow Ford Country-Squire station wagon with simulated wood grain siding, for a solid white, 1972 Ford Ranch Wagon station wagon. Near the end of moving day, Pappa and I drove two last, knick-knack trips from Hayward to Fremont. Both times we drive on

Mission Boulevard. After passing the historic town of Niles heading south, Mission Peak dominates the view. From this vantage point, Mission Peak looks like an Egyptian pyramid, triangular and pointed. The peak is fixed on the horizon, leading us to the promised land. A good sign.

Even though the move to Fremont means a commute for Pappa, they probably moved due to the crime and cramped quarters of east Palma Ceia. Not long ago, a break-in occurred at our Mantilla house. The robbers hit the garage only. In the middle of the night about the same time as the burglary, Pappa's Dalmatian, Bootsy, died of an alleged heart attack.

Jackson Street Neighbors A to Z

On Saturday evening, April 15th, 1972; the Moyers huddle around the large dining table. The dining table light hangs too low on a retractable cord that doesn't retract. The low-hung light illuminates our faces like an interrogation room from a black and white TV police drama; the garish spotlight on the suspect's desperate face as he is questioned by hardened investigators.

The family mood is giddy excitement, a mix of fatigue and joy. The first supper is spectacular, take-out pizza. We're not dreaming . . . it's real. We can see it and taste it.

It's near dark outside, twilight, inside I'm enjoying the best dinner of my life under the interrogation light, when a firm *knock-knock-knock* comes from the front door. Six jaws stop chewing, "who's that?"

The neighbor boy from across the street introduces himself to Pappa, "Hi, my name is Denny Zolanski, what's your name? Do you want to play?" Denny is three years younger than I; he brought his Lincoln Logs and wants to know if we want to play? Denny has a minor mental handicap. He is overly friendly and a little saliva hangs from the corner of his mouth as he speaks. Pappa shakes his hand, invites him in and we introduce ourselves. Denny has a couple warts on his face. Denny's laugh is loud and makes us smile and feel welcome. Denny is the baby of a large family. His father's name is Bernard Zolanski and his mother's name is Marlene. Bernard is a supervisor in the paint department at the General Motors automotive plant in south Fremont, he's worked there since it opened in 1963. Denny has two brothers and two sisters. Thomas is the oldest, then Patricia, Cheryl and Alexander. Alex is my age and grade and was born here. They live across the street, one house over. The Zolanski's have lived on Jackson Street since 1960.

Directly across the street and next door to the Zolanskis are the Lansings. The Patriarch, Ron Lansing is a handsome cool cat. He drives a custom black 1956 Ford pickup with vertical chrome exhaust pipes behind the cab. Mrs. Jillian Lansing goes by Jill and is nice and pretty. Ron and Jill have two tough, smart sons and three smart, pretty daughters; Dean is the oldest, then Jimmy, Donna, Charlene and Paula the baby. Charlene is my age and grade. The Zolanski children have dirty blonde hair like mine. The Lansing children have light to medium brown hair. There is a 30" high, cinder-block wall nicknamed, "the wall," in between their two front yards. The Lansing and Zolanski children's wide age spectrum, combined with their highly social natures, ensure a steady flow of lively visitors. The Zolanski/Lansing common wall (a 15' long bench) and Lansing's large shade tree create a social hot-spot.

The last important member of the Lansing family is Sonya, a german shepherd type dog, with a beautiful coat of shiny flowing long black hair, with brown highlights. Intelligent and highly trained, like a circus dog, Sonya does numerous tricks on command.

Sonya's black mane contrasts with her gleaming white teeth and pink nose, she lies on the plush green lawn in the cool shade, her long-haired tail wags slowly left and right, over and over in a calm way, waiting patiently to perform numerous tricks for any member of the family; a rich scene for a 10 year old boy, a sweet memory.

The Zolanskis also have a dog, Smoky. Smoky *is* a german shepherd, dark and light smoky gray colors, with a white muzzle from age. The funny thing about Smoky is, wherever Alex is; whether down the street, around the corner, or a 1/2 mile away, Smoky shows up. If Alex is there, four gray legs and a white muzzle quietly appear from nowhere. Alex always responds the same, "Smoky! . . . go *home!*" Smoky stops, stares at Alex, hoping for a change of heart or that a mistake has been made. No mistake Smoky. Louder this time, Smoky!! GO *HOME*!! For the 80th time in three days, Smoky dutifully obeys; he turns around and bee-lines it home, only to return a half-hour later and try his luck again again. A boy and his dog.

Next door to the Lansings and directly across the street are the Farmers, a family of fighters. Mr. and Mrs. Farmer have many children, Ross, a year younger than I, Charlie, eighteen and a sister two years younger are the three I remember. The Farmers move out two years after we move in.

From my bedroom window I can see most of the Lansing front yard and the entire Farmer home, but not The wall or the Zolanski home.

Ross, Charlie and their sister do judo too, so Ross and I hit it off. Their dojo is a converted garage in nearby Irvington. They invite me, so I go. I wear a yellow belt and still work out at the Castro Valley dojo. Ross Farmer is a yellow belt like me and Charlie Farmer is a brown belt. The garage is crowded and loud, with oppressive body heat. Centered in the garage, is a wood 4x4 brown painted post wrapped with foam, and it adds to the claustrophobia. A competitive fire fills the dojo. After a solid warm-up, no time is spared; I'm paired up with my first opponent and match. That night's workout was more like a tournament, than the lessons I'm familiar with. It's weird doing judo in a different dojo; the mats are too hard, you don't know who's who. Everybody seems anxious to show off their skills, challenge the new kid, beat him. Nippon!

Competition is fierce but I hold my own and Ross and I become friends. Charley's older so we don't talk. Ross is a year younger so our friendship is limited, plus the family is a little rough, hard overall. Oddly, in the shade of the Farmer's front porch, are two 55-gallon, sealed metal drums, *full of corn-nuts*! Corn-nuts of the utmost quality and freshness. How Mr. Farmer acquired 110 gallons of the salted, roasted delicacy is a mystery. The nuts provide the nutritional foundation for Jackson

Street's budding youth, a two year daily supply of protein and energy. This may help explain the above average physical strength and stamina of the male youth on Jackson Street. A theory based on nutritional science.

The Jackson Street community defines my world for the next ten years.

Kevin Finley lives three houses east on our side of the street. The Finleys moved in two months before us. Kevin is two years younger than I, as tall, sharp (deep thinker), musical and athletic. Kevin's got it all. The Finley's first names all start with the letter K; Mr. Keith Finley, Mrs. Kathy Finley, Kamela, Kevin and Kristen. Kamela is my age and grade, very smart and funny.

Kevin is older in his class and I'm younger in mine. So we're closer in age, than in education. Though two grades behind me, the high caliber, private education that Kevin receives, evens us up or exceeds me academically. Kevin and I share a lot in common: sports, the common creek area behind our houses, and a mutual creative penchant for trouble, so we hit it off.

Kevin's freedom is limited and well delineated, he plays outside within set boundaries, for example: not beyond Jeff Cardoso's house west and not beyond Troyer Avenue east. Mr. and Mrs. Finley are protective. They want Kevin to avoid trouble. Mr. and Mrs. Finley have religious convictions that I don't understand or ponder. Kevin and his sisters attend Prince of Peace Lutheran School, a private Christian school, kindergarten through eighth grade on Fremont Boulevard near Centerville; a fine school, in operation today. Mrs. Finley and the children attend Prince of Peace Lutheran Church on Sunday mornings.

Mission Valley Elementary School (public) is close to home and it's where most Jackson Street kids go to school. I finish fifth grade and did sixth grade at Chadbourne Elementary School. Chadbourne is one mile away from our new house, and Mission Valley is a quarter mile away.

Chadbourne has the MGM program and Mission Valley does not. During Easter break, Pappa bought me a very cool, stripped down, white Schwinn Stingray from the big flea market on Foothill Road in Hayward, so the extra distance to Chadbourne is no biggie. There's a couple days left for Easter break, so Mom suggests I do a trial ride to Chadbourne. It's sunny out and I have a good ride.

Jackson Street is full of great people. Ken and Olney Starr live next door west. The Starrs are ten years older than Mom and Pappa. The four adult children from Olney's previous marriage are named Croh, not Starr. William Croh is the eldest, then Fay, Wilma and Stanley. Fay and Wilma have one child each. Junior (Marja's age) is Fay's son and Donnie (Tessa's age) is Wilma's son.

William Croh is a popular local businessman who owns and operates the successful typesetting company Royal Type, located on Fremont Boulevard, near the General Motors Plant.

Olney's new husband Kenny Starr, grew up on a farm next to a river in Oklahoma, and is a union carpenter. Kenny told me once, he had it made in Oklahoma, 'room to roam, spacious skies, great fishing and a river to swim in when it was hot out.' And, 'farming wasn't hard either, just till the dirt in rows and pop the seeds in the ground yay apart, boink, boink, boink, easy." The Starr's backyard is deep like ours, but unlike ours, their extra south 50' is flat, fenced, cultivated and incorporated into the backyard; by far the most impressive vegetable garden around. The six foot high, wood framed, wire fencing around the garden is see-through, and provides a great view of the charming creek area and its sycamores, cottonwoods and willow trees. As sure as the turning of the earth, twice a year, Kenny Starr sows his garden of eden, reaping bumper crops. Great soil, dirty fingernails and the best garden in Fremont. A couple houses down live the Topper family. Salt Lake City Mormon transplants, the Toppers are another large family on Jackson Street. Mr.

Topper is a union carpenter like Mr. Starr and a retired rodeo star. As a young Utah cowboy, Mr. Topper traveled the rodeo circuit and enjoyed success. Mr. Topper drives an older, mid-60's, green Dodge pickup. The truck's round headlights framed in white trim, give the old truck a sagely, owlish appearance. Mrs. Topper is a seamstress for United Airlines and drives a luxury car to work; a new, gold Chrysler. The Topper children are, starting with the oldest: Valerie (Hannah's age), Marlo (same age and grade as me), and the twins, Tray and Macon, 5 years younger than Marlo and I.

Sport interest in Fremont is very high and suits me. My interest in basketball grows during its season. Marlo T. and Kevin F. have baskets & backboards, secured to their parent's roofs at the top of their driveways and I spend considerable time at both residences, perfecting my hook shot.

The Vanderbergs live at the west end of Jackson Street, on the corner of Olive Avenue and Jackson Street. Mr. and Mrs. Vanderberg have four children, John the eldest an adult, Bill who joined the Marines (A Marine becomes a real man fast), Darin, two years older than me and Vicky, three years younger than me. Darin and I are not friends the first year.

On our side of the street west, Jeff Cardoso lives three houses down. Jeff is two grades behind me, like Kevin Finley. Jeff's mother is divorced. Two and three houses west of Jeff Cardoso, live the Cortez family and the Wellbaum family respectively.

Stately Olive Avenue runs east and west in a straight line. Beginning at Washington Avenue, Olive Avenue heads east, crosses our little creek, passes Jackson Street and Chadbourne Drive, crosses Paseo Padre and continues to Palm Avenue. Turn right on Palm Avenue, over the new 680 freeway, immediately turn left and you're back on Olive Avenue, resume east and Olive Avenue ends at Starr Street. Olive Avenue's median from Troyer Avenue to Starr Street, is lined with beautiful and mature fruit-bearing olive trees.

On the southside of Olive Avenue, Jackson Street and Barbary Street form a loop. Jackson Street follows a seasonal creek bed, the same creek that runs behind my parent's new house. Continue six houses east past Kevin's house, and you can either turn left on Troyer Avenue and return to Olive Avenue, or continue straight three more houses and must go left onto Barbary Street which also leads back to Olive Avenue.

Marion Avenue runs parallel with Olive Avenue, between Troyer Avenue and Jackson Street, it tees into both. At the corner of Marion Avenue and Jackson Street is the Topper house and directly across Jackson Street is the Cortez house and the Wellbaum house.

Why the minutiae? Because it's here on Jackson Street and its congruous arteries, I grow up, we grow up. Within this finite suburban solar system my orbits spin; its planets, moons, sun and stars, await our discovery.

In this seemingly boring setting, the extraordinary can and does happen.

For my new friends and I, the world beyond Jackson Street, doesn't matter much.

This is where we laugh, grow, and learn about *one another and ourselves*. Where we live, love and die, stumble and fall.

Architecturally, Jackson Street residences consist of two types. The Zolanski/Lansing/Farmer side of the street, from Olive to Barbary are modest single-story flat tops, older homes, built in the 50's. Marion Avenue, Troyer Avenue and the south side of Olive Avenue from Jackson Street to Troyer Avenue, are also this type. On the south side of Jackson Street, our side, from Olive Avenue to Jeff Cardoso's house, are typical flat-tops. However, from Jeff's house east to Barbary Street,

Starrs / Us / Finleys the homes are newer, 1966-1972 with pitched, composition roofs. Additionally, both sides of Barbary Street are modern too. Interestingly the north side of Olive Avenue is a mix of older custom homes including a few estates.

On the south side of Jackson Street, across from Troyer Avenue is a field, two empty lots together. For the inclined, this field provides easy access to the creek, and the famous: *Jackson Street rope-swing*. This segment of the creek is deeper and wider, the banks rise 15' on both sides. Humongous Eucalyptus trees line both sides of the creek on top of its banks here.

An ordinary boy nearby, achieved the extraordinary. A young man, a brave soul, courageous like the conquistadors Columbus and Magellan, with enough David faith to strike down Goliath. His name is Christopher Peters; a skinny white kid from Marion Avenue, only a year older than me, he is this man.

With calculated reckless courage . . . Chris Peters, climbed the biggest, tallest eucalyptus tree on the planet, shimmied far, far out on its longest, highest, farthest reaching limb, to dizzying heights over the deep creek bed, and secured the thickest, strongest, heaviest rope any of us ever saw. The overall height from this tree branch to the bottom of the creek is a terrifying 60'! To fall would be to die, no more Chris. Why did Chris risk life and limb, to accomplish this amazing unselfish act?!? I don't know! But I'm lucky to live so close. What a feat!

The creek bed is wide, 20 yards. From the south bank the first-time-swinger stands and stares at the gnarly dark brown rope hanging in the middle of the creek bed, it's perfectly still, as thick as their arm, unholy. I lean way back, look up and squint, looking for the rope's point of attachment. There's the massive knot, secured to a magnificent limb, mechanically sound enough to swing an elephant. Eyes travel slowly down the rope's plumbed length. Wow. I can't believe this! There's no help around. I'd heard about the swing and Kevin Finley is with me, but seeing it for the first time, you know it isn't safe. This is dangerous! I begin to doubt whether I'll swing or not, I keep looking at it, searching for inner strength. I really want to. I *have* to do this.

From the creek bottom and a tight grip, the swinger takes hold of the massive knot on the rope's end, (looking up from here I'm dizzy by the distance to the knotted limb above) and scrambles up the south bank to level dirt. While going up, I feel the increasing weight of the massive rope's 60' length. There's more risk review before reaching full swing commitment.

There's no room for complacency, regardless of how many times you swing, the danger never subsides, it's only managed.

I straddle the 2x4 fastened to the end of the rope; once adequate courage is mustered, take a deep breath and swing . . . way, way, *waaay out there*, then back, 100' in each direction five or six times. Now what? Where should I jump off? You and Isaac Newton figure it out. Dismount at the starting point requires less work for the next jump, but the bottom works too (don't fall or trip or do something lame). We spend half the summer swinging on a rope. I haven't seen a swing close to this one. I don't believe Hannah, Marja or Tessa ever did *The Swing*, few girls did.

Later that first summer I met the 12 year old legend responsible for climbing and hoisting up that rope, high into the mighty tree's upper canopy. Chris Peters, only 12 years old, what insane bravery! And it's not hearsay, later, with my own eyes I watch Chris scale the giant trunk, shimmy out on that long horizontal limb to re-position the slip-knot farther out on the branch. The knot slipped back some, toward the trunk. It's hard to believe Chris tied such a thick rope so high above the ground, that anyone could do it. But seeing is believing.

Chris' swing never fails.

Chris lives on Marion Avenue, close to Troyer Avenue, just beyond my circle of friends. The reputation of Chris' swing is known throughout the land, visitors came from all over, most are grateful, well-behaved guests. Chris should receive a community achievement award, for his bravery and for the thrills and joy given to the youth of Mission San Jose, for installing the swing of our lives, the *pride* of Jackson Street.

My city-mouse past gives me a unique perspective of Jackson Street and Fremont. There's definitely a Tom Sawyer-Huck Finn undercurrent here.

The new Interstate 680 behind the house, opened two months before we moved in. Neighbors tell us, before 680 went in, it was a straight shot to Mission Peak. Before the freeway came in, every morning and evening, deer and other wildlife from the hills roamed along our creek, visiting Jackson Street backyards. The Starr's reflect fondly on the pre-680 critter sightings.

Every weekend the roar and thunder of the Fremont Dragstrip fills the air. Practically in our backyard, amateurs and pros race their cars down the famous quarter-mile. The professional drivers are colorful characters and immensely popular; "Big Daddy" Don Garlits, Don "the Snake" Prudhome and "Cha Cha" Shirley Muldowney to name a few. In their dragsters and funny cars they achieve incredible speeds, constantly breaking speed records.

Last but definitely not least, next door to and west of the Cortez's, live the Wellbaum family. Mrs. Wellbaum is a very nice, young divorced Mexican mother. Her four children are Guy, the oldest, two years older than me. Daniel or Danny, one year older than me. Curtis, one year younger than me and Julie, Tessa's age. Their German father Mr. Wellbaum, lives in Fort Bragg and is a commercial fisherman. He visits the boys once a year on Christmas and gives them each $20 (small fortune). Danny and I spend a lot of time together, riding bikes, fishing, and engaging in mischief.

Mrs.Wellbaum has a sister, Mrs. Aubrey, who also has three sons and lives on Fremont's east frontier; beyond the Aubrey home, are miles and miles of unspoiled wilderness. Her sons are David (Guy's age), Peewee (Curtis' age) and Gary (three years younger than me). The Aubrey brothers and Wellbaum brothers (and sister) are first cousins. Mr. Aubrey is a long distance trucker. Mrs. Wellbaum and Mrs. Aubrey are sisters and Hispanic, Mr. Wellbaum is German and Mr. Aubrey is Welch. Later I chide Danny, and call him a german brown, like the trout. With a wilderness for a backyard, the Aubrey boys grow up wild and fearless, like indian braves. They're unlike anyone I've met before or since. Their ability with a rifle and bow are legendary; uncanny, instinctive, *fast and accurate*. All day long the Aubrey boys roam and hunt the vast Ohlone Wilderness.

Mission San Jose High School's wooden Warrior Tower rises from the campus like an old frontier fort lookout, clearly visible from the hills across Mission Boulevard. I've never told Mom and Pappa or my nice sisters any of these things, such as the arrows stuck fast to the top of the old tower. Pointless.

Another Jackson Street friend, Wade Jennings, is my age and the youngest of another large family, Wade lives on Marion Avenue, three houses off Jackson Street. Wade's a tough hombre from a tough family. We did a lot together.

MGM Meltdown

Marja also tests for the MGM Program and is accepted, so Marja attends Chadbourne too. The fifth and sixth grade MGM classes at Chadbourne are full time. MGM all day, every day. Fourth grade MGM (Marja) is part time, once a week, like at Ruus Elementary School in Palma Ceia.

In Fremont my education, at least on the report card, struggles. In Hayward, I connect the dots. In Fremont I have to find the dots and connect them, but they're elusive, far apart, obscure. At Chadbourne from day one I feel left behind, because I *am* behind. I attempt to regain traction and catch up; I flail about but grasp air and slip further. Running within clearly marked lanes is replaced by confusion, and I lose interest in school.

In Fremont, fought-for-respect, and teacher discipline is gone. This freedom is new. The absence of the fear of discipline equates to disinterest in schoolwork. My new fifth grade teacher is great. Mrs. Vanderzee is so enthusiastic and smart, super talented in theater. If on an average school day Mr. Turentine spoke 1,000 words, then Mrs. Vanderzee 6,000! At Ruus, I'm familiar with a certain pace and the satisfaction of accomplishment. In Mr. Turentine's class, the directives were clear and orderly, delivered in calm baritone, upheld by a yardstick.

On the day I left Ruus Elementary School in Hayward, academically, I peaked. At Chadbourne Elementary in Fremont, the last two months of 5th grade, I start a long scholastic slide. I lack drive to achieve, no long term goals, no dreams. No legs, no lanes, no targets, no belief system, living inside my private moral vacuum.

Seven years later, I miss high school graduation. I don't walk.

I go from, top of the class, to the bottom. No alarm is sounded, no gong heard, no catch up plan implemented; what's a tutor? Deaf and blind to cause and effect, the principle of consequence. Awkward as hell.

At Chadbourne I try, but cannot get my head around the style of study in Mrs. Vanderzee's class. Where am I? Please give me an outline, a game plan, what's a syllabus? I wish I knew, I would have asked for one. I don't "figure it out." Speak directly, please be clear.

Yada, yada, yada, yada, yada, yada. All day long! Everybody gets it. I know they do. With a sixth sense the students interpret what Mrs. Vanderzee lays down. Mrs. Vanderzee can't go fast enough, the kids are almost bored! I'm thinking, "oh Jens, this is bad."

MGM, with all its promise, distinction, and recognition, is my failure.

On day one Mrs. Vanderzee asked me, "are you going on the field trip?" What is she talking about? "In four days we're flying to Sacramento, to visit the State Capitol." What is she talking about?!? 'You'll need parental permission and the cost is eight dollars." Eight dollars?! I'm getting 25 cents a week allowance Mrs. Vanderzee, where am I going to get eight dollars? I don't ask her to explain. I'll figure it out.

I think about stuff more than I talk about stuff.

Mom and Pappa sign the permission slip, pay the eight bucks and I fly with my new fifth grade class, 20 minutes by jet, to Sacramento. Flying is a dream. We tour the State Capital Building and the shipping canals and locks. We lean over the railing and watch the water level rise and fall, allowing the large boats to continue their voyage.

The MGM students in my fifth and sixth grade classes @ Chadbourne Elementary are beyond exceptional. Like a room full of noisy, intelligent adults, but in child bodies and higher voices.

They carry *so much concern*, spoken and unspoken. Half the class verbalizes everything on their minds, and it's a lot. Endless facts and opinions to whomever will listen, and someone *always* listens *and* understands. The energy! A few male students say little, almost mute. The quiet ones reserve speech for something clever, funny or critical.

The class works hard on their top-priority project: this year's, annual drama production, The Wizard of Oz. This is exciting, definitely my favorite thing going on here. OZ preparations dominate the day. Unfortunately, casting finished days before I arrived. Susan Singer plays OZ; Kay Kavash, Dorothy; Pamela West, the Wicked Witch of the East; Kris Temper, the Good Witch etc. etc. etc.

A serious red-head boy, James Kent, depicts lovable Toto. Red pointed ears, red whiskers, red freckles, and that's *before* make-up (jokey, jokey) a full body dog suit, the whole nine yards.

The only other rebels in the class (I didn't know I was a rebel until Chadbourne, must be the long hair), and both from the historic Níles area are, Neal Black and Linden Braningham. Sharp-tongued and very smart, angry Neal is the best artist in the class, in the school. The boy can draw, a cartoonist mostly but can draw anything, very well. Cool as a cucumber, ice-man Linden, a handsome rich kid, great hair. Quiet, not one to speak foolishly, Linden's comments are clever and funny, with a snobbish odeur. Linden and Neal are mouthy and rude to Mrs. Vanderzee. I've never seen rude behavior from a student to the teacher like this. Amazingly, their rudeness is tolerated by Mrs. Vanderzee - though she's visibly annoyed - stinging barbs uttered without consequence!? I want to see them try *that* on Mr. Turentine. That would be great. I'd pay 59 cents to see that.

Pamela West and Mrs. Vanderzee work on Pam's delivery of the Wicked Witch's evil laugh. "Try it like this," says Mrs. V. Pam nails it. So loud, so evil, perfect. I missed the casting, and by default am designated to stage crew, specifically lighting. Switching them off and on, on cue. My artistic contribution is the big tornado scene; I flick light switches off and on frantically, creating the appearance of lightning. OZ is a musical and while greedy songbirds sing solos to adoring audiences (three performances), Linden, Neal and I are hidden, in the dark, pulling curtain ropes and operating spotlight switches. Neal and Linden are behind the scenes by choice; I have no choice, bad timing, bad timing. Doesn't Mrs. Vanderzee know? I'm a Russian dancer for crying out loud, commie-trained, with stage experience. I'm no stranger to the stage Mrs.Vanderzee, the hot lights, the applause, I can take it Mrs. Vanderzee, I want to sing. I feel like the last kid to be picked for a baseball or football team, had that ever happened, which it had not. The kid who hides, who's afraid, stage crew. Ehh, maybe there's time.

Whaddya got for me Jon Voight?

Major disappointments fester with time. Minor setbacks like this, for the wise, patient, and understanding, *fuel* healthy ambition, motivate one to succeed, get up, get ready, prepare. "Own it and move forward." I sell it, torch it, roll it downhill over the cliff, and the whole kit and kaboodle plunge headlong into the black abyss.

The beloved playground, the place to play and compete with classmates and friends, show-off to girls, remains reliable and now becomes my only contact with non-MGM Students. 80% of MGM males don't engage in athletics during lunch and recess. Linden and Neal do however and we become friends.

My dirty blonde mane peaks at Chadbourne, past the shoulders. Crew-cut stud Mike Ventura harasses me about it, insinuates it's feminine. Mike got to me that day. I remember it now, so he must have. I wish it was longer, and I have no intentions to cut it, ever. My long hair is not related to rock music, or an act of rebellion, it's just me. My musical influences to date are Elvis, the Beatles and Motown. I like long hair.

Mike V's twin brother Ed (not identical) is a beast and Mike uses this to his advantage. Ed has the muscle, Mike has the mouth.

MGM students are separate from the general student body, and naturally ostracized by them. The Mike Venturas, Mark Munsters, and Bill Motts, are green with MGM envy and prove it with verbal persecution, but many others scoff *quietly*. I hear them, see them, *feel* them, everyday at Chadbourne. Not every acute sense blesses their receptor.

Oblivious to insult and envy, Chadbourne's MGM pride is conditioned for it; insular, thick skinned, barbs ricochet off. An academic aristocracy. Like, "of course the other students hate us." Bred and groomed to achieve in this life. Princes trained by kings, the art of rule; diplomacy, what to do, what not to do. What to say, what not to say. What is expected, how to react, how to deal with adversity and always, always, exhibit strength, not weakness. Fortitude! My fifth and sixth grade classmates are like that. Truly.

With the morning's Wall Street Journal in hand, David Bauser and Brad Rosendenza discuss the stock market, bonds and mutual funds, David flapping page after page; he wears a suit and tie! Not asked to speak, yet convicted to speak out, April Griffith stands up at her desk, seizes control and addresses the surprised class. April informs us of various plights and injustices suffered around the world and viable solutions. From the front row, Ruth Glinda stands up, faces the class and delivers a blistering, stand-up comedy performance, AD-LIB! What does ad-lib mean? Robert Gilbane is pre-destined for military greatness. Stephen Trump's (future attorney) office will overlook the sea, Susan Singer and Karl Waters become prominent doctors, leaders in their fields.

And Jens, the lost sad Viking who cannot reinvent the wheel and has never had an original thought in his life. I shouldn't be here. Sure, I can read alright and I enjoy it but I'm sorely unprepared for the rigor and pressure of greatness, the responsibility.

It's these students, these teachers. *They* are my textbooks, my curriculum. Their expressions, moods, depth, everything.

I'm in over my head and know it . . . drowning.

Ten years old, bolo tie made by Pappa

Direct from Italy and Jack's new Studio

Pappa has a weekday routine, come home from work, Cal State Hayward's Art Department, enter his studio and work on art projects until dinner time, eat dinner (planned by Mom, prepared by us kids) with Hannah, Marja, Tessa and I - exchange updates - return to the studio, work until 10 o'clock, clean up and watch the evening news with Mom.

Mom gets a part-time job at the Emporium Capwells department store. She works in the sleep department, selling mattresses and bedding for hourly wages plus sales commission. She does well and works there 20 years, until Capwell's scuttles her store. Inger forges lasting friendships with female co-workers. Because of Europe's excellent public transportation system, Inger never learns to drive. However she lives in the East Bay now and two big surprises are on the way.

I have my Jackson Street routine, wake up, walk fluidly to the kitchen bursting with animal joy and dig up breakfast. I prepare my own breakfast, cold cereal and cold milk. This delicious duo has been my favorite since I could pick up a spoon, chomp and appreciate the attractive box illustrations; for the next 50 years I won't change this routine. This morning is no exception, I jump out of bed, leave my room, ramble down the hall and turn right through the kitchen doorway. I pass the quiet living room with the red brick fireplace, wait, something awry, stop, pivot, freeze, stare, mouth open. On the brown, low pile, wall-to-wall carpet, sit two large wood crates. One crate is wider than the other. Both have colored labels stuck on the outside, *"Made in Italy."* Wow, wow! What *are these*??

Direct from Italy: a 1972 fire-engine red, 180cc Vespa Rally scooter for Pappa, And a 1972 canary yellow, 50cc Vespa Ciao moped for Mom. Pappa drives the new scooter from Fremont to

Cal-State Hayward everyday, (weather permitting) sporting a white full-face helmet with either a clear or tinted shield and a thick heavy black leather jacket emblazoned with a huge *Vespa* patch on the back. Inger commutes to Emporium Capwells on her new moped, wearing her signature scarf and sweater, no helmet.

Inger owns and operates the first moped in Fremont. 110,000 people, and nobody's ever seen one. Overnight, my parents become minor local celebrities. Mom finishes work at 9:30 pm. Pappa closes shop, uses solvent-based paint thinner to wash off the oil-based paints that cover his large hands, kick-starts the Vespa and buzzes off to their nightly rendezvous.

Under the Mission San Jose moon, Jack escorts Inger home. The pair with European flair glide on Paseo Padre Parkway, past Lake Elizabeth and the Hobo Jungle. Once or twice I ride on the back of Pappa's Vespa and join Mom's escort. The Italian 2-stroke engines harmonize and make a nice sound. At home they shake off the cold, jackets are hung, scarf folded and Jack and Inger snuggle on the couch. They watch the evening news together. Walter Cronkite talks about the Vietnam War and the ongoing horrible Easter Offensive, and all the young men getting killed. Inger dips her finger in the sugar bowl.

Kenny and Olney Starr

Our charismatic next door neighbor, Kenny Starr, known to many as the "King of Jackson Street," has a farmer's influence on Jack. Shortly after the crated Vespas arrive, Pappa purchases a brand new Sears Craftsman, 8-horsepower rototiller, *with reverse*.

Sharp looking and powerful, a highly-capable machine, Pappa tills our entire backyard, all three tiers, plus the west side yard, between the garage and the Starr's fence. No stone left unturned. After a short lesson, I till the farm. The next three seasons, I till our entire backyard, and the Starr's south-forty, twice. Mr. Starr paid me $20 bucks to till his south garden. Next spring, I till it again, but for free, as punishment for an iniquity I don't recall. Moyer's famous potatoes are the main crop; also artichokes, corn, asparagus, beets, carrots, various squash, pumpkins etc. etc. etc. For the squash and pumpkins we form a half dozen dirt mounds, four-feet in diameter and set a coffee can with holes on the bottom into the dirt on top of the mound. The top of the can is flush with the top of the mound. We plant squash, zucchini and pumpkins on the mound. We water the seeds by filling the coffee can with water every few days. It works very well.

Planting and harvesting strengthen neighbor relationships; produce exchanges hands.

A typical Jackson Street weekend starts this way; Saturday is fix the car day. Kenny pops a top on the first Olympia beer and either drives, or with assistance, pushes the patient onto the driveway, flips open the hood. Soon (if not under their own hoods) the neighborhood, repair and support-group trickles over, Mr. Zolanski, Mr. Lansing, Pappa, Robert Brown, Alex Z. and others. Moral support and jokes are given in abundance, while helping themselves to Kenny's beer, and eventually drift away.

If the repair is too complex, outside of their wheelhouse: an engine swap or transmission replacement, Lambert gets the call. Lambert is Jackson Streets' chief auto-mechanic, and dear family friend. Highly respected, when Lambert shows up, it's like Elvis has entered the building, it's a-happening. Many neighbors are employees of the General Motors auto plant. Mr. Lansing, Mr. Zolanski and others know their way around a car or truck. But when Lambert picks up the wrench, they're humble and eager to learn from the master; me and Pappa too.

They all drink. Pappa doesn't hang out long, but tries to make a showing.

Mrs. Starr *loves everybody*. Every adult and every child. Always an enthusiastic greeting, beaming smile, always something to eat and drink. All kids are treated like grandkids, if you're white.

My first exposure to flaunted racial prejudice is Fremont. My Hispanic friends, the Wellbaums and Lopezes, are fully aware of the prejudice against them. They obviously don't like it. I didn't notice it at first, (my Mexican neighbors are acutely aware). It's subtle, but after a while, I see it clear enough, the prejudice against them. For ten years I heard it. Not just Jackson Street, but at high school especially.

In the Starr's kitchen, the counter and stools are packed with visitors, young and old. Coffee drinking cigarette smokers, beer drinking cigarette smokers, and cookie chomping kids, soon to be cigarette smokers, all sit shoulder to shoulder. Behind the counter, Mrs. Starr buzzes to and fro, pulling something out of the fridge, pulling something out of the oven, big smiles and laughs for everyone. Until the hoods drop, the driveway is full of visitors, two-beer bennies, greasy mechanics, the kitchen is full of visitors, all day! After car repairs conclude, men migrate, depending on the season, either to the south 40 for more beer, cocktails and horseshoes, or, a rowdy game of pool, with beer, cocktails, cigarettes and Mr. Zolanski's cigar; every weekend, all weekend, no exception, no exaggeration.

Jackson Street swarms with pre-teens, and teens, playing in the street. At dinnertime parents send forth Apollos or Hermes with an urgent message: "Princes, return to your castle and feast." Mom sends Hannah or Marja to call me in. They either walk past the Starrs and spot me in front of the Topper's shooting baskets or in the street playing two-hand touch football, or frisbee, or hide n go seek; or up the street toward Kevin Finley's in his driveway shooting baskets, or in the street orchestrating the winning drive, "Jens, dinner!" Street games are played either up the street near the Finley's, or down the street near the Topper's. Jackson Street bends in front of our house forming a blind curve, risky for street sport.

I tell the boys, "gotta go," toss em' the ball and run home to eat dinner . . . way too fast.

Summertime Swing

Fifth grade's done and summer begins! Neighborhood friendships and alliances are nurtured. Summer fun includes Jackson Street's famous rope-swing, all sports, bike antics, fort construction, go-kart building, model building, swimming and much more. Summer chores include backyard gardening, front yard mowing and KP duty. I earn pocket money by mowing lawns.

Maurice Garza is a gifted athlete and basketball player who lives next door to Wade Jennings on Marion Avenue. Maurice is my age and grade but doesn't mix with us much. His father is a great big man who works at the Ford Auto Plant in Milpitas.

Maurice breaks his arm on the rope swing.

He loses his grip at the farthest point of the swing's pendulum, opposite the launch side (worst case scenario) and drops like a ragdoll to the creek bed far below. Maurice heals quickly (6 weeks) and his cast is removed in time for the CYO Basketball Season.

40' behind our back fence, in the creek area, a large, five foot diameter, 300' long, buried concrete culvert runs from our house, past the Finley house. The culvert is large enough for Kevin and I to walk through, if we bend our knees and lean forward slightly. Water and mud run through it but we straddle the muck.

60' behind our back fence is the new Interstate 680, Washington Boulevard off-ramp. A hill rises up 20' to the off-ramp with no guard-rail. We call it Horseshoe Hill. Long ago, boys formed a trail in the shape of an elongated horseshoe on the side of the hill next to the off-ramp. For hours, friends and I ride our bikes up and down Horseshoe Hill. We build a wood jump-ramp and position it at the bottom of one side. The daring ones race on the road over the culvert, ascend the left side of Horseshoe Hill and roll down the right side, launching off the homemade wood-ramp (collected 2x4s, plywood, nails). This is a typical 1970's activity my friends and I engage in and enjoy immensely.

A new family moves in next door, on the east side. Mr. and Mrs. Tyrell have three daughters, lovely, fun and a bit intimidating, Dorothy, Sherry, and Glenda. Sherry is my age and grade, Glenda three years younger and Dorothy four years older. Mr. Tyrell digs graves at Chapel of the Chimes on Mission Boulevard in Hayward. All three daughters are pleasant, spirited and cute. I'm *lucky.*

My friends and I are hands-on, but I'm not as good with tools or building projects like some are. We build tree-forts, ground-forts and gravity powered go-karts from wood. Wood is the building material of choice. Wood and saw, hammer and nail and always . . . made in the USA.

Kevin Finley, Marlo Topper and Maurice Garza are the neighborhood jocks. Football, basketball, and baseball. In addition, Kevin F. excels in gymnastics, high-jump, ping-pong, tennis, frisbee, Jokari and boomerang.

Only Kevin and I do Jokari and boomerang.

Jokari involves a 2 1/2" x 7" x 7" wooden block base and a handball-sized rubber ball, connected by a 15' long, strong, stretchy rubber cord. The wooden base has an anti-skid bottom and stays put to the street, unbelievably well. It takes Kevin F. and I an hour to master Jokari, but we finally do. With solid wood paddles the size of tennis rackets but on short handles, we stand side by side like in the game handball, and alternate crushing the ball as hard as possible in the same direction, forward. Our hardest whacks may cause the block to jump a foot, but that's it.

Jokari entertains Kevin and I for hours. A small group of fans enjoy the novelty. Try as we might, the stretch-band would . . . not . . . snap!

Bike jumping attracts all Jackson Street males (except Maurice and Bucky). I already told you about the horseshoe jump behind the house. To take jumping to the next level, we have to increase speed. We devised a two-prong plan: 1. Build a larger, stronger, Evel Knievel-grade jump ramp, and 2. Set the ramp on the street, in front of our house, to achieve maximum speed for maximum jump distance. The master builder, Darin Vanderberg, and I, design, construct and paint the ramp. Darin builds it strong, able to withstand a motorcycle. We position the ramp in the street off-center, so cars can pass. To measure jump distances, we get a 25' tape measure, make stencils for striping and numbering, get white spray paint, spray white stripes every foot and numbers- in multiples of five, up to 20 feet. We paint a straight white line up the middle of the ramp to help jumpers line their bikes up for the approach. Every boy with a bike, takes turns on the ramp. Ride way up the street (past Kevin Finley's house if you're serious), pause psyche up and with the help of Jackson Street's gentle downslope, sprint to the ramp and fly. A spotter mans the ramp to verify jump distance (spot at back wheel, not front). To entertain ourselves and attract interest, those able, ride wheelies up the street (me included). Daring souls lie belly-up in front of the ramp. Guys *and* gals do this. Such trust. Four, even five kids get jumped over! I'm pleased to report, nobody ever got hurt.

We'd been jumping for a while when Sherry Tyrell showed up.

Darin Vanderberg say's, "I'll go," and rides a wheelie all the way to Troyer Avenue, turns around and waits. Darin, 600 feet away, confirms Sherry's watching, then pauses a minute, letting suspense build. We all feel it.

There's a summer crowd assembled, Jimmy and Dean Lansing, Donna Lansing, Paula and Charlene Lansing, Sonya on the grass, Alex Zolanski, brother Denny and Smokey their dog, "Smoky go home!" Marlo Topper, Valerie Topper, the three Wellbaum brothers, Kevin Finley, me, Dorothy and Glenda Tyrell, Rose Pimentel and of course Sherry Tyrell. There's a sense something unprecedented and of utmost importance is about to happen.

Darin Vanderberg flies down Jackson Street, every muscle strained, possessed. The bike cannot be pedaled faster. The ramp welcomes the violent impact. Darin the Rocket Vanderberg flies through space and into the record books. There's no doubt, several eyewitnesses testify; Darin's back wheel clears the 20 foot mark! No one ever gets close, 50 years later, the record stands; as does Darin Vanderberg's other record;

Hopkins Junior High School: *Most Pull-Ups, 25.*

Darin Vanderberg, two years older, is many things; outstanding builder, workaholic, capable auto mechanic, audiophile, long term boyfriend, superior fighter and stronger than you. The long list of honorable attributes bring Darin V. respect, and we look up to Darin. Darin is well-liked and feared. Darin is that fight you don't want. That said, he is never a bully, but rather meek. Darin pokes fun, teases if you ask for it, but he's a leader. Darin's on your side, the walking definition of advocate. His ear for music and ability to set-up cutting edge audio systems for home and auto, is without equal and showers us with music bliss, when we need it most, while we're young. For perspective, Pappa's Ford station wagon has an AM radio. At home, Pappa's antique Telefunken AM/FM radio and ultra-basic turntable with ultra-low performance speakers, can't hold a candle to what I'm beginning to see out there.

Jack and Inger's vinyl collection remains my musical cornerstone, absolutely, but the Moyer TV is black and white. Because of my parents' advanced age, musically speaking, they're behind the times a smidge (and that's okay), but consequently so am I.

Darin Vanderberg fixes that.

As elementary school grinds to a halt, two things happen, 1. I kiss Rose Pimentel (my first kiss) and 2. I lose traction in school.

The gals from Jackson Street deserve recognition; in spite of every adversity known to women, they all graduate high school. The Lansing daughters: Donna, Charlene and Paula. Kamela and Kristen Finley, my three sisters, Julie Wellbaum, Valerie Topper, the Tyrell sisters. All strong women, all graduates.

In stark contrast, the Jackson Street guys in mass exodus, exit high school, and transfer to our district's continuation school; Williamson, in Irvington, then quit school altogether. These are my friends, my Jackson Street brothers I grow up with.

Irvington is one of five Townships that form the City of Fremont. The five Townships are: Mission San Jose (east), Niles (north), Irvington (central) Centerville (west) and Warm Springs (south).

Sherry Tyrell, my cute neighbor, is tall, slender, fair and blonde, my age and grade. Pretty and tough, a country girl. Did I mention, next door? The Tyrell girls ride horses. Glenda will become a national champion barrel racer. The family boards their horses on nearby Osgood Road.

In the summer of 1973, Sherry and I bat an eye. If you blink, you miss it. A few days at most. On the day of Sherry's birthday party, I got some red stuff in my hair, from running around the front lawn and brushing up against the large bottle-brush bush, in-between our front yards. Dorothy says, "Jens, the only way to get that red stuff out of your hair, is to wash it." Dorothy looks out for me and is absolutely right. It's Sherry's birthday, but I don't feel like washing my hair, so because I'm too lazy to wash my hair (shampoo lather, rinse, repeat), I skip Sherry's party. That ends that. Our last encounter was Halloween night that year. I knocked on the Tyrell's door and Sherry answered with a girlfriend, Rose Pimentel, both dressed in cute costumes. "Hi Sherry, hi Rose," "Hi Jens, happy Halloween," and smashes two raw eggs in my hair! The two explode in laughter and shut the door. I found the energy to wash my hair that time. I have to say, after that egg treatment, my hair's never been softer or more lustrous.

Darin on the other hand, is very interested in Sherry, and their courtship lasts five years.

By doing tons of free house & yard work for Mr. and Mrs. Tyrell, Darin ingratiates himself to Sherry's parents. Soon, the two are inseparable and Darin practically lives next door.

Darin V. enjoys work more than anybody I know. This is foreign to me but intriguing; building things, mowing lawns, raking leaves, house painting, accomplish, accomplish, do, do, do, the energy! Like Tom Sawyer, Darin makes work seem fun to others, but unlike Tom Sawyer, Darin honestly enjoys work. Darin's Uncle Tom owns and operates a successful landscaping business. Darin works for Uncle Tom often and this inspires my friends and I to embrace work. If we're willing, Darin hires us to help him do landscape jobs near home. Those jobs are cash-driven, the Tyrell work, *Amore*-driven.

Since Darin V. is next door every waking minute, we do more stuff together. Darin converts the Tyrell garage into a pool room. "Rack 'em up . . . eight ball, corner pocket."

Darin does it all solo, cleans out the packed-solid garage, acquires the pool table, the balls, the rack, the cue-sticks mounted cleanly on the freshly textured and painted wall, cue chalk, hand talc. Top notch, a first class set-up. And the best part? A powerful AM/FM stereo with a phonograph super-saturates the air-space, the latest rock albums constantly spin. Softer rock edges out harder stuff, better suited for Sherry and the Tyrrell family. Elton John's greatest hits I & II, Peter Frampton Live, Aerosmith etc. etc. etc. I love listening to Darin's music. Always clear, always stereo, and always loud, you can hear 200' in every direction. Darin and Sherry's relationship erase previous awkward feelings and I am 100% comfortable now with everyone there, and they with me.

Darin and I begin working together. Our first co-project is a fort behind my back fence; the fence forms the fort's north wall. Together after dinner, at dusk, we ride bikes through the creek, cross Washington Boulevard and up a short hill, a dirt road. New homes are being built there. The dirt road ascends from Washington Boulevard directly across from the Northbound 680 on-ramp. I don't know what the plan is, but Darin does. We each pick up a 4'x 8'x 3/4" sheet of plywood from a pile next to a new framed house. There are so many new houses being built and so many piles of wood, our haul is a needle in the haystack. Without hesitation, Darin V. and I each balance a single sheet of plywood on our backs, steady them with one hand, like a turtle shell, coast down the dirt road, across Washington Boulevard and drop into the creek out of sight. We go back for 4"x 4"x 8' posts, one each and 2"x4"x8's. Next morning, construction begins.

Darin's fort project is worthy of note. His first step is the raised foundation. Using a post-hole digger, Darin and I dig six holes, two feet deep, for six 4x4 posts. The two posts are cut into six equal lengths, then set 10" above ground, leveled and packed tight. Next, 2x4 floor joists are measured, cut and nailed down tight. Then plywood is measured, sawed and nailed to the floor framing, thus a raised floor is established, square and level.

With a single extension cord rolled out, a borrowed circular-saw, tape measures, sharpened yellow #2 Pencils (before, only for tests and homework) set smartly on one ear, we transform Darin's dream into a fortress reality.

For Darin, fort construction is serious. Quality counts. Like we're building a real house!

Would there be a door? Windows? Electric outlets, lighting? A *stereo*?? With Darin Vanderberg, anything is possible.

Build day 1 is strictly Darin and I. Intense focus, rapid progress. The foundation and floor are done. Curiosity shows up on day 2, friends pitch in, pick up hammers and drive nails. Guy and Danny Wellbaum, Kevin Finley, Marlo Topper and others. Framed walls are erected and yes, two windows are framed, east and west. The entire roof is a plywood sun deck complete with railing. The roof/deck height is flush with the top of the fence. We can stand inside without bumping our heads. A single front-door, floor to ceiling faces south. Mom and Pappa are impressed. In the 70's, housing is affordable.

Sixth Grade Synopsis

Besides kissing Rose Pimentel in the sixth grade, two other memories stand out.

A new public electric train arrives in the bay area, Bay Area Rapid Transit or BART. A Fremont station is built. The Fremont BART station is the end of the BART line. There are no BART stations south of Fremont. Schools organize field trips to ride the sleek futuristic trains. The BART field trips for Marja and I, scheduled on two different days, are both canceled for extraordinary reasons.

As my chatty, noisy yellow school bus nears the BART station, an eerie silence fills the bus. In plain view, a shiny new, brushed aluminum BART car, with large tinted windows, the end car, has *crashed through* the runaway barricade, and *sits lifeless,* marooned on the 30 degree earthen run-away ramp. The accident just happened minutes before we arrived. Brown dirt hangs in the air surrounding the disabled train.

BART's runaway train barricade works beautifully! And fortunately, it was only a test run, so no passengers. Yay!

30-11 year old MGM mouths hang open, wide-eyed glaring at the crash, then at each other, at the crash, each other etc. etc. etc.

Mrs. Splaingard makes an announcement: "today's BART field trip has been canceled."

Funnier still, when Marja's class goes to BART, and their noisy, chatty yellow school bus nears the BART Station, confused silence fills the bus, In plain view, an impressive row of long black limousines are parked in front of the new station, where busses are supposed to park. Men in black suits stand next to the limousines. Small American flags on the black hoods, flap in the steady

Fremont breeze.

30-10 year old MGM mouths hang open, wide eyed, glaring at long black limousines and men

in black suits, then at each other, then at long black limousines, at men in black suits, each other

etc. etc. etc.

President Nixon decided to visit Fremont's state of the art BART station, today!

Mrs. Brees makes an announcement: "today's BART field trip has been canceled."

Round two: Chadbourne's entire sixth grade class waits on the station platform next to the

tracks and the deadly, electrified third rail, for the next BART train to glide in and whisk us away.

At the BART station we each receive a brown bag lunch and are told not to eat yet, hang on to it

until we get to our destination. We're going to Fairyland in Oakland. As the first *moving* BART

train we've ever seen approaches, Mark Munster shouts loudly so all can hear and comically fake-

stumbles, as if he's about to fall onto the tracks in front of the oncoming train. To save himself

from being electrocuted and squished, Mark sacrifices his brown bag lunch, tossing it on the

tracks, to get squished in his place. The incoming BART car obliterates Mark's peanut butter and

jelly sandwich, carrot sticks and milk carton. Critics agree, Mark performed well.

A depart from BART please:

Mr. Bautista, a math teacher, coaches Chadbourne's flag-football team, and competes against

other schools in the area. Having started last year late, I was unaware the school *had* an organized

football team.

My fellow MGMrs and I are isolated from the athletic heart of the school, and its football team.

I don't recall a try-out. I'm on the outside looking in. Ahh, I want to play and I show up to practice. Chadbourne has some real studs, Mark Munster, Ray Weisbrod, Tony Clarin, Lee Sparks, Bill Hegland and many others. Lee and Bill are track stars. Ray is an everything star. John Matthews plays quarterback and has a good arm, but most important, he has the *confidence* of the coach and team.

Whenever I spot Coach Bautista during recess or lunch, I make sure to zip bullets and bombs around, hoping he'll notice. They lost the week prior and for the season's last game, coach Bautista makes me back-up quarterback! Not my first choice but second-str*ing* is better than no strings attached.

I watch the first half from the sideline, we're behind. The second half starts and coach B. says, "Jens, get in there!" I love playing catch at recess and quarterbacking at home, but organized play? Lead a *full-size offense*? Direct a *huddle*? I have no idea, I'm a rookie, a green-weenie.

I want three things: points, a win, and glory.

Nervous in the huddle, I try to speak right, "Ray, go deep; down the left side and slant toward the middle." I tell another receiver to run a short pattern, down and out right, "in case they blitz." Something else new, instant pass rush. Intense pressure to find an open receiver and complete a pass. I'll be rushed immediately, if not sooner! I encourage our offensive line to, "*stop* the rush, *give* Ray time to run deep." I set the snap count, "on three." We line up well. For show, I eyeball the defense.

I'm brimming with hope.

"Hut! . . Hut! . . Hut!" I take the snap, secure the ball while taking five steps back. Eyes on Ray, I instinctively spin the ball in my right hand aligning the ball laces to my fingers, when it feels right I lock on. While back stepping, I fake a look at my #2 receiver on the short pass route, sense the incoming pass rush and decide where to set. I look for Ray, find him and set to pass. He's

running the correct route, starting to slant inward and open just enough, leading his defender (he's

so fast), creating space. I can't underthrow, or I'll get picked off. I'm disrupted, pressure comes

from my right side, turn left, run three steps, to avert the sack. Ray races downfield in no time. I set

again to pass, Ray slant to middle, yes! Bomb it, lead him, a lofty spiral, it feels positive but he's

not wide open. Ray's athletic, gifted, a selfless playmaker. The strongest, quickest guy on the team,

in the school. The bomb gives the defense time to zero in, Ray's in traffic. Ray hauls it in! First

down and more! 35 yard gain! Yes!

"Great job." Let's slow it down go conservative, confuse the defense, mix it up and do a run

play. "Mark, line up right and sweep left behind me, I'll toss it to you.' "Block left, run left. On

four, clap (huddle hype) break!" I space out the count a little. Hut! . . . Hut! . . . Hut! . . . Hut!"

Snap, got it, good job center - what's his name? I don't know - turn right, look back, there's tall

jock, class clown Mark Munster, on cue, beautiful, alright Mark! Toss back to him, lead him,

stomach high, not too hard, not too soft, on the money. Mark drops the ball! No! No!!

The theatrical bobble looks *too* familiar. Mark, are you throwing this game? Mark? Mark?!?

Four years later, Mark and I have our day, a *battle-royal.*

Longest hair ever, football passes, long spirals farther than anyone in the neighborhood,

including Marlo Topper, Maurice Garza and Darin Vanderberg. There is one boy, the bully Chico,

from Denise Street below Mission Valley Elementary, who makes a rare, one day only appearance

on Jackson Street. Chico the bull, the Mexican equivalent of Darin Vanderberg, throws a football

as far as I do, then farther. Chico, you're kidding me, amazing. I strain to match him, and do.

Chico pushed me to be better. Thank you Chico, you're the man!

That summer I helped build a fine fort, to be discovered 2,000 years later, by a robotic archaeological team. I'm training at a big-time judo dojo in Santa Clara. I'm ready for Hopkins Junior High and my first locker. True, my grades aren't exemplary, but I'm looking forward to it. Yes, I'm looking forward to it.

Eleven years old

Me, Mom and Grandmother Tessa

Hopkins Junior High 1973

48 hours before the start of the seventh grade, Pappa drives me to the barber.

A crew cut!

I'm traumatized; like Samson, my strength is gone. Punishment for a forgotten cruelty? This really chaffs my hide, literally. Pappa says I look great, yet, I don't believe him because he's bald. Unexpectedly, I don't get razzed by friends, or the girls. The haircut is a serious downgrade, a violation, what a waste. My identity cut-off, swept up and trashed.

First day at junior high went well, smooth. I park and lock my white Schwinn stingray among many bikes to one of two, long unpainted steel bike racks; locate and *open* my assigned combination locker and find my classrooms, on time, before the tardy bell. The adjustment to junior high is significant: there's a dramatic increase in student population, I'm enduring older kids again. I recognize students from Chadbourne of course, however, the countless new faces funneled in from surrounding elementary schools, heavily outnumber familiar ones.

The girls are prettier than in elementary school, Ditto slacks, bright colored tube tops, stylish and sharp, a little taller, more curvy and cute. I gravitate toward other athletes, I'm more comfortable passing footballs and shooting baskets, than engaging in spirited and clever conversation with either sex.

MGM in the rear view mirror, almost, my English class is accelerated, and I'm there by default, not by choice. I'm over being, "mentally gifted" and feeling "good" about myself. I'm not buying it.

I need to succeed. My other classes are average, like before Chadbourne minus the fights. I'm a member of the general student body. Freedom. Free of tipped expectations. Equality!

In class I sit next to rude loudmouths. In World Studies, tall Prince Hokulani never stops talking out loud, razzing our poor teacher Mrs. Vargas, out loud. Prince makes disparaging, smart-aleck comments to the teacher. Old-fashioned rudeness. He's vocally critical of authority. Prince makes some students laugh, but doesn't care that he hurts others feelings. Prince drives Mrs. Vargas to tears. And nothing stops him! Prince Hokulani redefines my understanding of bad student conduct. He speaks his mind, with defiance. Daily outpourings of outrageous behavior. Mr. Turentine, we need you!

At junior high I half-expect a Jackson Street reunion. Marlo Topper, Alex Zolanski, Wade Jennings and Maurice Garza. Sherry Tyrell, Danny Wellbaum, Charlene Lansing, they're all here. Strangely, no Jackson Streeters are in my junior high classes. Transition from MGM to the general student environment is easy to manage and fun.

My English class is the only tough nut to crack. This is the first time I hear the terms: "thesis", "introduction" and "conclusion." The new terms build a wall of confusion for learning how to write. It makes writing *impossible* for me. This sounds like an excuse; it is not an excuse. For me to dislike writing doesn't make sense, because I love to read. Interpreting and adapting the mechanical terms of English writing structure kills it for me.

I should have ignored them, not ignored, but taken it with a grain of salt, just write, like I'm talking to someone, like now. Too many rules block the forest for the trees. Clarity hides.

Write what's accurate and sounds right.

Reading is writing's teacher, reading and life. Life writes.

Desperate to distance myself from MGM's stigma, I dive into the general student pool. Junior high is the perfect time and place for a reset. I'm ready for normal.

At Chadbourne, the MGM students *themselves* were my educational takeaway. Their ubiquitous intelligence and spark, their individuality, their topics of discussion, their mature interaction with the teacher and one another, I hold in highest regard. Whether I attain it or not, they *are* the bar. I know it sounds silly. My fifth and sixth grade MGM classmates were my teachers. The abilities and confidence I didn't have, but wanted, they had in spades. Teachers loved them, and why not?

Mrs. Splaingard, our sixth grade teacher, did not like me. I was her class' weak link and she let me know. Darn acute senses.

In summary, I had some smarts; minus work ethic, confidence and discipline needed to develop. Worst of all, dreamless. Proof? The majority of junior high students live on academic easy street, skating along. I trade in challenges for skates. I want to skate.

Before school and during lunch, the rebellious kids know exactly what they want, they congregate on the grass field, beyond the football field and baseball diamonds, near the creek. They sit on the grass, forming a circle.

The daily predictable gathering is known simply as, "the circle."

Everyone knows what they're doing: smoking cigarettes, smoking marijuana, rebellion 101. The circle's kingpin in training, Prince Hokulani, entertains all his girlfriends there. Prince enjoys a magnetic rapport with the ladies. He talks as much as they do. Tall like me, taller if you factor in his curly pompadour. Prince is exotic, pure Hawaiin. His parents are Hawaiian natives. Prince and I are cordial, in fact he lives on Chadbourne Drive, not far from Jackson Street. In World Studies (he sat behind me), Prince told me a story. When his folks were looking for a home in Fremont (same time my folks were looking), they looked at our house. His parents loved the backyard and said, "it's the perfect spot for a built-in swimming pool." I tell John, "instead of digging for a pool, the Moyers dig up potatoes."

Fishing Poles

Hopkins Junior High's eastern border and Mission San Jose High's western border are the same line. A seasonal creek bed forms the southern border for both schools. At Hopkins, vicious rumors circulate: a large group of disreputable high schoolers, loiter at the creek.

They're called, "Creek Rats."

Hopkin's circlers are creek rats in training, baby rats. The circlers are serving a two year creek rat apprenticeship. From our vantage point at Hopkin's, Mission San Jose High is not visible, blocked by the high screened fencing surrounding Mission's large tennis courts area. We can't see the nefarious creek rats, their existence is speculation, only rumor, yet, a nagging source of fear. Hyperbole I hope.

Beyond the tennis courts, high school beckons, waiting for my arrival.

Everyday after school, I unlock my stingray and race home; south on Driscoll Road, east on Paseo Padre Parkway, south on Chadbourne Drive, past Prince Hokulani's house, right on Olive Avenue and a quick left onto Jackson Street. Past Darin Vanderbergs' house on the corner, uphill past the Wellbaums and Cortezes on the right, the Toppers, preschool and Zolanskis on the left, the Starr's pink and white house on the right and up our driveway. I park the Schwinn on its kickstand left of the porch steps, on the narrow concrete walkway that leads around the side of the house on the Tyrell side. I enter our house and look for Mom. In the morning, after breakfast, the ride to school is the same, but in reverse and cooler.

Seventh grade is straightforward. Memories form outside the classroom more than in. Guy and Danny Wellbaum are both in eighth grade, and occasionally I see them at school. Guy and Danny are active members of the Hopkins circle.

Darin Vanderberg finished Hopkins last year and is a freshman at Mission San Jose High School.

Alex Zolanski, Marlo Topper, Maurice Garza, Wade Jennings, Bucky Cortez and Charlene Lansing are also seventh graders at Hopkins, but I rarely see them at school. At home we've been friends for 18 months, but at school there is not much interaction. My first Jackson Street - school mingling, never happens.

Kevin, Kamela and Kristen Finley still attend Prince of Peace School; a kindergarten through eighth grade private school. Kevin Finley's parents invite me to lunch a few times. Their everyday table settings are very nice and fancy, ornate, not plain.

I am never at ease during the Finley meals. I like them a lot, but they're intimidating. They enjoy a good tease, and I'm not used to it. Finley kids are smart and accomplished and excel in academics, sports and music. Kevin plays a recorder (flute-like instrument), can read and compose music. Mr. Finley works at a local cannery in Union City and Mrs. Finley works part time at the Prince of Peace office. K, K and K act every year in a large-scale, school theater production. I'm invited to Prince of Peace's production, The Mikado, an elaborate play, very well-done. Performers dress in colorful Asian costumes and make-up and perform in a large venue. It is well directed and a lot of fun. Unfortunately, I'm not familiar with the story, and the performance is wasted on me. The actors bubble with charisma and give a great show. Kevin stars in the play.

On Christmas morn I unwrap my first fishing rod & reel. Santa, aware I'm a novice, gave me a rubber weight to practice casting on dry land. Kevin F. gets a nice fishing rig too. Cast practice begins immediately on the lawn and eventually progresses to the street. Kevin and I make it a game and our casting gets precise. By Christmas, Kevin and I hit the broadside of a barn everytime. Guy and Danny Wellbaum are already good anglers, having fished for years.

I appreciate the guidance and wisdom I receive from Pappa; how to build models and the importance of following directions, how to throw a football, and for starting me slow with fishing, get good at casting first, learn how to tie a loop, then get worms and go to the lake. He did it in stages. The satisfaction I enjoy later is thanks to Pappa. His principles endure, I draw on them today, and not just for throwing spiraled bullets, casting on a dime and building award winning models.

Driving along Paseo Padre with Pappa, I saw the fenced swimming lagoon, but hadn't been to the lake behind the lagoon. I remember well, my first fishing trip to Lake Elizabeth.

Guy Wellbaum knows a shortcut and leads the way. The dirt trail starts at Driscoll Road, and cuts diagonally across a large grassy field to Paseo Padre Parkway, where the railroad track crosses. Two right hands hold two balanced fishing poles, four shoes walk on the narrow dirt trail. Guy talks the whole way. We cross Paseo Padre Parkway to Hobo Jungle and head east a half-mile along the railroad tracks. We turn left and work our way past several large trees. The terrain opens up to a large pond, then across the small train bridge over a creek full of water to the back of Lake Elizabeth, about 300 yards from the tracks.

The paved walking trail that completely encircles Lake Elizabeth separates the lake from the pond and creek. The creek parallels the Lake trail from Paseo Padre Parkway, to Catfish Pond. Guy calls it Catfish Pond, so we do too. This remote area is special for my friends and I, our go-to spot for the next five years and contains the best fishing. Removed from the lake crowd, it's quiet here, our own private fishing boy place.

Guy is a very good fisherman, Danny too. The Wellbaums are my fishing buddies. Kevin goes once in a while, when allowed. Kevin Finley is younger and Lake Elizabeth is a world away from Jackson Street. In stark contrast, the Wellbaum brothers enjoy complete freedom. I do too, if I keep my nose clean and am back home on time for dinner etc etc etc. For Guy and Danny: bow and arrows, fishing poles, firecrackers, knives, and BB guns are standard, brandished day or night. Another inescapable fact; Guy and Danny Wellbaum are good-looking, well dressed and speak with unique voices; harsh gravely tones delivered in funny broken sentence fragments. Physically fit, friendly, funny and fearless, Guy and Danny Wellbaum are good friends and very popular with the ladies.

Jackson Street residents young and old are lively, but in a group, an explosion of energy. I know them all by name, and they all know me. Older brothers fix, race and rev muscle cars, motorcycles and trucks, up and down the street all over town, sport sunglasses; their scantily clad girlfriends ride shotgun. Relationships last, but change eventually. Fast cars, long soft hair and porcelain skin, greasy hands, tanned to the max. Open hoods, chrome wrenches flash, tuned engines, engines being tuned, leaking oil.

Greasy faces act out real-life, award winning dramas on the stage called Jackson Street.

And the soundtrack? 70's and late 60's rock, plays with authority, rhythm and fun. Anthems blare from bedrooms, living rooms, broadcast through open windows spilling into front yards, backyards, the street; joyous to the ear, offensive to parents and teachers; pop and boom from powerful car stereos, owner-installed, custom speaker boxes, amplifiers and equalizers. The drugs are there too, but I don't want to know about it. Drugs, like God, are to be feared.

Learning to Cheat

Indoor pastimes include board games with the family. Pappa rarely plays. Like everyone else we get on this kick or that, this game or that. Mom, Hannah, Marja, Tessa and I like to roll dice and spin spinners. Friends join too. The huckleberrys play them all: Masterpiece, Monopoly, Inventors, Life, Clue, miscellaneous card games: Speed, Kings in the Corner, Poker, Blackjack etc. etc. etc. The Memory Game is popular, then forgotten.

For me it's simple, win. Where does that come from? Have to win. Are we born with it? Do we think a win makes us better? If we want to beat loved ones, not for love's sake, why then? Love of self? Why does everyone love a winner? Is winning by the rules noble or noteworthy? And what about the losers? Do we enjoy stomping our figurative foot on their necks?! Winning is not without challenge. The winner's job? Win graciously, stay humble? One little problem; as soon as humility is *acquired*, it's gone. Better luck next time ol boy. You're a good sport, bless your heart.

Where does cheating come from?

Marja is willing to play board games with me, one on one, when others won't. Bad judgment Marja. I take advantage of her younger age and cheat to win, but only if necessary. I don't remember cheating before that. I can win without cheating. Cheating is fun, taking advantage. After Marja wises up, I continue to "cut corners" wherever and whenever opportunity presents itself. Do you really believe George Washington and Abraham Lincoln didn't lie? Okay. It's not wrong if you don't get caught, many say. Marja plays an integral part in rounding out my education. My resourcefulness traumatizes her to this day. Sorry kiddo.

There is no money. Our neighbors watch super beautiful, 25" color TV. We watch 13" black and white. The Zolanskis eat Kentucky Fried Chicken or a delicious salisbury steak frozen dinner, in front of their 25" color TV, like breathing. We eat tuna casserole or Shake N Bake chicken (not allowed to eat dinner in front of TV). Mrs. Zolanski drives a new Buick. As a General Motors supervisor, Mr. Zolanski receives a substantial discount on any new GM car purchase. I wear clothes that embarrass, especially at school. I complained to Mom about it, and she got annoyed. Mom says, "I'll have you know, our combined incomes last year was $20,000 dollars." 20 grand, that's a lot. Being an artist's son sucks sometimes.

I'll stop and say, we never miss a meal, our diet is nutritionally balanced, but I'll add, I want more, not satiated, never satisfied.

Seventh grade academics went well. I don't recall any extracurricular sports that year, I did spend endless hours on the Finley and Topper driveways shooting baskets with Kevin and Marlo. Two-hand touch football games are played in the street six days a week in season. Marja wises up at board games, but pathetically harbors an eternal grudge. Hannah and Tessa are non-existent other than dinner time. I'm on call 24-7, for fishing adventures.

Mom works afternoon and evenings at Emporium Capwells, and Hannah, Marja and I are given additional responsibilities: dinner KP duty. The format is simple, each week we rotate to the next sibling. Say it's my week for example; I read Mom's written instructions for dinner, and cook it. Typically an entree, a vegetable, and dessert. I set the table, a simple setting for five: plate, fork, knife, and spoon; the spoon and knife set on a bi-folded paper towel on the right, and the fork on the left, and a glass. When the food is almost ready, I call Pappa from the studio and my three sisters, so they have time to wash up and be seated, then I set a steaming hot dinner on the table.

We sit, hold hands and are quiet for approximately 30 seconds - beside the aroma of dinner and the growl in my stomach, I think of nothing - then Pappa squeezes hands and we all squeeze .

I eat too fast.

After dinner, I clear off the table, hand wash the dishes in scalding hot water, rinse, towel dry and put them away in the cupboard and drawer.

Dinners I make include but are not limited to; Shake n Bake chicken, Hamburger Helper (I love), frozen spinach, frozen green beans, canned orange squash or baby corn. Indian style white rice (India), boiled potatoes with butter, salt and pepper, frozen fish sticks etc. etc. etc. Mom's dinner prep directions are clear and easy to follow. This routine continues for several years. Looking back, I learned practical domestica, and the chore schedule provided a framework to our motherless afternoons and evenings.

KP done; freedom once again, back to my glorious pursuit of happiness!

Reading for pleasure increases, specifically science fiction classics: The Hobbit Series, Wizard of Oz Trilogy, the Green Brain etc. etc. etc. My literary peak is too brief (peaks are brief). Between seventh and ninth grade, finishing a book in a day or two is common. TV is black and white, two-dimensional and grainy (what's that big box behind the screen?).

Books read in vivid color, flawless resolution and an infinite depth of field.

Puberty advances unnoticed, revealing itself slowly, in glorious ways; interests lose ground: sports, reading and music struggle to keep control of my throne.

The Moyers grab swimsuits and towels, pile into the station wagon and drive to the Hayward Plunge. The Plunge is a huge rectangular, indoor swimming pool, complete with low and high-diving boards, and the best, tallest, pool-slide anywhere. This is the pool-slide's answer to

Chris Peters' rope swing. The strong scent of chlorine cannot dampen the joy of these pool-side thrills. The slide's towering height is intimidating and requires courage. It's a long climb to the top. A fall guarantees bone fractures or worse. That's the last thing on my mind however.

Allow me to interrupt my "puberty dive." I have to review Pappa's driving.

The Moyers do not wear seat belts; the 1970's don't wear seat belts. We move freely about our station wagon, lying in the far back if we want. We never drive anywhere, without Pappa slamming on the brakes. "Hold on!" A powerful lurch forward. This is normal driving. These fits and starts don't bother Mom who often naps in the passenger seat. Pappa's parallel parking in the city includes a gentle but definite "tap" on the vehicles fore and aft. Again, nothing to worry about, the "tap" technique is on the verge of extinction; steel bumpers disappear after 1972.

Back to the "dive." My first order of business is not the high slide and its ladder, or the high-dive board. I begin with the low-dive. Start small, work my way up, gradually. Get some *good* going.

No friends that day, I'm flying solo. In situations like these, my sisters vanish from the earth's surface. They're here, I know, but I don't *see* or *consider* them. What I do hear and *feel* however, is the music; sweet hits play good and loud from the Plunge's sound system; it creates a party-atmosphere and fills me with courage. I climb the low-dive ladder, energized by the new music, and stand tall on the board . . . I *feel* taller, a new song plays; <u>One of a Kind Love Affair</u>, by the Spinners. The song has a fine *unique* sound. I feel *different*. The new tune stirs me in a *new way*, like a peacock or a tom turkey, fanning its plumage. The feathers are invisible, but they're there, in full color. After a couple low dives, I ascend the high-dive, the Spinners' song still plays. I don't want it to end, but after it does, I view life differently.

That song, <u>One of a Kind Love Affair</u>, felt like, "hey ladies, check this dive out. 'Hey beautiful!" I don't remember any bathing beauties in particular, just how I felt. In a strange way the love song and feather flapping together, broadcasts amore signals to the female birds splashing in attendance. Woah, communication.

With a nudge from the Spinners I embrace adolescence, a jack knife from the high-dive . . . take the plunge!

Fort Vanderberg, that bastion of freedom, serves us well, MOC, Mischief Operations Central. The sun-deck is a great spot for sleepovers. Kevin Finley sleeps over a couple times.

Our fort inspires; Kevin and his dad build a deck together. A steep drop-off behind their back fence requires 8' high support posts under the far end of the deck. Their deck doesn't have a railing; don't roll around in your sleep, you may wake up with a goose egg on your head! No matter, Fort Finley and Fort Moyer (name change) form a strong line of defense against the hostile wilderness, and are great sleepover spots. Creekside sleepovers include but are not limited to: smoking rolled up newspaper and pummeling the Tyrell house (within range and sight) with a dozen eggs.

The same 680 off-ramp that runs behind our house, runs behind the Finley home. During dinner once, a car exits too fast! We hear the tires screeeeech! Followed by Bang! BANG!! **BANG!!!**

Driver and vehicle . . . out of control! Car skids off the ramp, rolls down Horseshoe Hill!

Mr. Tyrell, in a stirring Oklahoman drawl, commands us boys not to ride on Horseshoe Hill anymore. "Jens, you can't ride your bikes behind the back fence anymore! Do you hear me?! No more Jens! No more damnit! Jens?!!? No more now!!" His pleas fall on deaf ears, nothing changes.

The State installs a steel guardrail on the aforementioned off-ramp.

Beyond the off-ramp and culvert, past the Starr's house, the creek returns to its original shape; where sycamore, cottonwood and willow trees grow so thick they blot out the sun. In its darkest recess, an antiquated automobile rots.

First time off the high dive at Cal State Hayward Pool.

Is this going to hurt?

Poison Oak Blues

Behind the back fence provides a generous slice of Huck Finn life for my friends and I. Noisy days in nature are spent here; among the birds, squirrels and evil that lurks, we forget about civilization. We sift the area for its secrets; I am extremely allergic to one of them, poison oak. How can an inconspicuous three leaf plant inflict such misery? A touch of its leaf or branch results in a heinous oozing rash, and I'm transformed into a hideous ogre. My face swells, my eyelids shut tight, I can't see! Legs, arms, hands, feet, fingers and toes, *private* areas, covered by a thick, wet and dry carpet of yellow crust. Help me!

I contract frightening cases of poison oak from behind the house. Chadbourne Elementary once, Hopkins Junior High once and Mission San Jose High once. I miss three weeks of school each time and am still disfigured when I go back. The Kaiser doctor says to Mom and me, "if Jens gets another case of poison oak, he'll die." He calls it, "Anaphylactic Shock." Poison oak ends a YMCA scuba-diving class I'm taking with Kevin Finley, at the Ohlone College pool. We got as far as the skin-dive trip to Monterey Bay and the buddy-breathing exercise with tanks in the deep-end of the Ohlone College pool (17'). I still have the mask, snorkel and fins Pappa bought me. My afflictions were biblical in scope and impact. God gave Satan free reign, sparing only my life. A living hell.

Mom signed me up for two different classes; tennis and sailing. Kevin F. has a racket, so we play at either Hopkins or Mission. The sailing class is at Lake Elizabeth. We learn to sail the small single sail Toro sailboats.

I set sail for distant shores, gliding effortlessly, in touch with my inner Viking.

Come about, jibe, daggerboard, tacking etc. etc. etc. Lake Elizabeth is known for its year-round sailing breeze; sailing *does* take me away, to where I've always heard it could be.

It's the summer of Danny, we have much in common. Not in the sport sense - though Danny is faster than me - but in mechanics; bikes, model building, mini-bike engines and eventually motorcycles. We both like the ladies and they like us, we're attentive and we get some attention; Danny's humor tips the social scales in our favor. Wherever we go, fun follows.

We build solid handling bikes from scratch, and set them up for road and off-road use. The low and wide BMX handlebar with cross-brace, helps us scramble on dirt, more control. Two foam tubes are added for safety (and style), one on the handlebar cross-brace, and one on the top tube of the frame. Looks cool too.

There are many different places for a kid to ride: Mill Creek Road, Hobo Jungle, Lake Elizabeth, Mission Peak, but the best is Honda Hills. Honda Hills is a deep, seasonal creek bed, bone dry in the summer, located on the corner of Grimmer Boulevard and Paseo Padre Parkway, directly across from the Hobo Jungle and Lake Elizabeth. There are no homes there, just a creekbed, trees, a grassy hill and dirt. The creek bed sits back 100 yards from the corner, well away from vehicular traffic and its trails entertain Fremont boys on bikes, all day long.

South of the creekbed a single trail rises gently, then steeper to the top of a brown grassy hill; from the top there's a nice view of Hobo Jungle and Lake Elizabeth, you can see the water. Riders gain speed from the hill down to the creek. As the trail meets the creek, it forks in three directions. The forks lead to the same creek, but in different locations. All three trails go between giant Eucalyptus trees and drop into the creek. All three options lead to similar results, bike and rider jump from the opposite bank into the air, landing on flat dirt.

Start from the flat area, make sure it's clear, that no one's coming down the other side, drop into the creek, pop up the other side, crank up the gentle slope until it gets too steep, jump off and walk my bike uphill. After choosing a start point on the hill, I point the bike downhill, facing the creek below, choose Jump 1, 2 or 3, and commit. I collect myself, breathe deep, and focus on the jump to come. When my head is screwed on tight, I start down. I'm approaching the split and going fast now. Brace yourself! Hit the precipice, soar down into the creek, re-engage dirt, roll the bottom and shoot skyward . . . *airborn*! If the rider sticks the landing (stays on bike), friends and onlookers ooh and ahh and the rider feels great. If he wrecks, friends and onlookers ooh and ahh and the rider feels pain.

Riders assess their own confidence and skill level, how far up the hill to start his descent from. The farther up the hill, the farther you soar. Physics 101.

How far and high your jump goes, is a guess at best. However, with each additional step up the hill, that calculation becomes less predictable. With every new step up the hill, the line between risk and reward blurs. Each step farther from the creek increases your speed and requires exponentially more nerve. Danny and I pay our dues, with scars and stripes to prove it. All jumpers crash at Honda Hills, not if, but when. Most find that sweet spot, thrilling, but not bloody. However, the danger available to us is unlimited; the farther up the hill . . . the farther you fly. Heck, you could jump to the lake if you want to. Wait, what?

Ronny Bobbitt and his merry band of delinquents show up at Honda Hills. 10 boys on 10 bikes. A wild and intimidating group; a lot of chrome and a lot of hair. The sun's reflection off that much chrome, forces us to squint and adds to the intimidation. Danny Wellbaum and I are side by side, Kevin Finley is here too, making his Honda Hills debut. The three of us cringe at the unfriendly invasion.

This volatile situation can go a number of ways: a simple challenge, a dare, a pushing match, or fist fight. Kevin, deceptively tall but young, puts the job squarely on me and Danny's shoulders.

We are outnumbered.

Cunning and aware, Ronny Bobbitt knows Guy Wellbaum, he knows David Aubrey and he knows Darin Vanderberg. He's grown up with Guy and Darin. Ronny Bobbitt (two years older and tough) lives halfway down Marion Avenue, past Wade Jennings and Maurice Garza, on the same side, across the street from Chris Peters. Ronny knows *exactly* who's who, and the consequences thereof and forthwith. Like Chris Peters, Ronny Bobbitt lives *just* outside my circle of friends. Today is our first, face to face.

Though Ronny Bobbitt lives on Marion Avenue, oddly his posse consists of boys from between Mission Valley Elementary School and Driscoll Road.

With Bobbitt's desperados all present and accounted for, one thing is certain; Ronny has a decision to make.

I must admit, Ron's final choice proves wise. Rather than risk future confrontations with Guy Wellbaum, Darin Vanderberg, or worse David Aubrey (nobody wants that), Ron Bobbitt calls on his fearless rider, Indian Daryl.

Ron's magnanimous act establishes; 1. His authority over the situation; 2. His benevolence toward the inferior opposition (few in number - us); and 3. Undisputed loyalty of his followers.

Daryl is my first Native American encounter: he's different: kinetic, animated. Not stoic, calm or sleepy, rather, a busy bird in motion. Daryl is striking, Hollywood good looks, wavy jet-black hair reaching his shoulder blades, two years older, solid muscle, sinew and bone. Daryl looks hungry and wild, half crazy perhaps.

The three jumps have different launch angles, producing different results. J3 is tame, for beginners, girls and children. J1 and J2 are most popular, J2 the favorite. J2 is fun, the arc trajectory is lower, the landing impact easier to predict. J2 keeps us entertained for hours. If Honda Hills were golf clubs, J1 would be a pitching wedge, J2 a driver, and J3 a putter.

J1's arc is straight up and straight down. To spice it up, we occasionally do J1, knowing to go easy, check your speed. Otherwise you may crack up on impact or endo on your head or back, break your neck. If you do J1 too fast, and the rider *does* manage to land and remain in the saddle, they bounce off, and break a wheel or bone.

Do not approach J1 too fast! Half speed!

Bobbitt stares us down, and commands, "jump this thing Daryl." Daryl's response is instant, soldier-like, fearless. He *hoped* Ron would call on him.

Bobbitt, satisfied, slowly closes his eyes, turns away from us and looks uphill.

All eyes on Daryl.

Daryl swoops into the creek, weightless and smooth. Neither Kevin, Danny or I fully know Indian Daryl's intentions; does Bobbitt know?

All eyes on Daryl.

Beyond the creek, Daryl rides up then jumps off and runs his bike uphill, like he's running downhill.

What is this?? Where am I?!

The mute 12 congregate around the landing zones not sure where Daryl will go.

Daaaaaaamn, Daryl's at the top!

Ron smiles for the first time and shifts from undisputed pack leader, to humbled onlooker. I randomly deduce: while I was staring through a window in San Francisco, watching the fog and sailboats with my mouth hanging open . . . Daryl was here, jumping Honda Hills!

In a secret place, soft drumming is heard, white smoke signals rise. The medicine man, the chiefs, the elders, the braves and all their families, respond to the drum. With solemn countenance and great anticipation, they hurry.

At blue water's edge, Daryl's ancestors gather; mostly Dakota Sioux from the north. Sitting Bull and Crazy Horse arrive. Braves carry bows and arrows, young braves race each other to the bank, women and girls dab their cheeks with vermillion and sing and dance their way. The drum is louder.

When all gather, out from the near treeline, White Buffalo approaches blue water and bellows, the people step back, make way; White Buffalo lowers his head and drinks. Children stroke his mane, smiles are seen and old women cry. Ancestors peer beneath blue water:

Daryl starts down. *Pedaling down!* Warrior on white stallion, Daryl's long hair a black flag, ripping from his own storm. Our collective breath is held . . . Daryl assaults . . . J1.

No way! No!! . . . *suicide.*

Daryl leaps from the top of the south bank, and freefalls to the creek bottom, BAAMM!! Daryl's white stingray holds *together!* Straight up the wall, rocket launch!

Time stops.

Braves shout and pump their bows high in the air! Women and children dance on clouds and *sing.* Chiefs and elders watch.

12 boy faces pivot, from looking down into the creek, to straight up; and watch Daryl seated in the air. Like a slow stroke of an artist's brush: Daryl seated on spinning wheels. Daryl and the bike are much too high, like the head of a giraffe at the zoo. He's gliding like a *bird above us.*

Daryl and his bike shoot straight up to the top of an arc, and level off. At the top of the arc, weightless and floating forward, Daryl and the bike are still, the frame, forks, handlebars and pedals are still, but the wheels are spinning producing a slow-motion effect. Daryl's bike is level, his eyes wide open look *forward,* not down.

Woaaah, Indian Daryl is enjoying the view.

Daryl's black hair (so black, a blue tint is visible) is blowing straight back. 12 pairs of eyes stare straight up. A startled driver on Paseo Padre Parkway swerves sharply, barely avoiding the curb. Our young necks tilt back easily, we gape at Daryl's Converse soles on the pedals and his blue jean cuffs.

The balance!

Feet on the pedals, legs straightened, Daryl stands out of the saddle, hands on the grips, wheels level, forward. His big brown eyes should reflect panic, we panic, no fear is visible, no jostling, no cries, *not a sound.* Graceful through the air.

Daryl soars over the boys.

Crazy Horse reels like a wild animal, Sitting Bull smolders. Women and children hug. White Buffalo's big eyes see everything and he scents the air.

Daryl's hangtime is forever, but like Blood Sweat and Tears and Isaac Newton said, "what goes up, must come down."

The fall is mesmerizing and painful to watch.

Daryl and the bike smash the ground hard. *BOOM!* Both wheels taco, Daryl bounces from his seat, his body slams the dirt, rolls twice, stops still and groans. Three seconds later, Daryl gets up and shakes the dust from his long hair. His bloody face and white teeth smile ear to ear. Ronny Bobbett looks around with a mix of arrogance, swelling pride, and relief

"Good jump Daryl."

White Buffalo walks away. Powerful medicine today, a joyous celebration begins.

Darin Vanderberg is Jackson Street's undisputed teen leader, certainly among me and my friends. When Darin V. isn't neck deep in major yard work and home improvement projects free of charge for Mr. and Mrs. Tyrell, neighbors hire him for their landscape and painting needs. For large jobs Darin turns to the Jackson Street labor pool, which I am a proud member in good standing.

Besides teaching my friends and I the benefits of hard work, Darin leads us through other manly rites of passage.

He organizes a group ride to the top of mysterious Mill Creek Road, 4.7 miles, deep into the Ohlone Wilderness. I'd never ridden in a car to the top, let alone a bike. Mill Creek Road symbolizes everything wild; the near five mile uphill, tests our endurance. Darin V. rides a light, high quality, custom road bike he built himself and the six of us ride stingrays or ten-speeds of medium quality.

Not old enough for a driver's license, Darin helps older friends wrench on their cars. Darin knows his way around a bike. He can strip one down to the last nut and rebuild it. Darin teaches us how to custom paint our bikes. After stripping the bike to its frame,and sanding it, Darin hangs the frame in a big garage door opening, then primes and paints the frame with a few cans of spray paint. They come out perfect. So we do the same; strip,sand and paint our bike frames, reassemble and ride with pride, thanks to Darin V.

Through uncharted territory, we follow Darin up Mill Creek Road. No maps, no odometers, no way to know the top is near. We might have got bad information, what if it's 20 miles to the top?! The trek feels endless. Is this how the Israelites felt in the wilderness, so far from Egypt? Kevin Finley isn't here, he's not allowed to travel that far from home yet. I'll take Kevin F. up Mill Creek Road next year. Darin and friends finally reach the end of the road, top of the hill. Our Mount Everest. A satisfying accomplishment.

The best is yet to come, the descent. Darin Vanderberg takes the lead. He goes as fast as possible. What a thrill to keep up! Each straightaway breaks another personal speed record. Our combined adrenaline rushes would resuscitate King Tut!

This was the Emporium Capwell era, the scooter and moped years, the weekly block-party years; the innocence, the fall, black-bereted Pappa in the studio, painting his heart out; Mom in the kitchen, in the family room reading her novels watching her favorite late-night shows, beating the daily San Francisco Chronicle crossword puzzle (12 minute average, 8 minute personal best) every morning. Bountiful backyard gardens, branches drooped with fruit. Day and night street games;

football, frisbee, basketball, baseball, jokari, war, freeze-tag, hide-n-go-seek, everyday till dinnertime and after in the summer. Preparing family meals, wash and hand dry dishes, set the table, clear the table. How to ride, maintain and jump a bike. How to say "please and thank you, please pass the butter."

Ride a wheelie.

How to block out and rock out, the advent of superior audio equipment. Friendship. Mothers in the morning, shuffling next door in their robe and slippers, armed with a cup of steaming coffee to visit another mother dressed the same way, everyday.

Big Blue

Eighth grade 1974, my final year at Hopkins is under way. I gained a few new friends, John Velasco comes from Gomes Elementary by Lake Elizabeth and is best friends with Devin O'Malley. My interest in fishing grows fast. I received a pocket fisherman from Mom and Dad for my birthday; 12" long folded up, this marvel of engineering fits in my school locker! Hopkins is halfway to Lake Elizabeth from the house, so, in addition to every chance I get, I fish after school, catch my limit of five rainbow trout and pedal home. Clean 'em, freeze 'em, fry 'em.

Charley's Market on the corner of Driscoll Road and Paseo Padre Parkway is directly on my way home from Hopkins. One fateful day on the way home from school, I slip into Charley's Market, with evil on my mind. Clad in an oversized, faux-fur lined blue parka popular at the time, and hungry, I utilize peripheral vision developed from varied sport participation and slide a small box of Pop-Tarts into my parka; strawberry with icing. High on adrenaline I pedal fast from the crime scene and gorge on the tasty and popular pastry. Speeding along Paseo Padre Parkway, my countenance brightens, I fling the evidence (Pop-Tart wrappers) to my right onto the grass strip between the street and sidewalk. I hang a quick right on Dorne Place, a left on Apricot Lane, and into the safe arms of suburban badlands.

That first *pit-stop* at Charley's Market, that single moment of weakness, evolves into a routine. A *quick-stop* after school. Not long after this, whatever I want, if it fits into big blue, I steal it. My targets are limited to but not exclusive of: candy, bait or tackle. Payless Drugs Store downtown is well known for their impressive fishing tackle selection; In one shot I take 13 bottles of Pautzky's salmon eggs, Premium Red Label. I'd torn open the bottom of the blue parka's right side pocket, allowing access to the entire bottom of big blue. B.B. is converted to a big blue sack. Wade Jennings proves to be a dependable partner in crime. His mother likes to go to K-Mart to shop and browse. I rarely get there so when Wade invites me to tag along, I jump. We drive away with a record haul, big blue is bursting at the seams, the laden weight pulls down on my shoulders

John Velasco lives near Lake Elizabeth and likes to fish as much as I do. I eventually hang out at his house. John's room is very impressive. A shotgun and rifle hang high together on a wall (I don't own a BB gun yet). He has a nice stereo too. John plays a couple records and within five minutes, I hear Black Sabbath and Led Zeppelin for the first time. This is my first exposure to hard rock and I like it.

John has three pretty sisters at home. John's parents are divorced and I meet John's father a little later. His father had been in a bad work accident. John's father is an Iron Worker and was accidentally hit on the job by a piece of falling building steel. As a result he became a paraplegic and is confined to a wheelchair, but even so he drives a beautiful, white, Lincoln Continental and looks like a movie star. Mr. Velasco steers and brakes the car with a custom chrome hand-control. John has an older brother, Don, who is gone most of the time, but comes around to eat and sleep. Don drives already, he owns a sharp white, Chevy step-side pick-up with a white aluminum camper shell, mag wheels and glass-pack exhaust.

Japanese trucks don't exist, only full-size American trucks.

Heavy metal rock n roll posters soon adorn my bedroom walls and ceiling.

John and his brother Don sometimes gang up on me during sleepovers, razzing me about my stinky feet. One time Don insists we wrap them up with newspaper, then scraps that plan and says, "lets bag them up with plastic bags and rubber bands." They do neither. Don and John Velasco are quite funny. They fight sometimes, but not often. I begin to see a pattern develop between brothers: fighting.

I'm still involved with judo, working out at the renowned Santa Clara Judo dojo on Bascom Avenue in north San Jose. Pappa has two fine books about Judo, so I chose judo as the subject for a writing assignment. The best judo school in the world is the Kodokan in Tokyo, Japan. Several black belt sinseis at the Santa Clara dojo, were trained at the Kodokan, including the dojo's owner, a ninth-degree red belt.

I'm in a training match with a Kodakan trained sinsei and he does a move I'd never seen, - a judo match starts from a standing position, but often during the match, if an attempted throw doesn't result in a win (Nippon), the match may go from standing to wrestling, or matwork - the sensei lays on his back, knees bent and keeps rotating toward me, his feet toward me. I'm still standing. If I jump left, he rotates left, if I jump right, he rotates right, so I am forced to jump over his legs to get to his torso and try to pin him. When I do, he grabs my torso with his legs and swings me this way and that way. I see how strong legs can be. A very effective technique. During the same match, he does it again, while I try to figure out the solution, a different angle of attack, he covers his eyes with his hands. My judo pants slid down! Ahh! Embarrassing. I yank them up, tie them mid-match and keep going. I never got past the sensei's legs for the pin that night. I trained at the Santa Clara dojo for three and a half years, learned a lot and received a green belt, but, with all the surrounding distractions, I lost interest and quit.

I try not to look for trouble. I don't pick fights, but I can be provoked. That said, I know who not to mess with and who not to back down from. Nobody messes with Darin Vanderberg, and to his credit he does not provoke. It's good when both parties understand the potential damage one party can inflict on the other, and leave it there. Alex Zolanski on the other hand, does his best to get to me and we face off numerous times, a double push or single punch but nothing escalates beyond that fortunately.

Alex Z. is the master harasser. With alarming regularity he unleashes his prodigious teasing skills on ones he loves. Marlo Topper? He doesn't provoke, and we never go to blows. I respect Marlo's basketball skills. We did eighth grade wood shop together; we both received A+s for our maplewood gun racks; sanded to perfection and finished with a wax buff. Danny Wellbaum and I never get fist fight mad. I won't mess with Guy Wellbaum, unless absolutely necessary. However Guy is very good-natured, loves to have fun and in 10 years it never comes to that. Danny Wellbaum's humor is in a class by itself and we hang out quite a bit. Kevin Finley and I get along great, laugh it up non-stop and have each other's backs too.

I made a new friend in the eighth grade, Gary Forest. 5' 10", athletic, good looking with dirty blonde shoulder length hair, smart and funny. Gary lives around the corner on Paseo Padre Parkway with his youthful and fun aunt and uncle; Gary's father's brother and wife. They live close too, a right turn onto Paseo Padre Parkway off Olive Avenue, about four houses down on the right. Their nice new home backs up to Interstate 680, like ours. In addition to Gary, the couple have two young boys of their own, ages four and six.

Gary likes to have fun, he is very funny, he loves to laugh, he makes me laugh. He wears the thickest prescription glasses ever. Because the glasses are so thick, Gary suffers from mild to severe razzing at school, from everywhere. The boys on Jackson Street keep him at arm's length and chide him the hardest, but for the sake of our friendship, Gary puts up with it. As our friendship grew there were the classic sleepovers. Gary's aunt is very cool and pleasant. She discusses with Gary and I the lyrics to our favorite song, Led Zeppelin's, <u>Stairway to Heaven</u>. She says the last line,"To be a rock and not to roll" means: "be a leader, not a follower." Oh yeaaah, I see what you mean.

I let my hair grow since "the butch." Much better, but Gary's hair is a bit longer than mine. John Velasco's hair is black, thick, wavy and long, 3" beyond the shoulder, like a lion's mane. Kevin Finley's hair is straight and thin, growing steadily, but still short. Marlo Topper's hair is dirty blonde, thick but very straight, getting longer, but still conservative. Alex's hair is dirty blonde, a little wavy, a little scraggly, but conservative length, like 1964 Beatles. The Wellbaums, Guy and Danny; both dark brown with light brown highlights, thick and wavy, shoulder length. Danny's is a bit longer than Guys, Guy's thicker than Danny's. Danny's hair blows around on a windy day, getting in his eyes. Guy's stays in place during a hurricane.

Wade Jennings is tough, he likes to get in my face and push me around a bit, then laugh about it. He enjoys dominating. He has many older brothers and one sister; one brother is in prison for manslaughter. Not in the first degree, but Larry did a couple years. Wade let me read a letter from his brother in jail. I remember reading, "it's a shithole Wade. Don't ever end up here." Suffice it to say, the unpredictable result is not worth a real confrontation with Wade. By and large when Wade and I hang out we have a blast, but there is always push-back / a quick fist display in the face thing, from both of us. The punches aren't landed, just thrown. A rapid succession of hand slaps to the head and chest area. Not meant to inflict pain or provoke reprisal, but to let the other guy know, "hey buddy, I ain't afraid of you."

This summarizes life on Jackson Street. Whenever we hang out, which is daily, there are constant displays of one-on-one aggression, to let the aggressee and anyone else hanging around know, you're not scared, not chicken. A few quick n' lite face slaps in rapid succession is all,

enough to back your buddy up a bit, from the momentum of your whirling advance. We're all

going through puberty and this is how we deal with it. It's natural, we don't analyze it, just react to

it. Sleepovers include fantasizing about certain girls we know, whoever is front and center in our

little brains; mention so and so, imagine making out with her, then fall asleep. Kind of funny.

There are sleepovers with Alex Zolanski, Kevin Finley, John Velasco, and Gary Forest. But not

with Danny Wellbaum, Darin Vanderberg, Jeff Cardoso, Wade Jennings or Marlo Topper.

Big Blue, and flares

CYO, PPK and Church

CYO basketball season is about to start and I want to try-out. Marlo Topper and Maurice Garza played on the same team the last two seasons on Saint Joseph; a very good team. I'm taller, 6' 3", and play constantly in driveways and school playgrounds, so I go for it and sign-up for CYO.

Last year's seventh grade St. Joseph CYO team did very well, league champions, and remain intact as the eighth grade team this year, but enough additional boys want to play, so they form an eighth grade B team. We're not as good as the A-team team, but have a good head coach and assistant coach, a weekly practice schedule and a complete game schedule, so we're not a self-pity-team. Our uniforms and knee-high socks are the same as the A-Team. The B team is legit, just shorter and less talented. Nevertheless, we have standouts and I improve as a shooter. Playing basketball inside on a hardwood floor court is the ultimate.

We practice at Saint Joseph's gym, next door to the old Mission San Jose. Saint Joe's gym floor is tile, but league games are played on wood floor courts, in real gyms. I enjoy practice and love game day. We have a couple good shooters. Jimmy Allen and I become friends and go to each other's homes once or twice. His dad is a fireman, and his mother is pretty. Jimmy and his younger brother are excellent baseball players. Both can throw a baseball really hard and both are Pony League standouts. I played three-way catch with them once but I didn't last long. Daniel Lopez,

Monty Boucher and the assistant coach's son are good friends. Six boys attend Saint Joseph's Catholic School. I'm a non-Catholic outsider, on the team's social fringe.

At season's end, a teammate and I are awarded All-Star plaques with our names engraved, and played in the All-Star game. Maurice Garza, a neighbor from the A-Team, made the All-Star team also. So we got to play together one time and it was great.

Maurice has this unique, fade-away jump shot; unconventional with zero arc, yet extremely effective and exciting to watch. From 15-18' anywhere on the floor, Maurice fires-off these crazy jump-shots with a bullet trajectory, and bamm, sideways net jerk, two points!

Through the season's league play, I see how Marlo Topper earned his spot on the A team. His play is consistent and gritty, a dependable ball handler and passer; a guard who provides a high flow of assists to his teammates in every game; an accurate set shot and a tenacious, drive to the hoop lay-up (like on his driveway). Marlo's set shot is cool under pressure and accurate, but he holds the ball low, in front of his neck. It's easier to defend and limits his opportunities to shoot. This year I learned to hold the ball above my head and shoot; it's harder to defend and gives an unobstructed sight-line to the basket. I love it.

Alex Zolanski attends Saint Joseph Church every Christmas and Easter. They go to confession throughout the year. I went to confession with Alex, just him and I. Alex confessed, I did not but should have. I try to do the hand crossing thing in front of the chest, I like the humble gesture, it looks reverent and respectful and I want to do it, but don't. Kevin Finley's family attends the weekly worship service at Prince of Peace Lutheran Church. Kevin, Kristen and Kamela also attend the private school there. Kevin and I won't attend the same school campus together for three more years, when I'm a junior in high school, and Kevin a freshman. The Finleys attend church every week, except Mr. Finley. He prefers spending his Sundays unwinding, watching sports and science fiction movies on TV and smoking Pall Malls from his favorite living room chair. The Wellbaums, Toppers, Jennings, Cardosos, Vanderbergs, Lansings, Starrs, and Tyrells do not attend church. On a sleepover, Gary Forest showed me his paraphrased Bible, The Way, he said, "I enjoy reading it at night, it gives me comfort." Comfort from what?

In Hayward, the Moyer's began attending a Quaker Friends Meeting. Our attendance is not optional. Pappa grew up a single child in an unequally yoked home, spiritually speaking. Back in Pennsylvania, Jack's mother, Tessa, is the pianist, organist, music minister, choir director, and worship leader of their neighborhood Church of Christ. His Father, Norman, was a Catholic and attended Mass at a Catholic Church; I do not know the frequency of his attendance.

I'm not sure where Pappa stood spiritually before or after his service in WWII. Did he attend a church? Was he a member of a Christian denomination? Did he believe in God? Did he pray? Based on his upbringing, and serving in the War, maybe.

In the 1972 white Ford Ranch Wagon, Pappa wedged between the windshield and dashboard, a three inch tall, rubber Buddha. When Danny Wellbaum rides with us in the Ford, he pokes the Buddha's belly while laughing out loud; Buddha springs to life and experiences great joy. Danny kept us in stitches for 10 years, and I smile now.

On Sunday mornings, before we leave for the Quaker meeting, Pappa pulls a very large book off the shelf, The World's Great Religions. He gathers the children and we take turns reading out loud about Hinduism, Buddhism, Confucianism, and Christianity. This activity doesn't rank first, second or third on my favorite things to do list, neither is attending the Quaker meeting. I hide a long face and endure. Pappa says he doesn't want to influence us toward one religion or another.

He says, "you need to decide for yourself what you believe," and, "that's why I want you to read about the different faiths." I like Pappa's logic: freedom of religion.

Before the weekly Quaker meeting begins, adults chitty-chat, chitty-chat a while. At the set time, two dozen folks take their seats and . . . quiet. No talking, but lots of quiet, waiting for a divine message, a pleasant thought, a friendly spirit or enlightenment from above? De-stressing from life's hassles? All the above?

The quiet storm lasts an hour.

The good news; younger people endure 20 minutes, then we can (do) leave the meeting. One adult accompanies us (supervision) in the earlier Hayward years.

On the drive home, we might stop at Emil's Villa Barbeque Restaurant on Mission Boulevard in Hayward. Pappa parks on busy Mission Boulevard, directly in front of the restaurant and its large plate windows. Mom and us kids wait for Pappa in the car, and watch patrons enjoying incredible lunches. Pappa steps inside and buys an order of french fries to go. The amazing steak-cut fries are kept piping hot in a foil pie tin with a cardboard foil-lined top, the top is kept secure by the pan's edges crimped over the top. Back in the wagon, Pappa removes the lid and digs in. We each get a few.

One sunny Sunday afternoon, while waiting in the wagon for parents and fries, I notice tucked in the door map-pocket, a loose french-fry-lid from a previous fry-stop. Bored, I grab it. The foil lid reflects an intense, wide beam of sunlight. In any direction I choose. The power of the sun, to wield at my will!

I start small, blinding my sisters separately, then collectively. Shrieks and screams are contained within the vehicle, "stop it Jens. *Stop it!!!*" Empowered, I pinpoint the full strength of the sun, into the satiated eyes of the restaurant's gorging patrons. So fat and happy with their barbeque-sauced cheeks and white cloth napkins hung from their collars. Fire and brimstone sent from the heavens, devour all gluttons! Gorging burgers, gulping shakes, and I'm lucky to get a couple fries?!?

Justice!

Mom storms out of Emil's Villa waving her arms, "stop it Jens!"

How do you like your fine dining and city view now big boy?

Later that year the Hayward Quaker Friends meeting moved from its dreary Hayward location to a private family estate; the property borders Lake Don Castro Park.

What luck!

The Hayward Quakers, loan to members Norman and Alice Jean, the $5,000 they need for the down-payment and they purchase the estate for $110,000 (deal!). In exchange, the Hayward Quakers would meet Sunday mornings, in the Jean's living room, in perpetuity.

The Jeans are a racially mixed couple, Norman is black, and Alice white. This is unusual then. Norman is a retired Marine and Alice a longtime nurse. Their place is great, the living room centers around a huge fireplace, always bright and crackling during winter meetings; Norm tends the fire during the meeting. The meeting's keynote speaker: the roaring fire, uplifts, inspires, and comforts. After twenty minutes, the kiddos slip out.

Most importantly, the Jean house is next door to Lake Don Castro which provides good bass and crappie fishing, and eventually a new fishing buddy. Six months later, a black foster child, Garrett Montaine, moves in with the Jeans. Garrett is 14 like me. We have a lot in common: music, sports, girls and fishing. He's tall like me and Garrett and I are instant friends.

Gary Forest lives with his aunt and uncle because his mother can't afford to raise both him and his younger brother Christopher. "They live in Niles," Gary said.

Gary loves to eat. I do too, but Gary even more so if that's possible. Gary can cook, he's a good cook. I don't notice, but Mom says later, "Gary latches on to people." He did ingratiate himself to our family, way more than any other friend has. He's around constantly. Gary spends quite a bit of time with us, especially mealtime. Gary the leach, barnacle Gary. It's okay because I enjoy his company. Gary's my age, a good basketball player, shorter than me but not as short as Danny W., an inch shorter than Marlo T. and Alex Z. the latter two, two inches shorter than me.

Punt, Pass and Kick PP&K is a football (not soccer) skills contest for kids, it still is. Today, PP&K winners get a ribbon, that's okay but in 1974, PP&K victors receive trophies. A foot tall, the trophies resemble an Academy Award, except these wear a helmet. PP&K trophy-man stands goal-post straight, chest out, stomach in, perfect posture, eyes straight ahead. His right hand holds a football firmly to his side. Bronze for third, silver for second and gold for first, oh yes.

The PP&K trophy resembles an Oscar, but for me it's better. A symbol of outstanding achievement for things I love to do; punt the football far, pass the football farther and straighter than the other guys, and kick the football off a tee, straight away.

As insurance, I plan to send up my first prayer to God. A real prayer. A specific prayer: to win the Punt Pass and Kick gold trophy for 13 year olds. And to move on to the next level. Win gold twice and advance to the Regional Championships; held at half-time at an Oakland Raider game in the Coliseum! PPK's final destination? Super Bowl half-time! That's right, Super . . . Bowl. I want to advance to the Oakland Raider halftime level, beyond that? Pipe dream.

Winter is here, fog, rain, wet leaves on the frosty ground. Football assumes its rightful place in the United States of America; center stage. Boys young and old, on snowy fields and streets, in front of countless TVs, in every corner of the country, regardless of weather or ability, gather to play and or watch football.

Big Saturday.

Pappa and I drive to Mission San Jose High School, to the 1974 Punt, Pass and Kick Competition. The air is cold, I can see everyone's breath including mine. Everything is damp, it's foggy and it's early, 8:00 am. I play after school, when it's warmer. There are several 13 year old boys here. Of the three skills tested, I feel best about the pass. Throwing a football is my best thing. My hopes are pinned to a spiral.

I want to win.

Pappa helps me warm up with some catch.

Pappa suggests I ask God to help me do well. I'll try anything, and nod.

A long tape-measure is strung out, straight away from us, to measure each contestant's punt, pass and kick distance. A field-judge, spots the ball, notes the distance and calls it back. In addition to distance, the field-judge measures how far left or right the ball is off centerline, the tape measure being the center line. For example if I throw the ball 50 yards, six feet right of center, six feet is subtracted from 50 yards, my throw score is 48 yards. Same for the punt and the kick etc. etc. etc.

There's a boy I don't recognize, Dave Hengel. Dave recently turned 13, in December and is in the 7th Grade, my 13th birthday was back in August. So Dave H. is an older seventh grader, and I'm a younger eighth grader. I'm not sure which is better. One thing I am sure of, Dave Hengel threw the football farther than I did. Choke! No! I don't grip the ball well from the frost, the ball is wet too. These excuses don't bother big Dave however.

I forgot to pray.

Next up, the punt. I'm stung, unable to deliver my best pass when it mattered, and *painfully* aware that gold and applause has slipped away. I remember Pappa's advice: "pray to God for help Jens." So this time, I *do* pray. Better late than never?

I pick up the ball, hold it a moment, look down and say to myself, "God, help me punt this ball." Not in a demanding way, but with fear and humility I make my supplication.

In slow motion, arms down, right hand on top, stabilizing the ball, and left palm underneath supporting the football's weight. I spin the ball quick, laces up and place them lightly between my right forefinger and middle finger. Then I slowly lift the ball high in front of me and hold it high, chin height, take two steps toward the line, remove the left hand, ball drops. The football explodes off my right kick foot, a high spiral, great hang time, perfect ratio of forward thrust and height. My best punt *ever* finally touches down . . . the tape moves! I hear reactions from boys and their fathers looking on. I feel good. God heard my prayer and answered. No doubt.

The silver trophy stands on a wall shelf, it's behind me now, eyes dead ahead.

Dave Hengel stole the gold fair and square. Ten years later I feel better, when I buy Dave Hengel's rookie card. Dave played for the Seattle Mariners for years. Yes, I feel better after that.

Lucky Boomerang

For Kevin Finley and I, a boomerang makes every Christmas and birthday list: third on the weapon of choice list, after bb guns and wrist-rockets. Because Kevin F. was so good this year, direct from Australia, via Santa Claus, Kevin receives an authentic wood boomerang. Christmas vacation provides the necessary boomerang training time. On the 26th, early, Kevin and I stride up Jackson Street, toward the empty lot, armed. The Jackson Street swing is directly behind the empty lot - we cut through the empty lot, to access the swing - The empty lot is large, two home lots side-by-side, located eight houses east of the Finley house and directly across from where Troyer Avenue Ts into Jackson Street. These are the last empty lots on Jackson Street. I guess no one wants their house T-Boned by a dumb kid or drunk driver, racing up Troyer Avenue.

This is not the cheap, plastic boomerang; rather, Santa gives Kevin a genuine, Outback approved, Aborigine tested, Aussy hardwood boomerang. So lucky! A whirling messenger of death, a kangaroo kill machine. Oh man! We can't wait to take this baby for a test-drive, get in touch with our inner-Aborigine.

A warm east breeze blows; a Santa Anna, unusual in December. Kevin and I position ourselves at the west end of the lot, 20 feet past the last house and 30 feet into the field from the sidewalk. We don't know how this will turn out (pun intended). Kevin experiments, I observe, no pressure, it's Christmas vacay, let's have fun. The goal is for the boomerang to fly away, then return, like hungry hunters in Australia do. Kevin tries a side-arm throw, like skipping a stone. The boomerang spins away, lifts, sputters and drops to the field 60' away.

Kevin alternates throws. He tries a 45 degree throw, in between overhand and side-arm. This works better rising higher at the end, but the boomerang won't return. We start to doubt the premise and its learning curve (pun intended).

Persistence pays off; we discover an overhand throw, combined with a wrist snap-release, works much better. It has to be thrown overhead.

The boomerang's trajectory runs level for a considerable distance, like a line-drive in baseball, the boomerang's spinning end over end, like a pin-wheel on the Fourth of July. The spinning boomerang flattens like a frisbee and climbs suddenly. It gains maximum altitude at the farthest point and spins vertically again, while at the same time arcing sideways left toward Jackson Street. It continues its U-turn and returns halfway back to us, before touching down.

"Kevin, you're getting it." Encouraged and loose, Kevin goes for it, fires it out there, overhand with 100% more velocity, and a sharp *snap* of the wrist, and guess what? The flat, bent, kill stick returns straight for us! We hear the thing spinning and slicing the air, wop wop wop; WOP WOP WOP! Look out, *RUN*! "That thing would have nailed us." 'Kevin, let me try." I mimic Kevin and pop it hard, across both lots, then up, up, up, left, left, left toward the street, then back, back, *back*. Here we go again, wop wop wop wopp, WOPP WOPP WOPPPWOPPWOPPPP!! "Kevin duck!"

. . *CRASH!!* The sound of breaking glass! The boomerang smashed the gas-meter glass on the side of the house behind us! "Kevin, that boomerang almost took us out!" 'Yeah, guillotine!' From the pile of broken glass and dirt, Kevin snatches Santa's apt gift and we disappear.

Yellow Boat Rotten Plums

Inspired by industrious Darin Vanderberg, I mow lawns and save for my first big purchase. A beautiful, bright-yellow, two-man inflatable raft with oars. The cost? $35.00. It takes several weeks, but I save up. The maiden voyage guest list includes: Kevin Finley. The big yellow boat is set afloat on Lake Elizabeth, the fishing tackle and lunch loaded and Kevin and I board. The strong plastic, new boat smell, increases our excitement. All summer we have a blast in Big Yellow. When fishing slows and the sun heats up, we jump in, flip the boat over and swim underneath it. With our heads in the seat space; we stay under there breathing for five minutes if we want. The goal is to alarm passersby, but it never does.

Jack brings Mr. Boni to the lake and he photographs Kevin and I in the boat on the lake. Mr. Boni is an accomplished professional photographer. The picture quality is superb, the 11x17 and 8x10 black and white prints are striking. Kevin and I tack a Boni print to our bedroom walls, a dear memory. Mrs. Finley is sole possessor of the last surviving prints.

By summer's end the Kevin and Jens boat trips morph into something else entirely. We employ a fishing rod and reel to fly a kite. The kite design is a classic: the Jolly Roger kite, a white skull and crossbones against a black background. Lake Elizabeth's reliable sailing breeze doubles for superb kite-flying. I recently filled my reel with new line and in 15 minutes the kite is so high, we lose sight of it for minutes at a time. Soon, it's gone for good, lost-in-space, like the TV show, except in color not black and white, wait, the kite is black and white. They say, "if you love something, set it free." If it's meant to be, it shall return. I yank the rod back hard and the kite breaks free, never shall it return. In mad glee, Kevin and I run from tree to tree, winding 1,000' of 6-pound test fishing line around their trunks, weaving a world record: fisherman's-tangle.

In the early years, if parental supervision is absent, however brief, our worst natures are unleashed. I'm older than Kevin the Good, so I blame myself.

There are many, many fruit trees dotting neighbors' backyards and something's always in season. Often neighbors allow us boys to pick a bag full of fruit. We had a couple brown grocery bags full of delicious ripe plums, way more than we could eat.

The Interstate 680, Washington Boulevard, south bound off-ramp is located directly behind my house, *and* Kevin's house. The off-ramp is closer to Kevin's back fence than ours.

I cannot overstate the importance of sport in our lives. Not watching sports on TV, but *doing* sports, throwing things. Everything is a target, especially if it moves.

Kevin, what are we going to do with all these sweet juicy plums?

The off-ramp is an endless stream of moving targets. The distance is considerable, 50 yds. By the time the car is visible, it's too late. The car is rolling away during the wind-up. The road angles away from us and only the roof is seen.

Too much persistence.

We connect a couple times; there are consequences. After a solid squish, Kevin and I dart to the front of the house shaking like wet Chihuahuas, resume our basketball game in the driveway, then walk to my house. Kamela Finley shows up, "Mom says, come home now Kevin, you're both in trouble." The target surmises which house the ripe plum originates from and knocks on Finley's door. Serious punishments are given to Kevin and I by our parents.

Thankfully, cars were tough then, solid American steel, instead of thin foreign crap. Or instead of extra chores and grounding, Kevin and I would be on a chain gang like Cool hand Luke.

I must have been good, part of the year, because on Christmas, wrapped with a bow, Santa brought me a wrist-rocket. With near BB gun power, the wrist-rocket is the ultimate slingshot, not as accurate as a BB gun but with practice, close. Wherever I go, the wrist-rocket goes.

On one of countless fishing trips to Lake Elizabeth, Kevin F. and I spot some ducks, in the creek on the other side of the Lake path, way out there, but within range maybe. With a sling and a small stone, I nail one. The duck is spun upside down, head underwater, above, orange legs and webbed feet kicking furiously, non-stop. Kevin and I shift from hunters to bird advocates and start rooting for the fellow at full volume, "turn over, turn over!!" After much too long, *finally* . . . the duck uprights itself. With head up, he looks around and rejoins his family. Woah! We release huge sighs of relief, and wipe our brows. I consider myself extremely lucky.

While shooting baskets in Kevin Finley's driveway, as we often do, we notice up the street on a front lawn, a group of boys our age, engaging in a loud and rowdy game of tackle football. They're having a blast . . . without us. This particular corner lot is six houses east, on the west corner of Jackson Street and Troyer Avenue. The corner lot is big enough for eight boys to play. We recognize them, John Audi lives there. John, my age and height, for reasons unknown, does not associate with me or my friends, they won't even look at us. We have fact-based theories for their continual snub. An invisible line exists between the Finleys and Troyer Avenue; we can't see it, but it's there. We don't know why that is, it just is.

They're too good for us. Kevin and I are ignored, not asked to play.

I recognize John's good buddy Richard. Richard lives around the corner on Barbary Street.
Little Richard looks down on us, says things; that's a matter of verbal record.

It's football season and cold; Kevin stops shooting and looks longingly 6 houses away, toward
the boisterous, tackle football game. We'd been watching John's last drive develop, his team is
doing well, moving forward. It's a big yard, a corner lot, it's third-down, John's lined up at
quarterback, his left side toward us. He takes the snap, stands up straight, pigskin in hand,
positions to pass, drops the ball, grabs the left side of his neck, shrieks once and drops to his knees.
We evaporate.

Before WWI, Kaiser Willhelm II had never been invited to Paris.

For the past 45 years, I have suffered chronic neck pain; it kills me now as I write; no cure.

Coach Anderson

Swishing ten free throws in a row in front of your teammates and coaches at basketball practice is the best.

Academically stagnant since leaving Mr. Turentine's watchful eye and straightforward teaching style, education's fragile shell is cracked, the yolk scrambled. I'm happiest when competing in sports. The eighth grade CYO basketball season went well, although not a winning season; I can picture their faces, practicing hard, breaking a sweat, the teamwork, the team's ebb and flow, our mistakes and successes on the court. The maple hardwood gym floors, the poleless backboards, hovering in mid-air. Bright orange steel rims and bright white cotton nets. The rim is the gateway to ball-net collision, swish! But not an easy thing, it takes me years to get to this point. Driveways, schoolyards during and after-school, weekends. Seven days a week during basketball season, I feel the dribble, hear it. I can almost palm the ball.

This year has been a turning point in my skills. I learn, to reach the next level requires a concentrated effort. In a word, training. *Training* is the *vehicle* to improve, and get where you ache to go.

This will be my last year of league play.

Coach Anderson is Mission San Jose's varsity basketball coach. Tough and accomplished, his reputation is well known, his name synonymous with excellence. The summer before high school, Coach Anderson runs a basketball camp at the high school; I signed up. At camp, the boy's ages range from my age, to incoming seniors. Intimidating.

The Mission San Jose basketball gym is huge compared to Hopkins. We train five days a week, three hours a day, 9am-noon, for four weeks. It's a big difference, playing in the morning versus the afternoon, the first 15 minutes I'm stiff and uncoordinated. But after the warm up I feel good. Drills and more drills, Coach Anderson directs over the din. At one end of the court, he lines us up in four lines, hands everyone a special visor, and says, "wear these visors *below* your eyes". We can't see the ball as we dribble. He says, "dribble out to half court and back, as fast as you can." The front guy of each line takes off, balls go flying, it's awkward and frustrating at first. Coach Anderson isn't smiling. We get the hang of it. "Right hand! . . . left hand!" You're forced to rely on timing and trust the ball will be there, where you need it to be. Head up, eyes look at teammates and play development, rather than the floor and the ball. I remember that drill the most, the hardest to learn.

I'm tall, but not the tallest. I'm not fast and don't have a good vertical leap, my strongest attribute is definitely my arms. With basketball, shooting and passing is everything for me. Same with football, I have a quarterback arm. Not John Elway strong, but Joe Montanish. Accurately, about forty yards on a rope, fifty on a lob. My shoulders and chest are lean, underwhelming, and no wheels; all my muscles need development. I lean on the dribble, the pass, my height, shooting and aggressive rebounding.

A sneaky tight bounce pass, a full court overhand pass and a quick two points in transition, I love that! A tight spiral, the accurate bullet or bomb. Short or long pass, thrown as hard as the receiver can handle, or a soft timing pass. Doing what it takes for the score. Not giving up. Whether the receiver is quick or slow; throw the ball so it lands, right there, in his outstretched arms, in the perfect spot, so he has to catch it. No excuses, that summer before high school, that's what life is. Coach Anderson's summer basketball camp is fun, hard work. I learn basic nut and

bolt basketball stuff; working as a team and playing strategy. A fine continuation of the eighth

grade CYO season. Dribbling my way to high school, eyes straight ahead.

The summer before high school is basketball, fishing and girls. Earlier, I mentioned Garrett

Montaine, my age and friend, a full-time foster child of Norman and Alice Jean. Norman and Alice

Jean are caretakers of the Hayward Quaker Friends Meeting (the Jean's home). My family and I

attend here on Sunday mornings. The Jean's home/Friends Meeting is located next to Don Castro

Lake. Every Sunday, as soon as we are excused from the meeting, Wes and I go fishing.

Perfect.

During the summer of 1975, I'm invited to a sleepover at the Jean's house. Mr. and Mrs. Jean

take Garrett and I to the drive-in movies. Norman Jean, a retired Marine, is always moving,

physically moving, lean, strong and working, rarely still, other than during the Sunday Meeting,

and when he sits and listens to his favorite music with stereo headphones. We pack into the van,

and arrive early, we're the first ones there, so Norman gets the perfect parking spot, close to the

immense screen, dead center. The early bird *does* get the worm. The drive-in is empty. Wes and I

pull two folding chairs from the van and in the parking spot next to the van, set up our own venue.

Neither Wes nor I know which movie we're about to watch, Norman didn't say. There's no

dialogue back at the house or in the van regarding tonight's movie. It's a secret. This is strange, but

as an invited guest, I stay out of it. "Garrett, do you know what's playing?" 'Nope." Whatever's

playing, we have a great spot and are ready for a good time.

Within 30 minutes the drive-in is packed, not an empty spot, *anywhere*. What a sight we must

be; two young 6' 3" guys, in lawn chairs at the drive-in, taking a parking spot, a speaker attached to a lawn chair, ha. What did people think? What, these guys don't have a car? Did they walk in, with lawn chairs?!? Nobody hassles us. No clue which movie is playing, but we did hear, tonight is opening-night for a new movie. Which is cool and rare.

The other movie premieres I'd seen were Soylent Green in 1973, with Neal Black and Linden Braningham in the sixth grade. Neal and I were guests of Linden, celebrating his 10th birthday. Linden and Neal both live in Niles and are close friends.

And in 1974, to a small theatre in the quaint fishing village of Fort Bragg, Ca. - Mr. and Mrs. Boni invited our family to tent-camp on their property in Fort Bragg - Mr. Boni took Bombe and I to the premiere of Godfather Part II.

Soylent Green and Godfather Part II were the most violent movies I've seen.

Opening night explains the full-house.

After a couple cartoons, the movie finally starts and looks innocent and fun; a group of young adults on a beach at night, gathered around a crackling fire, talking, singing and laughing together, one guy plays a guitar. A scene from my future I hope.

A pretty lady and guitar guy sneak off from the group for a private roll in the sand when the young lady decides to go for a swim (in the buff). You don't see much, because it's nighttime. You can barely tell she's bare out there, swimming on top of the black ocean in the dark.

A pulsating bass beat starts; metered and menacing. Quiet at first, steadily increasing in volume and tempo; bump bump, bump bump, bump bump, Bump Bump, Bumm Bumm, loud now, faster BUM BUMM, BUM BUMM, BUMM BUMM!! I hadn't noticed, but it got dark at the drive-in, a cold breeze blows and I tighten. The nice young lady pauses her swim and treads water. She calls to the young man to join her and he struggles on the sand.

WHAMM!! "Oh my God," the lady is violently yanked down below the surface. Quiet . . . she resurfaces. Two seconds later, BAMM! Another groan, down again! "What's this movie rated?!" Quiet again, moments later she floats back up, bobbing like a buoy, BAMM!! Again she disappears beneath, for good. Nooo!

Garrett and I are horrified. Our mouths stuck open, gasping for air, hearts racing. Woaaaah! Woaaaah, hoh, hoh!

We're watching the premiere of Jaws, and just got bit!

Jaws scares the hell out of Garrett and I. From the opening scene's first bite, Director Steven Spielberg and his 25 foot Great White Shark terrorize the shocked audience and fill us with fear, fear of the ocean. Many who watch the film stay out of the ocean for the remainder of their lives; the damage is permanent. Exposed to the cool night air makes Jaw's ocean colder, the shark real, and Garrett and I exposed and vulnerable. I wonder how many 14 year olds watch the premiere of Jaws; exposed to black, windy night?

Trust the ocean? I will not.

High School Freshman!

The summer of 1975 winds down. I will be a freshman at Mission San Jose High School. This is really going to happen. Mission San Jose has a reputation for the best cars and the prettiest girls in Fremont. This proves true.

Hopkins Junior High School is located along the busy 4-lane Driscoll Road. Hopkins, built on a rise, looks down over a long straight section of Driscoll Road. A day doesn't pass that young drivers don't roar past on Driscoll Road. They're loud and fast, and force you to hear and look. Here, Driscoll Road is straight like the Fremont drag-strip; that combined with an audience of 1,500 impressionable junior highers looking on, encourages reckless displays of vehicular exhibition, show offs. Drivers and junior highers are only separated by a couple years; there's a connection. Showing off to young brothers and sisters, cars and motorcycles punch it full throttle past Hopkins. The daily speedshow causes junior highers to salivate in anticipation of getting *their* driver's license.

Two years ahead of me, Darin Vanderberg is already making his Mission San Jose exit! Students who bottom out at Mission San Jose High and Irvington High, wind up at Williamson Continuation School. Darin prefers work, cars, girlfriends, stereos and music, CB radio, things like that. Shortly after his junior year starts, he transfers to Williamson. Kevin Finley is two years behind me, so he's not in high school yet. Gary Forest moved from his aunt and uncle's house in Fremont to a foster home, location unknown. Danny and Guy Wellbaum are at Mission, both sophomores. Curtis Wellbaum, Paula Lansing and Marja are two years behind. They're back at Hopkins. Charlene Lansing, Marlo Topper, Alex Zolanski, Wade Jennings, Maurice Garza and I, fresh-faced all, will start high school together. Hannah, an incoming sophomore, is doing great. Dean Lansing just graduated. Jimmy Lansing a senior, and Donna Lansing a junior, both doing great.

I ride my custom white Schwinn stingray to high school; I'm punctual, I get to campus 20 minutes before the bell, lock up the bike and hang out with friends, never late.

The campus is big, 2,500 students. Cliques abound, and are noisy. You gradually learn who's who, who drives what, how they drive. When muscle cars rumble through the large parking lot, you hold your breath, anticipating the next burnout. V-8 engines rev and race, cars pitch sideways , white smoke fills the sky, the toxic rubber smell permeates the parking lot. The excitement for a young man is total. I feel no shame in riding a bike, the bike racks are long and full of bikes.

Besides, I received rainbow tape for my birthday and decorated my Schwinn with it; a serious upgrade, cutting edge stuff, very attractive. The all new rainbow tape is extremely popular; we saw it first on cars, on the bumper or around a window; a metallic reflective tape flashes different colors from different angles. Bright and dynamic, a multi-color show, very hot. Pappa is intrigued by it too. I roll up to Mission San Jose riding the *only* bike with rainbow tape.

High school debut.

I got my first look at the notorius creek area, at the southwest corner of the parking lot. I had to see for myself. Were rumors true? This congregation of ill-repute we heard so much about? This Shangri La, Nirvana, Lost City of Atlantis, did it truly exist?

Yes . . . the rumors *are* true.

Each morning before the first bell, a boisterous throng of "Creek Rats" gather there. A devil's den of iniquity, high school hellions gather in impressive numbers. Smoking cigarettes, smoking marijuana, they sit in and on their cars, stand in small circles, wear bright or dark, puffy down-jackets or dark blue parkas like mine. Everything's *real*. Loud rock music is thicker than the smoke: Ted Nugent's Stranglehold, Aerosmith's Dream on, Foghat's Slow Ride, Lynyrd Skynyrd's Free Bird, preside over and through all; throughout high school and years beyond. Led Zeppelin's Stairway to Heaven rules supreme.

Hopkin's smoking circlers are kindergartners at snack time compared to the creek rats. The "creek rat situation" is not limited to before school, or only lunchtime. Rats live this life, *full-time*. A different mindset, happy and nasty, angry, rebellious, hilarious, on edge. Upset they only have two middle fingers.

A unique aspect of Mission San Jose High during my era, 75-79', was the school's class scheduling system. Modular-scheduling is cutting-edge but never makes sense. The system creates blocks of *dead* time for every student. Dead zones; some for all, more for some. Freshmen have less "fun time," maybe one 20 minute block of free time between classes. Older students have a 30-40 minute block, or an entire hour not including lunch. I remember Steve Clay's older brother, Dave, a quiet, tough hombre - a grown, hardened man - having an hour of dead time with nothing to do.

Danny and Guy Wellbaum are well established creek rats. My contemporary, John Velasco, jumps in there. John's older brother Don graduated high school last year and drives a nice white Chevy Stepside pick-up with a camper shell. We see Don Velasco at school occasionally, there to harass John or give him a ride home.

Creek rat attendance (loitering) is bolstered by modular-scheduling. "Hanging around" is not exclusive to the creek area only, creek rats loiter at the boy's bathroom (time honored tradition) and kill "free time" with cigarettes, pot, and make-out sessions with cuties. The vigilant MSJ Staff

conduct daily boy's room raids, "break it up!" Their comments are either laced with tough cutting

humor or disdain, depending on which staff member shows up and which creek rats are

confronted.

Coaches are mixed. Unless you're working for a letter jacket - throughout high school, I don't

understand a letterman jacket's significance - they have no love for you. Coach Randle was my

sixth grade summer swimming lesson instructor. Coach Freitas is a joker, Coach Anderson is

awesome. Coach Marten, the track coach who runs 20 miles before breakfast - his son Jack, my

age, is a star sprinter, he wins State twice as a junior and senior - hates all artists, musicians,

underachievers and definitely creek rats.

In hindsight, modular scheduling resembles a college class schedule. The mature and

self-motivated college student handles idle time better, more responsibly, than a high school

freshman. "Hey, I don't have anywhere to be for an hour." "Want a cigarette?" "Yeah." Marlboro

Filters?" "No, Camel Filter." "All riiiight." "Got a light?" Flip open a chrome Zippo lighter, a big

flame and the stench of butane.

Enough about modular scheduling, I have bigger fish to fry. I stay far away from this creek rat

stuff, *I know it's bad, not good, a costly mistake, the worst of decisions.*

Tryouts for Coach Anderson's varsity basketball team are next week. Fresh off a solid CYO

season and Anderson's basketball camp, I beam with confidence, real and imagined.

The day arrives, I sign up, show up, am confident, capable and tall. Yes, there are taller, faster,

better players, better athletes, but I'm undeterred, I like to shoot. The try-out scene resembles coach's summer camp a month ago. Same gym, same coach and same students. The older guys, still intimidating, real whiskers, developed muscles, knockout girlfriends and painted muscle cars. These economic disadvantages and social divisions I hate, but am getting used to. Some stuff is out of my control, heck they're older. I get that, the varsity team is for the older kids, and the freshmen team for me, but we try out together as one group. Varsity and junior varsity selections aren't made solely by age, but by ability, effort and merit, I think.

Coach Anderson's tryout cut system is strange, would not happen today. The varsity team is formed first. After the third day of try-outs, the following morning, a name-list is posted in the boy's locker room, posted publicly. If your name *is not* on the list, you have *not* been cut from the varsity team; and are supposed to attend the next day's tryout. This daily cutting back (less boys each day) continues for two more days, the third list being the last. The names *absent* from the third and final list are the varsity team. Confused? On the final cut, my name is not on the list. I look again, not there, again, no, not there. What the hell? Must be a mistake.

The absence of a name to indicate you make varsity, is a crappy way to receive big news. Very unclear, it feels like, I'll go to the next practice and the coach will probably say in front of the whole team, "Hey Moyer, what are *you* doing here?" I don't like fuzzy or obscure directions, especially for something important. In hindsight, I should have approached the coach privately.

I made the Mission San Jose varsity basketball team, as a freshman? Impossible.

WHAAAAAAT!?!

I never found out.

I mention it to no one. I hold it inside and attend my classes. Art class is the *last* class of the day.

Too much too soon, too much too soon.

Four students sit at each art table. Two guys face two guys on either side of a rectangular table, big enough to plop down clay or whatever the medium. Two seniors sit across from me, Jeff Gable and his sidekick, Mike McCormick. They both tried out for the team. I asked Jeff if he made varsity and he said, "yes." I told him I made it too. He lit up and congratulated me. His good friend, Mike McCormick looked forlorn, he tried out but no luck. His name was posted that morning.

What was I thinking? Is this my out? Do I want an out? No, I want this, I hope to make the freshman team. Coach Anderson sees something in me, I don't see. Too impulsive!

"Hey Mike, you want my spot?" "Huh?" "Uh, yeaaaah . . . thanks."

Why, why, why did I do that?!? No good reason, bad decision, only bad, taking it upon myself to do that? I don't know what came of it. Yes I do, nothing. Why did I think I could replace myself on Coach Anderson's varsity roster?! Ludicrous! Did Mike McCormick get on the team or not? It doesn't matter. Why did I throw away my shot? I want to play basketball, to grow, strengthen and mature into my best self (or ride the bench and never meet expectations). I quit judo last summer; there's no physical development in my future, other than crappy PE classes. This debacle is unknown to my parents and sisters, no one knows. It's more than unsettling, more than sad, worse by writing it down. I don't want others to know. Too bad.

One million unshed tears.

What have I done? What did I do? Why didn't Coach Anderson talk to me, pull me to the side, or call me? If he believed in me, he could have called, defended his choice. No time for flake management. Too many guys chomping at the bit to take your place, for a shot at glory. Jeff G. must have told Coach A. what went down in art class. What does the coach think of me?

Not understanding then (I do now), I liberated myself from the commitment of healthy pursuits, to pursue my heart's desire . . . creek rat?

Three days after high school starts, before basketball tryouts, a thief peels & steals *the rainbow tape* from my bike! I'm furious and start the investigation. Within 30 minutes I corroborate witness testimonies, and the bandit is identified.

Freshman Mark Brassi, doesn't live too far; just west of Mount Olive, where Olive Avenue runs into Washington Boulevard, above the Old Winery on Bruce Drive. Mark's gnarly older brother, Steve Brassi, is out of high school, driving fast cars and jet-boats, has a cute girlfriend, long hair, muscles and works construction. I have my Guy and Danny Wellbaum alliance, but that's it. It's revealing how teenage boys from two neighborhoods nearby and familiar, dislike one another without cause.

Unbeknownst to me, weasel Mark Brassi, did the dastardly deed with the foreknowledge of prearranged back-up. Back-up from older creek rats.

The boy with older brothers has the advantage over the boy who doesn't.

Mark Brassi in addition to simply desiring the hot cool rainbow tape (enough to steal it) was probably encouraged, manipulated by a wiser senior rat, Kent Bailey, to steal the tape just to pick a fight. I do know Kent Bailey's younger twin brothers, Creg and Dave. The twins are freshman too, smart, tough, affable; but for an unbeknownst reason, the Bailey twins and their comrade and neighbor, Jerry Cranks, keep me at arm's length, and any attempt at friendship is abandoned early. The mysterious older brother, Kent Bailey, lurks in the creeks' shadows. Kent the senior is hard like Steve Clay's older brother; acne, stiff whiskers in clumps, white T-shirt, bell-bottom blue jeans, sheathed buck knife worn on his belt, girlfriends, muscles and driving . . . an unpredictable and scary druggy.

The instant I know for sure Mark Brassi stole the tape, I march toward the creek. With each step, the battlefield is in better focus and reassessed. I'm flanked and encouraged by eager to fight, Guy and Danny Wellbaum, they smell blood. I don't know Mark Brassi. Long, frizzy, blonde Robert Plant hair, well past the shoulders, I've seen him when passing the creek in the morning, at the boy's room, and pitching quarters. Besides being the thief who ripped me off, I've had no previous dealings or conversation with Mark Brassi whatsoever.

Calling Mark a thief, that's rich.

Mark Brassi sees me coming a mile away. Rats look alive!

An unexpected turn; Kent Bailey is there, with Mark. Kent has Mark's back! I hadn't factored senior Kent Bailey into the fight plan. Bailey's lowered, gold Chevy SS with chrome mag-wheels is parked in between myself and Mark Brassi, next to the creek. Worthy of note, generally speaking, white kids raise their cars up and Mexicans lower their cars. The fact that Kent Bailey is white, but his car lowered, and that he drives *extremely slow,* adds to the tension.

Battle lines are drawn. Waiting beyond the pulled-down chain-link fence, on a dirt field off school property, Mark Brassi wears a light blue puffy down jacket, with no shirt, just his skinny tanned torso, (Mark's signature look). Mark is extremely animated and struts side to side, 20' feet in each direction, his very long frizzy blonde hair, bounces with each step and animates the scene. His body points left and right, his face and eyes stay fixed on me. He's egging me on, is a gross understatement. To Mark Brassi's immediate left, my right, Kent Bailey stands statue still, composed, mute and wearing a clean white T-shirt. Kent with tattooed muscled arms folded, bristles, stares me down, daring me to come closer.

Kent dominates the scene. Nefarious.

Danny, Guy and I stop, just short of the 30' section of chain-link fence laying on the dirt, and conduct a final assessment. Clearly, any fight will include not only Mark Brassi, but back-up Kent Bailey as well. Flanked by the Wellbaum double team makes the fight seem fair. Kent Bailey is two clicks above Guy Wellbaum in strength and hardness. Mark Brassi is very doable, not problematic. His lion-pacing show does not work on me.

I like the tension.

My focus shifts from Brassi . . . to Bailey. I switch from hot wrath, to cooler head. I compute a risk versus reward analysis; do a sanity check. Is honor, self-respect and rainbow tape, worth being beaten, stabbed, or shot?! Yes.

Within the fraught stand-off, I sense a disturbing vacuum of fairplay. I don't want to look over my shoulder for the next four years. Turning away from the creek rats, I say to Guy and Danny, "it's not worth it, let's get out of here," and we retreat.

Surprisingly, there's no name calling from the rat camp. It's a sensible decision. No taunts are slung, no stones hurled, verbal or literal. The withdrawal isn't rushed or void of honor. There was a lengthy pause, an ample opportunity for either side to initiate a fight. We were close, 20' apart, Mark and Kent got a good look at the dealio, with plenty of time to attack. There was not a word said by either side.

I'm accustomed to a fair fight. I do not see that happening here.

In defense of my withdrawal, a large folding buck knife in a black leather case worn on the belt, is standard male creek rat issue, Brassi and Bailey no exception. Additionally, senior Kent Bailey, rules the rat colony, he's the kingpin. It doesn't make sense to challenge that. That's how I see it. I'm not looking to be crowned rat king, I'm not a creek rat. I just want my rainbow tape back. They show their true colors: thievery and a gang mentality.

This time, justice will require patience.

A Whisper

After the sticky rainbow tape incident and quitting basketball, my bike breaks down and I'm walking to school. Not in the snow like Pappa, but Jens n'friends in the California sunshine. The friends? Yup, you guessed it: Guy and Danny. The shortest route to school (path of least resistance) takes us directly through the infested creek rat zone and its minefield of mysteries.

Near school, we cross the dry creek bed and walk across a flat dirt area, half the size of a football field, the same spot where the Mark and Kent stand-off occurred a month ago. Numerous rat packs dot the area; guys and gals huddled close, passing around lit marijuana joints. The scene is smoky, emotional and . . . *musical*. It's cold, you see the breathing. The puffy down jackets are common, many with telltale cigarette holes burned through the outer nylon shell, some patched, some not. The rat colony (a few I recognize, most not) is dispersed along the dirt-packed sidewalk (along the 16 foot high tennis court fence) and next to their cars in the parking lot near the creek. There are twenty groups or more. A happening spot for sure, excellent loud rock n roll broadcasts from high-end car stereos, acoustic guitars are out, strumming and picking the latest rock anthems, and all before 8am! A lively spirit is here, a lot of heart. Creek rats in good standing, Guy and Danny smile, laugh and invariably join their group of choice. They start tokin' n jokin', shuckin' n' jivin', I watch them for 6 seconds as I think about what to say and how to get away. They take a puff and Guy invites me to join, "cmon Jens, it's greaaat, tryyy it," 'no thank you and walk to class.

The daily, morning walk past creek rat packs routine, continues for two weeks . . . then . . . I . . . stop and stand just outside a circle with Guy and Danny. Just to listen for a minute, so as not to be rude. A raucous torrent of humorous one-liners, irreverent zingers and lighthearted cussing are interspersed with longer urgent human interest stories. Stories from home, situations they're dealing with, problems with parents, or the "old man." I hadn't heard that reference before. I had zero interest in participating in their conversations or competing for air time. I have no earthy jokes to tell. It's 15 minutes before the bell. Beyond showing up to class on time, I have no scholastic pressure, nothing pressing, nothing difficult to plan for, execute or perform.

So much emotion at the creek, drama they call it today. The reality drama makes the panoply of rock song lyrics much more important, emotionally supportive. Interest in music is intense down here, through the roof. A lot of kids know all the lyrics and understand their meaning, they comment on them. *Rocker Central*. The music I love engulfs me, blasting clean and clear from expensive quality stereo equipment, not weak junk.

I hear music like never before.

In the circle a joint is lit.

Like I said before, the daily pot circle on the field at Hopkins Junior High is child's-play compared to the creek rat congregation at Mission San Jose High. I attended the Hopkins smoke circle once. Once was enough to get the gist of it. Various regulars produce sandwich baggies full of low-grade pot, full of seeds, referred to as grass. A "lid" or an "ounce" fills the baggie and only costs ten bucks (a fair amount then). The 'grass' is rolled into joints or stuffed into pipes and its effect is mild to nothing. During my freshman year however, pot's potency increases 10-fold. The transition to stronger pot happened before my eyes, during my freshman year.

The new potent pot shows up at the creek: columbian gold is light brown in color, not green, and more expensive; joints are two dollar a piece. The herbicide, paraquat is allegedly contaminating batches of Columbian Gold in Mexico and complained about frequently by rats, causing sore throats etc. etc. etc.

In addition to english, math and science, we sign up for elective classes, classes of interest: art, music, homemaking etc. etc. etc. I signed up for Elementary Guitar. Hannah's been taking private classic-guitar lessons at home; and guitar classes at school as well. Hannah plays folk and classical guitar very well.

On the same morning as my initial "creek experience," in guitar class, I pick the opening notes to Stairway to Heaven for the first time. Our guitar teacher Mr. Smith, is short and leprechaunish, full-beard, no mustache and spry. His passionate teaching style is infectious. Mr. Smith employs an easy-learn method for guitar, called notation. Notation dramatically shortens the learning curve; the laborious process of learning to read music is sacrificed for same-day gratification. The hope is, by learning a favorite song quickly, the student's interest in his or her instrument will grow. Why waste a year learning how to read music, when you can jam in three weeks? Mr. Smith has 50 popular songs for his students to choose; songs from the late 60's, to today, all printed in notation form. The student chooses a song printed on a single sheet of paper, and gets to work. Within a semester, students perform two songs for Mr. Smith (midterms), and a third song performed to the entire class (final).

It's difficult to convey the feeling, when I pick the opening notes of Stairway to Heaven, on a tuned Yamaha classical guitar (on loan from Hannah); hypnosis submersed in goosebumps. It's not work, it's not play, it's a legal drug and I'm hooked. Mr. Smith's song choices are hot; Neil Young, Fleetwood Mac, Led Zeppelin, Paul McCartney and Wings etc. etc. etc. If I really like a song, I play along with the album at home.

Notation does create interest. We quickly learn a few songs and mimic countless song fragments recorded by our rock heroes. With notation, Mr. Smith produces a generation of mediocre guitar players, me included.

Guy passes the joint to me, I take it, pinch it slightly and feel the weed's texture through the Zig-Zag rolling paper, purse my lips and take a hit. Per instructions I inhale and hold it in as long as possible, hack-cough exhale and everyone laughs. It works its way around again, I listen to endless jokes, laughs and stories, I take another drag, a little less, inhale, hold it as long as possible, then exhale smoothly. Easy.

Ten minutes till Admin, time to go. "See you later, thanks."

Admin is the morning daily roll-call for the entire school. We're seated alphabetically based on last name and report here every day. My admin spot is the basketball gym. A straight shot from the creek, along the dirt-packed sidewalk past the tennis court area, six courts. Up a few wide cement stairs, across a concrete patio, through one of eight, side by side, tall wood and glass doors, into a large roofed courtyard that is access to the gym, the pool and the student locker dressing rooms. Hang right through a tall solid wood door into the gym, immediately right to the bleachers, walk up to the seventh row and sit with 50 fellow students. Had the one taking roll, been musically inclined, instead of Coach Marten, we could have stood and sang as a choir. Robert Muela sits to my immediate left and a pretty girl, Sydney Mowery, on my right. Although Sydney is pretty, I don't recall a friendly connection. I don't know why. Maybe I was intimidated by her or distracted by the blackjack or poker game with Robert and the guys.

In PE, Robert Muela serves me a slice of humble-pie, and confirms the inevitable; I'm slow. The PE class for that 8 week segment is track. We're paired up alphabetically to do the 100 yard dash. The coach is timing us, taking notes. I'm paired with Robert Muela. Because Robert is stockier and shorter than myself, I'm sure I'll win. I start ahead, however, a determined Robert slowly but surely pulls ahead and wins. Ahh, reality check, disappointment, embarrassment.

I make my way to admin, to my bleacher seat. The weed hit me on the cement steps leading to the gym vestibule. Blurry vision accompanied with distorted depth perception and for the first time, paranoia. Sitting on the bleacher in the gym, Robert says, "your eyes are red." I glance away. I'm not doing this again, I thought. How long is this going to last? Robert seemed surprised mixed with concern. John Marten, Mission's track coach, conducts the daily, 20 minute call and response roll-call.

My first class of the day is beginner guitar. There are a half dozen stoners in here. Paranoia continues. We get in shifting cliques of four, and tinker and tune our instruments. Mr. Smith starts class with fingerpicking exercises, Arpeggios. Up to this point, my guitar career is uninspired, ineffectual, until I pick the opening notes of Stairway to Heaven.

In those defining moments, my guitar interest sprouts. I practice and play along with Jimmy Page on the record I bought days ago. I strive to play without mistake and match Jimmy Page note for note, and express the spirit of the song. I want listeners to hear what I hear, to enjoy it like I do.

Jimmy Stanford, a sophomore, lives in Mark Brassi's neighborhood and the two are good friends, they grew up on *their* Jackson Street, Bruce Drive. Jimmy isn't confrontational and abrasive like Mark. Jim's a good drummer and loves to play acoustic guitar too; if he's not in class, or in an elongated make-out session with his girlfriend, Jim can be found sitting stoned on the curb, at the creek, working out a song on his guitar. Long n' wavy strawberry blonde hair, an inch past the shoulder wearing a medium blue, puffy down jacket, Jimmy and guitar are ready to play. Funny, he spends more time tuning his guitar than playing it. A creek rat fixture and enrolled in advanced guitar with my sister Hannah, Glen is also an experienced stagehand for the Mission San Jose Drama Department with rookies Kevin O'Malley and John Velasco.

I learn guitar from Jim, he shows me song after song, at either the creek or the boys room, the Rain Song by Led Zeppelin being the most memorable. Rain Song is in Mr. Smith's song catalog and I choose it for my 2nd midterm later in the semester.

Stoned before school, report to admin (roll call), and float to guitar class happens twice the first week, a few times the following week and nearly everyday thereafter. The initial experience becomes a routine, then a lifestyle.

During the initial week I heard a firm inner voice warning, "don't do it again, you'll get hooked. Don't be a creek rat. Don't smoke pot. They will ruin your life."

The inner warning is at first clear, but soon grows faint, eventually becoming a whisper, easily silenced.

I toke my way to class, no one stops me, I don't stop me. In three weeks I shift from passionate, insecure athlete, and academically responsible student; to hazy, goofy grinning rock disciple. I can't go back. The creek life is my choice. I wasn't drafted, I enlist willingly; music, a smorgasboard of smoke and pretty emotional girls; the unpredictable buzz. Every previous relationship amongst the straight and narrow is released, abandoned, forgotten; trashed by my indifference.

In the next four years, I do not attend a school football game, basketball game, any game; not a school dance, no junior prom, no homecoming dance, no Sadie Hawkins dance, no senior prom. Mom and Pappa's only son, never earns another A, or gives them cause to rejoice.

Ten-in-a-row free throws at a basketball practice, a second place punt pass & kick trophy, and an eighth grade CYO basketball all-star plaque with my name engraved, mark the peak of a dead athletic career. What is a letterman jacket? I don't know. I see jocks wear them but am clueless of their exact meaning; they look cool, and must mean something significant. No personal skills, no social skills, nothing but stoned rock n roll bliss.

The din of other's progress encircles me, rings in my ears all around. Young people moving forward, noisy and enthusiastic, deafening. While I commit Led Zeppelin's oeuvre to memory, my ambitious classmates earn letter jackets, learn Spanish, French, discuss colleges etc. etc. etc. They look great, dress in vogue. I shun theater and english. No journalism, photography, auto-mechanics or hotrod building. Not even the roaring Fremont Dragstrip piques a response.

I prefer stupor.

A simple life, no challenge or effort, no confusion. Pick out hot songs on the guitar, that's it for me. I pay attention to new music coming out, but only specific genres. I rock to Eddie Money, Tom Petty, Aerosmith, Yes, especially Yes. Rush, UFO (live), all Led Zeppelin's albums front to back, every song, beginning to end. Every note from every instrument, each drum and cymbal strike, each word . . . memorized. I don't sort out obscure lyric meanings.

My Swedish grandmother came to visit during our country's Bi-Centennial, the summer of 1976. She gave me the album Physical Graffiti for my 15th birthday! My interest in music never finds a constructive outlet. Nothing comes of it, no physical or mental development whatsoever.

I do love it.

D- in Chemistry, D- in Spanish. During freshman year, 90% of the guys take the four trade classes. One each quarter; wood-shop, drafting, metal-shop and auto-shop. In wood-shop class at

Hopkins Junior High, Marlo Topper and I both received an A+. At Mission, my shop teachers hate me, especially wood-chuck Mr. Grinley.

My sophomore english teacher, Mrs. Sousa, in front of the entire class, tells me to quit high school and go to work. In her defense, I was head on the desk when she said that.

I push the envelope as far as it will go.

As a sophomore, I sign up for advanced-guitar. For a final, on my tuned Takamine steel string (first guitar), I play *and sing* Stairway to Heaven all the way through, stoned bad. The class loved it, I made sure of that.

By 1977, pot triples in potency again; gone was columbian gold. Sinsemilla, thai stick, hash and honey oil take its place. Sinsemilla is $10 per gram, and comes in a mini-ziplock bag, enough for two joints, three pinners, or one bone.

I smoke sinsemilla, right before my final; I play Stairway to Heaven, the three year old monster classic, in front of the class, sitting on the edge of the stage, legs dangling, my feet don't hit the floor; - guitar class was held in the Little Theater - I play *and* sing the song. The intro verses go well, the audience is relaxed and they feel it. I'm *too* relaxed however, a long drool grows slowly down from my open mouth, then falls to my shirt. I wipe it away and don't miss a beat. I got an A+, yet am extremely embarrassed.

Springtime brings sun and fun to the creek. I get proficient at frisbee (letter jacket for frisbee?) and pot smoking at lunchtime, rampant truancy ensues.

Mission San Jose High is an open-campus. The perfect compliment to modular scheduling, cigarettes, pot and filthy lucre.

Students are better off locked up, like private schools.

I beeline it to the pool hall in gritty downtown Irvington.

The pool hall is next to a topless and bottomless bar. I never get in there, I'm happy to report.

The draw for me is not pool, but pinball. After sacrificing education, for endless hours of flipping shiny steel balls, flashing lights, the bang-clang and *POP*, I become pretty good at it, not a wizard, but no slouch (I tend to slouch). The goal is to play as long as possible on the least amount of coin. For a quarter (earned pitching quarters (filthy lucre) before lunch & during scheduled breaks) (lunch paid for by pitching quarters (filthy lucre) before lunch) you get two games, five balls per game. With skill and chaos, if the required score is reached, a loud *POP* is heard by all and a free game credit is earned.

My harsh, and fragmented writing style reflects my lousy life choices.

Ink and Glue and Justice

Aside from the music, fishing, girls and pinball, there are two pleasant though skewed frosh-soph memories.

My favorite class is Model Making (yes, it's offered). Remember the time period and setting. If the 70's era is the sun, Fremont is a kid playing with a magnifying glass under that sun, burning things; muscle cars, dragsters and funny cars race at Fremont Drags *every* weekend, custom car shops are as numerous as the stars. General Motors Plant, the Ford Motor Plant and all their employees, Fremont's fathers, are in their prime. These concentrated, dynamic forces *ripple out* into surrounding neighborhoods. This intense refracted beam of automotive celebration burns *deep*. We live and breathe, inside this auto hot zone, in the fire.

Model building is a big deal among my contemporaries, in my town, in the western world. A stepping stone, a tangible promise of the day we drive for real. Before we're old enough to drive, we obsess with the automobile; model making is hot.

Though buying power peaks in the 70's, like it or not, the Moyer's exist (happily) near the lower end of the Bay Area standard of living. A State of California employee draws a consistent monthly salary, but is three clicks below a GM employee making union wages working bookoo overtime, two clicks down from a construction worker and two clicks above welfare. This isn't unusual on Jackson Street. Without thinking about it, I gravitate toward other boys of equal means. Nothing is doled out, except on Christmas and birthdays; that's why those celebrations are so damn important. Jackson Street youth work for a living. There's nothing beyond room and board the rest of the year (very much appreciated Pappa and Mom), which is fine.

I learn later that modest means is the best way to begin this life!

I built models for years, so the model class at Mission is perfect. The mid-term project is, you guessed it . . . a car model. The final class assignment is . . . wow you're good, another car model.

And, there's an annual model contest, *hot diggity*.

Competition is *fierce*, there's three model masters; Bailey twins Creg and Dave and their lifetime next door friend, Jerry Cranks, throw their hats into the ring. Mission San Jose's annual Model Contest is a big deal, wildly popular and a legit opportunity for frosh-soph to shine. In the quad area (quad is antithesis of creek) is a large, glass front, oakwood display case, mounted on steel supports at eye level. The case is beautiful and has been standing in the quad since the school's founding in 1964. The model contest entries are proudly displayed in the case for the *entire* school to scrutinize. This gets me pumped up. Based on the mid-term models, I know Jerry Cranks and the Bailey twins are the main threats, I mean, primary concerns, I mean "friendly competition."

There's no way I'm *not* winning. And I know *exactly* how. We didn't have a say in our mid-term model choice, they were doled out by teacher discretion. My first model was a dog; a 1975 Mustang Mach 2, arguably the worst Mustang ever built. I got an A+. The next model will be both our final, and our contest entry (if we participate). The good news? The final model is *our* choice.

I think, to win, would recover some warrior pride and hopefully recapture a little respect, admiration, a girlfriend . . . all the above. This is a tall order and I know that. Only the best looking vehicle on the planet will fit the bill. Fortunately, I am qualified to make this decision.

The 1940 Ford pick-up truck, in candy-apple red, is like Elvis, nothing both looked *and* sounded better. Sexy and practical, 1940 Ford trucks have it all; and made by Monogram, the best model manufacturer. Yes, that works.

There are three model classes competing, not just mine. I keep it quiet, for as long as possible, until after the other contestants reveal their picks. I don't need any copycats. Obviously, models have to be built flawlessly, additionally, we add custom details. For example, thin bare solid copper wires used as spark-plug wires to add realism; that engine looks hot!

First place is decided by the most votes, a student's choice award! I may be a stoner outcast, but if I'm into something, I perform. And I am into this. By the way, the non-identical twins, Creg and Dave Bailey, and Jerry Cranks are straight, clean, not to be seen at the creek.

Jerry Cranks and I are the top vote getters, by a mile! Forget the rest. I don't remember Jerry's model, but I remember Jerry. I tolerate Jerry and the twins. I got along fine with Dave and Creg before, however, since the rainbow-tape rip off, not so much.

Why the teacher allows Jerry, myself and the Bailey twins to tally the votes, I'll never know. Regardless, nice guys or not, the Bailey twins are guilty by association with older brother Kent; Kent Bailey-senior creek rat kingpin, protects Mark rip-off Brassi, and justice is denied.

Jerry Crank's only crime? A friend of the Baileys, thereby culpable. And I like Jerry. They must have heard where that rainbow tape ended up. During the vote-tally, by quick-talk and slight-of-hand, I assure the count, win the contest and the school's eternal love for a week, maybe two.

Guilt by association: Jerry Cranks is the sacrificial lamb for sticky fingers Mark Brassi and his menacing bodyguard Kent Bailey. Their theft of Pappa's gift in broad daylight, in front of peers and in my face?! Two wrongs *make* it right.

The other sweet sophomore memory thrust me into some sweet company, in Coach Ruiz's geometry class.

Incredibly popular, more than anyone should be, and still a stud athlete: meet varsity wrestling coach, glam-darling of Mission San Jose, Coaaaach Ruuuizzz! Medium height, Yul Brynner shoulders and exotic look; Mr. Ruiz' God-given looks are a Puertorican, Latino, Polynesian fusion. A full head of bouncing, medium long, curly Polynesian hair, he drives to school a 1957 fire-engine red Chevy Corvette convertible with white painted sides, a fire-breathing classic; a knife driving down the road. Before becoming a teacher and coach, Mr. Ruiz was one win shy of wrestling in the Olympic Games.

To say Coach Ruiz is a hit with the ladies, (Mission's entire female student body) is understatement of the year.

So, I'm in Coach Ruiz's geometry class, a springtime sophomore, stoned out of my mind, head on the desk, the iconic Farah Fawcett poster tacked to the front wall, next to the chalkboard. The class is riddled with popular class clowns, serious jocks and the prettiest cheerleaders. I lift my head momentarily and catch the class hottee, miss ultra-popular brunette senior cheerleader, she's turned facing the back of the class, her chin cradled in her left hand and left elbow supported by the back of her chair, staring at me, unembarrassed. Oh yea, a ray of sunshine! So I stare back with salmon-egg eyes and awkward grin; she compliments me to her friends! I sit up erect and eat it up. The bell rings, onto the fourth period.

Rewind two weeks: I'm burned out, crispy around the edges, it's end of day, basic art class. It's hot outside and inside the classroom. The instructor suggests a silk screen project; (our paths cross again after senior year). Reluctantly I agree. A silkscreen is the ultimate way to decorate a T-shirt. T-shirts and tank-tops with a cool rock design are *wildly popular*. I like to wear a T-Shirt with a design on it, something clever or edgy. For my project design, I chose an image of Robert Plant from the <u>Led Zeppelin III Album,</u> off the inner album sleeve. Robert's wearing a large cross-necklace. It's not a photograph, rather a negative image, just 2 colors.

In class there's an overhead table camera in a dark room, to project the image onto a special 2-layered film. The image size is adjustable and after enlarging it just right, a photograph is made onto the top emulsion layer. Now I have an 18x18 piece of 2-layered film, with Robert Plant's image on the orange colored emulsion layer. With an exacto knife, I gently cut through the top orange emulsion layer, along the image lines, peel off the sections where I want the ink on the shirt to go, the remaining emulsion film is adhered to the silk screen. Now the silk screen is ready to print high quality Robert Plant silhouettes, to an infinite number of T-shirts, or more.

I either brought an extra shirt, or, removed the one I wore; it's hot out. The silk screen frame is secured to a hinged press. The shirt is positioned on the press, the silk-screen is swung down and secured; a small amount of paint is squeezed out of a tube onto the screen; squeegee the paint across the screen in different directions, to get solid coverage, lift up the screen and voila.

The shirt design is hot; teacher and students are impressed. I'm pleased. In deep hush the teacher says, "you can sell these Jens." So I do, $5 bucks a piece. Customers provide the shirt. I sold ten. Do any of Jens'- Robert Plant shirts survive? Let me know please.

Work begins ASAP on the next design, the Led Zeppelin ZOSO symbol, and the three rune symbols underneath. True to the original designs, the Robert Plant shirts are orange, the ZOSO shirts are black and white. They both sell well, timing is spot on; Zeppelin's appeal is massive and my uni-shirts are popular with guys and gals. Especially the girls, a pleasant surprise indeed.

Some of the finest girls in school, including the starer in Coach Ruiz's class, wear them!

After winning the schoolwide model contest and producing popular custom shirts, I strut around campus with a natural high. Thanks to me, this creative spurt and industry, not unlike my athletic and academic development, stall and die.

Friends and Family

I consider the boys that live nearby, who remain outside my friend circle, and wonder why. The divide may be economic. Chris Peter's and Maurice Garza's fathers have high-paying jobs, the Audi's too. My friends and I lean on each other. Pappa is strict but our home is peaceful, Mom is happy. Among my friends however, a common denominator seems to be trouble at home. Darin Vanderberg's home life is fraught with tension I don't understand. Mrs. Vanderberg is a prolific seamstress and needlepointer; her home is stocked to the rafters with colorful textiles. Mr. Vanderberg works hard somewhere, drives a pale green Mustang and a very large green Dodge car. Darin's oldest brother, John is a shiftless drifter and puts the parents through hell. John lives from town to town returning for short stays. Older brother Russell joins the Marines, Kevin is on a fast track to get out of the house ASAP.

Mr. and Mrs. Topper seem strained to the breaking point. Mrs. Topper is a seamstress for United Airlines and works a ton of overtime, and is gone all day. Mrs. Topper suffers from exhaustion and duress, which leads to short bouts of mental breakdown. She checks into a mental hospital for a week, a couple different times to recuperate, very traumatic. Mr. Topper is a short, broad-shouldered, crass, ex-rodeo star and a union carpenter. Part and parcel to construction, there are a few short lapses of unemployment, but by and large, work is steady. Once a week Mr. Topper gets drunk at the Shamrock Bar

I find myself day or night, down the street, loitering with the gang (imagine Little Rascals, 8 years older) in front of next door neighbors: Cortez & Wellbaum. Twice I'm there late enough to watch Mr. Topper return from the bar; a 66' Dodge pick-up slow-rolls up the street, one tire at a time crawls up and over the curb onto the flat dirt spot next to the driveway. Mrs. Topper uses the concrete driveway and carport for her new car. Mr. Topper and the squeaky Dodge finally come to a stop, the engine shuts off. 15 minutes goes by, nothing, then the door opens, Mr Topper exits the truck very slowly and stands in the driveway.

After dinner on Saturday when he leaves the house, Mr. Topper is dressed to the nines, button up shirt, clean new Wrangler blue jeans, a huge shiny metal rodeo belt buckle and dress leather cowboy boots. The ends of his very long mustache are evenly curled and held in place with mustache wax, and tipped smartly, a beautiful cream colored Stetson cowboy hat.

Dark, cold and very early: 2;15 am, Mr. Topper stands in the driveway swaying, disheveled, no hat. Though reeling, his stance is solid, impressive. He cuts a masculine figure. His short bowed legs - strong as iron from rodeo, hard work and good genes - keeps Marlo's dad upright.

Every Saturday night Mr. Topper gives his best to the Shamrock Bar, three miles away located on Blacow Road and Fremont Boulevard; he's their four-leaf clover.

In those days, drunk drivers were expected, graded; spotted weaving on roads *every* Friday and Saturday night. Weee! "Watch out for the drunks." "Will do, thanks." Hic.

Wellbaums and others slowly cross Jackson Street to taunt Mr. Toppers for laughs. He's happy to see them.

Life is sunny and cruel on Jackson Street. Many times the human tragedy used to amuse, eventually afflicts the amusee.

Too smart for his own good, Kevin Finley, a cutting wit and talented teaser like his father, gets everybody to laugh, a real crack-up. However, a lot of tension resides in their home. Tight nerves, heightened senses mixed with fear equate to the Finley version of family peace and order. Mr.

Finley doesn't pick a fight, he's a great guy, but he's *edgy*, and *ready* for a fight; verbal or physical, whichever. We respect those qualities, but keep our distance, careful not to provoke. Uptight, on the brink, funny quips and highly intelligent, he entertains himself and family by ridiculing those that ask for it, making them feel stupid. The whole family has this chip; revels in smart aleck celebration. I didn't know being smart could be problematic, but it can.

When not working, from his living room chair, in front of a small, grainy, color TV, Keith Finley chain smokes Pall Malls and watches endless sporting events and science fiction movies (I'm wired the same way). The family walks on egg-shells and gives him a wide berth, me too.

Keith Finley grew up hardscrabble in the beautiful Black Hills of South Dakota, Indian country. Keith and his brothers were rough and tough. To stay entertained, the Finley brothers often engaged in friendly games of chicken; taking turns to see how close they could shoot their 22 rifles at one another, or how close they could throw a knife near one another, and not move etc. etc. etc.

Keith served in the Korean War.

Thank you Mr. Finley.

On a freezing moonless night, Private Finley drives his assigned army motorcycle along a Korean dirt road, he spots two buddies on their military motorcycles, heading straight for him! Keith decides to have a little fun, play some chicken, like back home. I'll ride between these two boneheads, and scare the crap out of em'.

But they ain't motorcycles . . . it's an army jeep! Private Finley celebrates his win from inside a body cast.

The rumor went, Mr. Finley got mean if he drank. If he does drink, everyone clears out. So he doesn't drink. During my 10 years on Jackson Street, he only drank once. Family members vacate for a day or two, then life goes back to normal.

Mr. Zolanski, beloved pillar of Jackson Street, is a longtime employee and supervisor at the nearby General Motors Assembly Plant. Bernard makes a good living and buys an enormous Winnebago RV; a massive refrigerator box with huge tinted windows on wheels with all the creature comforts, a rolling adventure palace.

Next summer I'm invited by Alex and his dad to go camping in Yosemite and I accept. Alex, younger brother Denny, Mr. Zolanski, a co-worker and I, head east in the Winnebago. This is my one Zolanski family vacation and only RV experience. There are several fun firsts on this guys only trip.

Bernard and his friend sit up front and divy up the driving. Their topics of discussion include; which line on the road, yellow, or white, does each one tend to drive the massive vehicle closer to? The white line on the right shoulder? Or the center yellow line on the left? Results reveal each driver favors the other line. We three boys have the run of the place, aft to stern, in the biggest RV Winnebago ever made.

It's a very hot day in California's Central Valley; sciroccos scorch fertile fields and desolate wasteland, equally. We zip by field after field of 16 foot tall corn. Mr. Zolanski pulls Winnie into a hamburger stand in Oakdale, California and buys us all lunch. I savor the delicious burger and french fries, and my first and largest, chocolate and vanilla soft-serve ice cream cone - in a dipped chocolate shell - I've ever had.

What a beauty!

It's 110 degrees outside; I feel the hot black asphalt through the soles of my sneakers and attempt to hose a skyscraper of soft *bliss*. The cone, woefully inadequate to support the significant weight, disappears, buried under vanilla and chocolate.

A sweet race.

In vain I try to keep up with the melting tower, licking and chomping my way. I've met my match! Broken sheets of chocolate shell shift down covering my hand.

A 12" tall tower of swirled chocolate/vanilla soft serve, encased in a delicious chocolate shell, on a 3" cone. A sweet mess!

Mr. Zolanski laughs and laughs as ice cream covers my hands, wrists, clothing and face. Sweet defeat! Bernard's laugh is deep, gravely, loud and real. Mr. Zolanski is very generous and I begin to understand why he's so beloved by his family and all of Jackson Street.

I mentioned Mr Zolanski's skin condition before; large warts cover his entire body, face and head, down to his feet. This is difficult to look upon at first and I believe the years of ceaseless gawking his father receive(s)d, has had a profound effect on Alex.

As soon as Alex is old enough to speak he confronts his father's vulturian-assailants with spine tingling wrath. After a decade, Alex's reaction to insensitive strangers has developed into a sword of fire. Rude onlookers don't know what hit them. Alex fires off an unbroken string of expletives, knocking the guilty off-balance, then buries their spirits in the dirt. His fiery tongue stings, and you hope the worst is over, but it is not over, it's only beginning. The sword swings wildly; after tears of repentance, Alex walks away. If that takes 15 minutes, so be it. When Alex's verbal fusillade stuns the cruel men, women and children (every time in public) a physical challenge is implied as well. If lazy parents' mouthy brats say something mean, the child *and* parent pay. The rudely insensitive are made very, very sorry, no matter their age. Alex's gatling gun of rebuke, combats the human cruelty of an innocent impairment.

Beyond the Sherman Tank response (only when needed), Alex is as nice as his dad, generous, friendly, forthright and . . . hero. Yes, hero. The following year, Alex, only 16 years old, saves his father's life.

Bernard's long and heavy (Cadillac heavy) American classic is up on jackstands in the driveway. The long driveway angles up from the sidewalk and levels out along the side of the house to the backyard. The jacked-up car is situated on level-driveway, just before the decline. The raised front-end faces the street. I noticed the car on jacks for a day or two. From the street, you can see the chassis underneath. This is commonplace everywhere; a raised vehicle, propped up on jacks in a driveway, awaiting the blood, sweat and curses from their mechanically intuitive owners.

Bernard is doing another brake job, the front wheels are removed. Though he's done more brake jobs than he can remember, they never bore him. He turns on the small portable AM/FM Delco radio plugged into an extension cord and tunes in the game. So begins another typical, 1970's working man's weekend: the All-American mechanic dance, the weekly ritual performed up and down every working class street in the country. With an enthusiastic quick-step, Mr. Z. darts back and forth, collecting the new brake parts and necessary tools. Bernard wears a dark-blue mechanic's jumpsuit, selects the correct forged steel tool and slides underneath the massive General Motors vehicle. Weekend life on Jackson Street: noisy, perilous and grimy auto repair; the car needs to be running by weekend's end, to get to work on Monday.

Bernard scoots underneath the jacked up car on a rolling creeper; a piece of varnished plywood, supported by four steel casters and an attached cushion for his head. He stares up at the car's belly and its myriad of mechanical systems, impressed by the engineering. Bernard recalls how the car looked in his GM paint booth 10 years ago; as new as a new car can get. The game announcer says, "strike two! Three and two, a full count."

The car above him is *not* blocked.

Bernard gets the breaker bar to loosen a stubborn nut. The leverage applied to the nut silently shifts the car's immense weight forward. The nut is uncooperative; Bernard applies more elbow grease. The mute jacks leeeean . . . topple! The two and a half ton car frame (front wheels removed) lands squarely on Leonard's shoulder and pins him, crushing him.

A single cry rings out!

Alex is home, he races out front. Dad is dying! Adrenaline surges through Alex, he kneels and grabs the front left bumper (no gloves) and with Samsonian strength, lifts the 5,000 lb. car, just enough for dad to escape. Alex saves dear dad! Alex is a hero!

Denny has a much milder version of his father's skin condition. Thomas, Patricia, Cheryl and Alex are not afflicted. Denny laughs like his father, loud and genuine. On our first night on Jackson Street, welcome wagon Denny Zolanski, brought his Lincoln Logs to play.

If Kenny Starr is the king of Jackson Street, Bernard Zolanski is the heart and soul.

When we arrive at Yosemite (my first time) and move into our campsite, Alex pan-frys steaks on the Winnebago stovetop. My *first* steak is compliments of Mr. Zolanski, cooked by Alex Zolanski and the best thing I'd ever tasted.

Alex and I are smitten with the same cute girl from a nearby campsite. Long, soft dark brown hair, and black-framed glasses like a librarian, she has a tiny, hairy, white dog that follows her everywhere.

After a successful morning of trout fishing on the beautiful Yosemite River, Alex, myself, the pretty camper and her dog take a short hike back to the same deep pool, where we caught the fish. It's warm out, but the river is freezing cold. Do *not* step foot in that river. *Splash!* The white dog jumps into the middle of the freezing pool! Tree debris blankets the pool's surface, only a pitiful tiny dog face is visible above the water, two ears, two eyeballs, a nose and mouth, like a big rat. The drowning dog responds to his owner's cries and paddles valiantly, but in vain. The debris and current hold Toto fast, paddles slow, the little head starts to sink. The sobbing young lady is frantic. Kersplash, Alex jumps in! He's neck deep! Alex's intelligent eyes get really, *really* big, and they're already big. He scoops up the canine and with his own furious dog paddle, the two flop safely on shore.

Alex Zolanski: hero, again.

Back in camp, we wrap Alex like a big cocoon! Robin Alex Hood saves the dog and wins Maid Marion the librarian's heart.

The fishing here is fantastic. On the Yosemite River we limit out for trout, both days. They taste great too. Winnie smells like fried fish, mmm.

On the drive home, I drink my *first* beer. A can of Olympia, "it's the water."Alex has one too. Neither of us care for it. Denny wisely abstains.

Walking home from Mission San Jose High on my typical route, Covington Drive to Paseo Padre Parkway left, to Olive Avenue right, Barbary Street left, Jackson Street right. I walk past the double empty lot (Jackson Street rope-swing access and Aboriginal boomerang training ground) and notice a lot of unusual noise and busyness there. What in the H-E-double-hockey-sticks?! Two new homes are being built!

Our sacred land, desecrated.

I shuffle along, head down - my pants are too long, they drag on the sidewalk (intentional) - miffed about losing convenient swing access, when calling from the gutter, a crisp green $20 bill! Stealth-mode engaged, step into the gutter, kneel, scoop, slip small fortune ($20 bucks big deal in 1975) deep in front pocket, safe. Eyes glued to gutter, three more steps, *another* $20 bill, crisp and green. Adrenaline rush, repeat kneel and scoop, transfer weighty windfall to forementioned pocket, four steps more? . . . a, a new, crisp, exotic green, oh say can you see? . . . *$100 bill!*

Cash on the ground ($900 in today's value)!

From rags to riches, in eight seconds. Now I know what Solomon felt like.

Dammit, I'm *RICH!*

Well the first thing you know ole Jens is a millionaire,

the kinfolk say, 'Jens move away from there!'

They said, 'California is the place you ought to be.'

So he loaded up the truck and they moved to Jackson Streeeet,

hills that is, swimming pools, moovie stars (heavy-metal banjo riff*).

First order of business: open a savings account at Downey Savings, next to Charley's Market. The ladies in the bank are very nice to me. I deposit one hundred dollars, and keep forty in cash. Next weekend, I take Gary Forest to the brand new Great America Amusement Park. I know Gary will keep his mouth shut.

A 13 year old just changed his lucky stars.

Time to catch up.

From the minute we enter the new amusement park in Milpitas, to the minute they close, Gary and I ride rides, non-stop. Yes Six-Flags, America *is* Great!

This last frosh-soph memory seems random, obscure, out of order. A pool party in a friend's backyard? Reason for the party? No idea. During this writing, I'm not sure exactly where or when this happened. So call it "the forgotten party."

During these years, hormones fly around like swallows from Capistrano. But when it's happening to you? Friends and I, don't *see* hormones, or discuss puberty in *scientific* terms, what you *do* see is a football jock shoving his hand down a girl's pants in the middle of a science lab. Crazy stuff like that. Honestly, I only see one guy and one gal do that a couple times. That's not status quo. We're not in Kansas anymore, lengthy make-out sessions out in the open, anywhere on and off campus are common.

It's the end of a school year, a hot day, a freshman pool party; a good turn out of my contemporaries.

The memory is so clear - hormonal displays are memorable if nothing else - lying on a clean concrete pool deck, drying in the sun, wet from a swim moments ago. I lie alongside two other kids, John Leon and Carol Acevedo. Neither are friends, but both are familiar and affable schoolmates, we're all on a first name basis. We share one class together, and I'm comfortable sunning next to them, and them me. John Leon is not handsome per say, a little fleshy but very funny, great hair, athletic and popular with everyone, a class clown/jock combo. Carol Acevedo is similar to John, likable, slightly dingy, and likes to laugh. But unlike John, Carol is sexy in her black bikini.

John starts in with the Leon charm, moving his hand along her back, Carol giggles and wriggles and pushes Johnny's hand away from her backside. John is persistent a couple more times, but with feminine fortitude and strength, Carol keeps Johnny the cad at bay.

That's all I recall. I remember that with fondness. Carol defends her honor from John Leon. Yeah, that's alright.

The only class Carol and I had together at Hopkins was World Studies (history). Carol got teased mercilessly by Prince Hokulani, once for using spray-on tan stuff that got a little peely, and other kids laughed too. I felt bad for her.

Later I hear Carol's family is well off and lives on a large Fremont estate at the end of a long straight road off Mission Boulevard; Witherley Road rises gently, a consistent mellow grade, not undulating. The Acevedo estate is at the end of the quarter mile, arrow-straight road, located between the two year old Ohlone College and where the Nuns from St. Joseph's Church live, next to the old Mission San Jose.

Carol's Estate is completely surrounded by a red brick wall, its entrance secured by an impenetrable black-iron gate.

The pool party was at the Highland Swim Club on Palm Avenue across the street from Mission San Jose High School. I don't remember the occasion, but I sure remember the swallows.

Loveable Rats and Hairy Apes

Established now at the creek, I meet some interesting people. Jim Stanford's older childhood buddy, Buddy Duke, is a junior and plays lead guitar faster than anyone else around. A white fair Irish complexion, long, wavy straight, raven black hair down to the middle of his back, Buddy isn't your typical, skinny as a rail musician type. Stocky and stolid, very (Buddy's violent past is well known) strong, not someone to trifle with.

By the time I meet Buddy, he's mellowed so I'm told. I never see Buddy engage in a fist-fight. Though extremely cynical, he likes to laugh and carry on. Buddy changes the lyrics to every popular song, to something crass and earthy. Buddy lives with his aunt near Jim Stanford and Mark Brassi on Bruce Drive.

The drug culture is still new to me, I tend to kick back, stay quiet and listen to others, and enjoy their passionate, clever antics. The island of misfits. I learn about life from them. Education is where you find it.

Dolly is a hot topic at the end of my freshman year. Dolly is a baby ape who lives at Buddy's house! Buddy and Dolly are raised by their aunt. So strange and wild. At the creek, Buddy's friends retell their Dolly encounters. They say, "Dolly spit at me!" or "Dolly did this or Dolly did that." All this confusion in a smoky, stoned haze, basting in iconic rock anthems. I didn't meet Dolly during high school; the apes on Bruce Drive are outside my social circle.

Life on campus: the basketball teams, games, the standings, football season, cheerleaders, school dances, wrestling? What's that?? I have no idea, none. The limited opportunities of youth, so fleeting, and by some, discarded like dirty socks. These foundational building blocks, critical for later in life, are put in a sack, tied around my neck and thrown overboard into an bottomless ocean of toxic smoke and heavy metal music.

Jack and Inger are fun loving too, I never feel suffocating pressure from them to focus on after-school sports, little-league baseball, college-prep etc. etc. etc. Pappa the artist, has his art and Inger has her job at Capwells, selling bedding for an hourly wage plus commission. They're hooked up.

In mid-70s California, a life outside of college still works. College isn't a prerequisite for a happy life; surviving and thriving does not require a college degree and a high school diploma certainly has more weight. If there's a college graduate on Jackson Street, I never met them.

I love the smell of Marlboros in the morning! Smoking starts slowly, first, steal Mom's brand (More's) puff, puff, puff. Bum them from creek rats, "gotta' smoke?" puff, puff, puff. Finally, buy your first pack, puff, puff, puff . . . puff, puff, puff, get sick to your stomach for two days, puff, puff, cough. Then you're good to go. Smoke anytime, all the time. I'm paying 50 cents a pack at the Rotten Robbie self-serve gas station. Marlboro man, what else? Most people smoke Marlboros, Winstons, Marlboro lights, Camel Filters etc. etc. etc. I don't understand to this day why black people prefer to smoke Kools, Newports and other menthol brands.

Located on the corner of Washington Boulevard and Roberts Avenue, The new Rotten Robbie gas station is the first self-serve gas station we ever saw. 50 cents a gallon for regular leaded gas and the premium leaded gas? Oh man, that purple color, so beautiful and powerful.
I love the smell of premium leaded gas in the morning!

A pack of cigarettes from a machine is between 75 cents and a buck. There is a machine at the Cloverleaf Bowl on Fremont Boulevard and at the Irvington Pool Hall where John Velasco, Devin

O'Malley and I smoke and play pinball by the hour. I buy my smokes from gas stations and liquor stores for less.

To our credit we stretch a buck on most of those pinball machines. And do I need to say it? The pool hall's sound system blares loud rock; a familiar theme everywhere I go, except the dentist office, an elevator, or place of worship.

Now, my typical high school day is: loiter at the creek before school, smoke cigarettes, pot if available (9 times out of 10 it is), rock out, work on some guitar songs with Jim Stanford, play and show off to interested girls; go to admin (role call) stoned, then to guitar class, stoned. Then kill time: (dead time-modular scheduling) smoke cigarettes in the boy's room, pot if available, and pitch quarters against the concrete planters in between the boy's bathroom and the gym. I win two-seven bucks frequently. Go to another class or two, math, english or history; head on the desk 50% of the time. Buy lunch if I score pitching quarters, always the box-lunch option: hamburger, shake and fries. Buddy Duke puts his fries in his hamburger bun, smart, meat and potatoes together, but I've never tried it to this day. I eat my hamburger and fries fast, my stomach cramps and I have to sit down and breathe until it stops burning. The meal comes with a chocolate shake, I drink it too fast and get a brain freeze, stop for another minute. After hosing lunch and recovering from stomach cramps and brain freeze, I make my way to the creek. Sunny spring weather brings renewal and the creek crowd is really fun. The same friends, characters and antics, but frisbees sail, new music is on and restrictive winter wear is exchanged for tube tops and shorts for the gals and T-shirts for the guys. The vibrant scene shimmers under the Mediterranean sunshine.

Stoned after lunch, my English teachers detect my mindless state and are rightfully annoyed. Two try to reach me, they work hard to connect. Mr. Howell and Mr. Callio are great, inspirational and funny teachers, they keep their students in stitches. Yet, I fail to grasp basic writing structure

theory: introduction, thesis, main body, conclusion. The layout is too rigorous. Yes, too

compartmental. I don't grasp it, can't make it go, make it burn. I can't fit books I read into their

correct writing theory structure boxes. I want to be creative and free; not abstract or obscure,

something legible, feasible, logical, mechanically sound. Word talk, simple. Explain, show, sell,

twist an arm. Write too much, too little, right or wrong but not forced to follow writing laws. Why?

To conform? This isn't 1952. Crew cuts work, but not for me. Sanitize, homogenize, condense?

What am I milk? Sentence structure mechanics? Smoke and mirrors. Grammar analytics are lost on

me. I get the who, what, where, when and why of journalism reporting, that registers (not pursued

but understood) but I can't wrap my head around the connection between English grammar

mechanix and a good story or a report.

Not then, not now. And if I wait for that light to come on? I may never try.

Instead I do what I want to do, enjoy doing. The rest: science, english 101, endless math

problems, no. Should the word math be capitalized? With time, screwing up gets easier.

Cause and effect lose impact. Consequence? What's that? I'm lazy and lack foresight.

Homework? No way, little to none. Long term consequences? No. The impacts of my bad

decisions surround me, but I'm deaf, dumb and blind to it.

Do the last two paragraphs define a fool?

I'm shunned now by the non-creek rat student body, cut-off. I don't pay attention to basic

concepts; self-respect, social grace or reputation. Social-economic differences may have a hand in

this, but I know plenty of kids from modest circumstances, who succeed in many areas, sports,

academics and civics, popularity. They shine. Like the tortoise and the hare, I raced to finish, finish first, then roll around in the dirt, rock and roll in the smoke. Mr and Miss Tortoise walk right by and don't pay Mr. Hare any mind. Man, they don't even know he's there.

For the disregard of personal behavior and my pending freefall, I have no excuse. I refuse to manufacture one. A self-seared conscience finds no excuse. I blame me; right answer, right? Music and girls are enough.

On Jackson Street, we lift weights. Guy and Danny Wellbaum, all the guys. Marlo Topper, Kevin Finley and I *still* shoot around in their respective driveways. I can still toss an NFL football 50 yards accurately. The fish still bite at Lake Elizabeth, life is *still* good and I spend a lot of time laughing it up. If I'm due home and my parents are there, I don't go home freshly stoned. Pappa is usually in the garage and I slip into the house, to my room, listen to music, or start dinner if it's my week for KP duty.

Rivers to Oceans

For a month Mission San Jose kids have been going nuts about an upcoming show; April 25th, 1976 Day on the Green #1, starring Peter Frampton. His insanely popular, <u>Frampton Comes Alive</u> double LP and cassette, is heard at the school parking lot, and Jackson Street all year. Everyone is going. I don't have a ticket, or pursue one. Half the school wears Peter Frampton Day on the Green T-shirts. The concept of a stadium-sized concert is new. I'm not ready yet, too much.

That summer, the only guys in the neighborhood getting stoned were the Wellbaum brothers, Darin Vanderberg, Marlo Topper and myself. Everyone else is straight.

So the summer of 76'? There are a couple significant developments. Nick Peters, Jack's coworker and fellow artist, inherits his father's mountain cabin, 'Pop's Flop', and invites Pappa and I to spend the night, do some trout fishing.

The small mountain town of Long Barn sits at an elevation of 5,000' and has few amenities. Not even a little market. If you forget bread or milk, you're out of luck, and that's cool. Within walking distance from Pop's Flop, is the Slide Inn. The bar contains a few bearded men on stools, lifeless statues with skin. A kid can go in and buy a candy bar, a soda and a pack of cigarettes, that's about it, maybe some old salmon eggs, or a Rooster Tail. If you need anything else, tough; no big deal, because I don't notice.

A wood plaque over the cabin door reads, 'Pop's Flop.' It should say, "Heaven." Behind the cabin and down a hill, is a small creek you can spit across. We attempt to fish it with nary a nibble. Next morning the three hopefuls pile into Pappa's white Ford station wagon loaded with fishing gear, Pappa and Nick use solely flies and lures. My faith and hope is firmly placed in salmon eggs. We drive three miles downhill on North Fork Road to the Tuolumne River North Fork.

Every angler clings to a small handful of memorable fishing trips; memories that last a lifetime. Fishing on the sublime Tuolumne River is one of these.

At 15, I consider myself a capable angler. I've caught flopping stringers full of rainbow trout, crappie and bluegill, some bass and a few catfish. My casts are accurate. I can tie a loop or knot that won't fail and can switch from bait to lure, lure to bait in a jiff. I'm intent on employing my stringer.

Today is my first time fishing in high altitude, on a wild and rushing mountain river. The river is only 20-30 feet across. The scenery is spectacular, but the narrow river itself is underwhelming and I expect nothing in the way of fish. Jack, Nick and myself split up, go our separate ways up and down the river. After reading countless <u>Field and Stream</u> articles, I know wild trout can see us and spook easily. Stealth is paramount, that's why we split up.

I find a large granite rock outcropping on which I can maneuver out to the middle of the river. I set up next to a deep pool created by the rock; I keep a low profile on the granite surface lying on my side and lower a salmon egg on a #14 gold hook, weighted by a small lead split-shot into the five feet deep pool. I want the egg to move around with the swirling current.

Three minutes nothing, five minutes nothing, seven minutes nothing, bored. It's as I expected, nothing in here. Not enough water, only five feet deep. I pinch the line against the rod with my right forefinger to feel the slightest nibble or bite.

I'm not bored to the point of abandoning rod and reel to chase butterflies, I always hold the rod or at least keep an eye on tip and line. The rushing water is loud and keeps me awake. My first high-altitude, mountain-river fishing trip is turning out to be Pappa's flop.

Dink dink dink, hey, bump, bump, bump, rod tip up set hook, nothing. Egg gone, rebait, lower into pool . . . bump, bump, bump, set hook, fish on! Wow he's a jumper and wild! A feisty fingerling. Another jump and mr. wild trout throws the hook. Wild rainbows have triple the energy of a stocked rainbow! Electricity flows through them, great fighters. *I'm* hooked!

After landing and releasing a couple tiny-tuna, my confidence soars. The search for their grandaddy is on. I hike three hundred yards upstream, up and down along a narrow track, into land that time forgot. I'm grateful for a recent gift, leather Red Wing - Irish Setter boots.

To prepare for this excursion, I studied how to read a river, to identify where the fish are, their lairs. With renewed enthusiasm, the search is on for that perfect riffle and pool.

I found it.

20 yards upstream, large granite boulders form a nice pool, downstream from that pool, a swift 60' long riffle, runs over the deepest part of the river past me. Pool and riffles are on the opposite bank. I figure the distance will help avoid spooking the big one. Tall granite boulders to my immediate left, hide me from the pool upriver.

The perfect spot.

My plan is simple; cast two salmon eggs threaded on a single #12 hook, weighted with two tiny split-shots, 13" above the hook upstream, to the head of the pool, in front of the granite boulder that forms the pool. The river current gives the bait natural movement to trick the trout. I'll reel in the slack as needed. Weight is necessary to cast 70' upstream; I don't want the egg to skip on top of the water, rather, I want the egg to sink, near the bottom, where the big boys hang out. I hope the bait flows submerged down the entire riffle. Too much weight though, and I'll snag the bottom for sure.

Cast too hard, snag the trees, too soft, bait's in shallow water.

A gentle cast is made, stressing accuracy over distance, bait stays on hook, salmon eggs hit where I aim. The egg sinks in the pool, the line moves slowly toward the riffle, I retrieve the slack. The swift water picks up the bait and speeds it along, no snags. The emerald green trees and brown dirt connect the white and blue river below, to a sapphire blue sky above, creating a gorgeous panorama.

My eyes dart back to the riffle, underwater a silver flash streaks *upstream*. A red salmon egg is visible! The rod tip yanks down as the flash disappears and swims back to the casting pool. The strong fish u-turns downstream, in my direction and makes two spectacular leaps, five feet high! The hang time affords a fine look at a magnificent rainbow trout. Splash! He returns to deep water using the strong current to his advantage. I keep the rod tip high to avoid snagging the channel's edge and let him swim where he pleases. For fear of breaking the line (my first attempt at patience) I resist a rushed landing.

Upstream, downstream, more acrobatics. In the air he doesn't vibrate like the small ones did, rather he leaps to maximum height, and freezes, posing for unforgettable memories. When I hope he's worn out, I hoist the 15" *lunker* rainbow out of the river, rod creaks, and swing him over the massive granite bedrock I stand on. Doink! He falls off the hook and hits the granite between me and the river's edge. Bend knees, left palm down, pin him to the hotrock. Under my hand his body twists hard, not fast, left . . . right . . . left . . . right. Each slimy twist is harder than the last. King of the river! I tighten my grip, at last, I have him. What a battle. Ahh!

Get the stringer, keep your catch cold and fresh. Where's the dang stringer?! I forgot it! Now what? I have a zip-lock plastic bag my sandwich was in (new invention), so I use it to bag my trophy. After fishing 30 more minutes with no luck I head back to find Nick and Pappa and show the rainbow. I pick up the three pound bag and stop a second to admire the mighty fish.

The plastic bag under full sun, cooked the magnificent fish to a soggy goo. Crestfallen, heart sinks, not fair.

Young man and the river.

Mechanically Unsound

Released to our summer devices, a few stories unravel. They involve Garrett Montaine from Quaker friends meeting and Jaws fame, and neighbor Kevin Finley.

Mill Creek Road, that near 5 mile, single lane road, winding through the heart of the Ohlone Wilderness, is a lightning rod of adventure for my comrades and I; last year's rite of passage: summit Mill Creek Road on bikes, opened my eyes (and adrenal glands) to future possibilities.

Reliving Jackson Street is sad and sweet, fun and difficult. It's hard to revisit bad decisions, stupid decisions, life altering choices etc. etc. etc. Reflecting on one's shameful acts does not stroke one's ego. Doing or saying anything mean, for a laugh? Woah tailspin, time out, it's not that bad yet.

I still go home when I'm told, usually by dinner time. But beyond the constraints of dinnertime, kp duty, and family outing, summer break is my oyster.

Mill Creek Road, that beacon of freedom, is as far from parental supervision as two Fremont (non-driving) teenage boys can get. Kevin Finley and I devise a plan: ascend Mill Creek Road on our bikes . . . then descend, Tour De France style. Having performed this feat of strength and skill once already, I'm the authority on all things Mill Creek. This will be Kevin's first time. I'm almost 15, Kevin 13. I ride an old Schwinn Varsity ten-speed, nothing fancy, a repaint that doesn't create envy, but a ten-speed nevertheless and mechanically sound. Kevin F. rides a bike of questionable quality, past its prime if it ever had one. Gold in color but suspect mechanically. Mr. Finley built the bike from old parts and hardware, drawn from various coffee cans in the garage. A mish mash of flotsam and jetsam, riddled with shims and stripped threads. A Frankenstein bike.

Upright chrome handlebars, obsolete two years ago. Shims used to compensate for a stripped stem bolt; that critical mechanical link between handlebar and fork. So you could straddle Kevin's front wheel holding it still, and apply the strength of a girl to the handlebar left and right and it moves! A death-trap. Kevin F. re-tightens and we're off.

It's a beautiful day and mechanical integrity is soon forgotten. Up Jackson Street, left on Barbary Street, right on Olive Avenue. Cross Paseo Padre Parkway, continue east on Olive Avenue, right on Palm Avenue over Interstate 680, immediate left back onto Olive Avenue (Olive Avenue is offset due to the new I-680). Continue East on Olive Avenue to the end. Left on Starr Street past nice apartments with a built-in pool, uphill to Mission Boulevard. Carefully cross busy Mission Boulevard and continue straight onto Mill Creek Road which rises sharply. The one and a half miles to this point seem longer due to the elevation gain and takes about 30 minutes. Up Mill Creek Road takes two hours give or take and the whole way is up, up, up.

We packed peanut butter and jelly sandwiches for a mountaintop lunch.

The gearing on Kevin's single-speed bike is too high, too hard to pedal uphill. Forced to stop halfway, Kevin's rite of passage is put on hold.

At the top of a long straight-away we park and devour our sandwiches. The PB&Js hit the spot and brighten our countenances. This respite concludes the day's fun aspect.

The descent will be a blast, it's why we endure the challenging uphill; wipe away the crumbs and start down. The ten-speed goes fast down the ¼-mile straight away and I'm way ahead of Kevin. The right side of the road is the uphill side, the left side of the road drops down to the creek bed and an excellent view to the south; a row of brown grass hills rise gradually in the distance, culminating at the majestic Mission Peak. Beautiful. Jens, don't stare at the scenery too long, you might become *part* of the scenery.

I'm at max-speed, from behind Kevin screams, "JENS!! . . . I'M GONNA' WRECK!!" I grab both brake levers, swivel my flexible neck behind, and witness four seconds of the pending disaster. At high speed, Kevin struggles for control of his bike, jerking his handlebars hard left, right, left, in quick succession.

In vain!

Kevin's front wheel disregards Kevin's desperate pleas and decides to go where *it* wills. The fork declares mutiny on Kevin's handlebar. When Kevin steers left, the wheel goes right, when Kevin steers right, the wheel turns left!

The front wheel turns 90 degrees and Kevin goes over the handlebar, down hard! As Kevin's tall body is thrown headlong to the pavement, I'm forced to return my sight forward, before *I* become part of the pavement. I stop, toss my Varsity aside and run back to the accident. Kevin is wailing, my friend's a mess, bloody head to toe. No one drives by.

Kevin's legs are strong however and after an injury assessment, we limp three and a half miles home. Kevin's sobs subside and he steels himself for the painful trek.

The floodgate of tears is reopened at the sight of Mrs. Finley. Kevin took a beating on Mill Creek Road, but survived. Mother's loving comfort and hearty cooking returns Kevin to full-health; the gold bike is never seen again.

Garrett Montaine, the adopted foster child of Norm and Alice Jean, and I were in the Payless Store on Castro Valley Boulevard to get needed fishing supplies. While Garrett shops, I shoplift.

After gathering candy, bait and tackle, I exit the store. I'm immediately apprehended by a young, white, clean-cut employee, about 25 years old with straight, thin short hair.

It was a good run, two years. The silly notion that I'm too smart to get caught, proves *incorrect*. Crime pays, until it doesn't. The security agent is in his prime. Dang, I'm scared of what Pappa will say, think and do, Mom too. They'll look down on me and hate me forever. I'm ushered into a small office inside the store, four small walls, a cramped space. They call Pappa, we wait.

Mr. Jean arrives first, to pick up Garrett. Mr. Jean says, "you don't need to steal this stuff Jens, work for it." Point taken. Norman Jean takes Garrett home. Garrett is not in trouble; he didn't steal anything. Ahhh, the wisdom of Garrett. Pappa shows up and drives me home. I don't remember anything specific, a quiet uncomfortable ride.

I receive serious punishments and lose key privileges temporarily. My sisters appreciate the extra kp duty I receive. I have to rototill Kenny Starr's, south acre garden for free. I survive the ordeal and resolve not to get caught again.

I purchased a pellet gun from Tri-City Sporting Goods on Grimmer Boulevard, just west of the Cloverleaf bowling alley and Ronald McDonald's place.

I pause; McDonalds is my favorite place to eat, our family's favorite place to eat. We get a kick of "# Billion Burgers Sold" posted on the golden arches out front. In 1972 the sign read: 2 Billion Served. Such an impressive quantity! Ten years later it reads: 4 Billion Served! Jeez, there aren't four billion people on earth. Only 110,000 people in Fremont. Woah, four billion?! Astronomical. Golden arches indeed.

Once a month, on Friday or Saturday, Pappa says, "let's go to supper!" Pappa calls lunch dinner, and dinner supper because they say that where he grew up, in Sayre, Pennsylvania. Sayre,

Pennsylvania is next to the New York border where the Susquehanna River comes through. A world away. Expeditiously we pile into the shiny waxed, snow white 72 Ford Ranch Wagon and drive to McDonalds. Six Moyers walk inside, soaking in the novelty of it all. Pappa orders and pays cash. We don't offer individual input like, "no mayo, hold the pickles please." There's no perusing the menu board on the wall, no, "I don't want McDonalds mommy, I want Taco Bell Pappa," 'okay, we'll cross the street after we leave McDonald's and get you Taco Bell Jensie." We're not doing that.

My folks insist on orderly conduct. We rarely have a say in decisions growing up. I don't mind, life is good. Not just good, but good enough. Mom brought my sisters and I to coffee shops many times, and allowed me to blow spit wads from my beverage straw at various harmless targets, but beyond that? A tight ship. Like everyone else, I love McDonald's. It never occurs to us that Ronald McDonald may require our help, to make a better hamburger.

I am the happiest kid in town. I hope to meet Ronald McDonald in person some day. Ronald McDonald appearances are rare, but they do happen; in San Jose typically, or some far away place; too far to go.

The pimply teen wearing a McDonald's paper hat, hands Pappa the bag of piping hot food; the family exits the restaurant and re-enter the spacious, warm and cozy station wagon, sit quietly and wait for dinner to be handed out. An exercise of faith. We're hungry and happy. The aroma intoxicates us. Without exception, I receive one, tightly-wrapped hamburger, a small fry, and a small coke. I hose it. "Jens, *slow down.*" ``Jens, no one is going to *take it from you.*" Wasted words on deaf ears, I guess they don't understand what McDonalds means to me.

I withdraw the last red cent and close my savings account forever. Danny Wellbaum and I ride to Tri-City Sporting Goods, just past McDonald's on Grimmer Boulevard, lock up the bikes and stride inside. We're there for one reason, to purchase my first air rifle. With utmost care and patience, we scrutinize all the options. They're on display 10' high on the wall, out of reach behind the counter. Real bullet rifles are up there too, on the same wall. A long row, 100 rifles of every type, lined up for 100', secured to the wall behind an equally long glass counter. That's a lot of glass! The air-rifles are grouped together at the end of the rifle parade. We exhaust the salesman for input, wear him out and he leaves. Painstakingly, with Danny's help, I figured it out; the most accurate, the most powerful, and the most expensive.

The 5 mm Sheridan Silver Streak pellet rifle is the best. The pellets are larger than the common .177 caliber bb guns everybody else has and only slightly smaller than 22 gauge (20 g) ammunition. Eight pumps will shoot a hole clean through a fence board! A Blue Streak model is also available. The Blue Streak's barrel is typical rifle color, the Silver Streak boasts a beautiful silver barrel. Both models cost the same, $80. No brainer, Silver Streak. Additionally, I purchase a small yellow plastic box full of 5mm. pellets. The box top opens to dump out many pellets, or a smaller opening allows one pellet at a time. A very practical design. The box is heavy for its size, heavier than a carton of cigarettes but half the size of a deck of playing cards. The pellets are lightly greased and cost $5 bucks. Not cheap, but worth it. The 5mm pellets are locked up inside the glass counter. Smart. On my bike, one arm holds the long box securely to my side, the other hand grips the handlebar. The box O' pellets push down on the bottom of my jeans pocket. We pedal directly to Jackson Street.

Danny, Hi Ho Silver and I, waste no time, we're on safari. Armed and dangerous finally. With a heightened sense of awareness, we trepidly step through my back gate, into the jungle discovered by John C. Fremont's famous scout, Kit Carson.

The Sheridan Silver Streak is a true beauty; it has a maple hardwood stock and a 12" long maple air-pump handle located under the barrel. You grab the pump handle and pull down 90 degrees with little resistance and pull back feeling the pressure pump into the barrel and repeat. The pressure accumulates with each pump. The pumping action requires teenage boy-strength. The user manual says: minimum two pumps, maximum eight pumps. I pump 'er up eight times, twist the bolt-action lever up, pull back with purpose, until it clicks, then load a single pellet - pellets are shaped like a drinking cup; load the open end back, so air pressure propels pellets out the barrel to target - slide bolt-action in, with respect, careful not to jam it, until it "clicks" and twist the bolt lever down. You're ready to shoot. Keep the safety-switch on, until you're ready to pull the trigger.

Pappa took me to a gun safety course at the Fremont Gun Club when I was 12. I learned to shoot Pappa's old 22 gauge Marlin rifle, from his Navy days during World War II. As an instructional aid, the gun safety instructor used an old cowboy boot with a large hole on top of the toe. He said, "this guy accidentally shot his toes off with his own shotgun." The boot worked, we got the message. I don't want to hurt myself or anyone else, do something I'll regret forever.

We cross the creek, turn west onto the narrow dirt track and meander slowly up and down through tall brown grass and large oak trees along the creek. The trees are thick and shield us from Jackson Street backyards. We're well below nosy drivers on Washington Boulevard and the 680 off-ramp. We hunt unseen.

Danny takes the lead, sets the pace; a synchronized slow stalk, searching for movement, for life. I'm 20' behind, cradling Silver, my right hand near the trigger area. Like a pointer, Danny freezes; he's done this before. I freeze. He crouches, turns slowly back, his forefinger in front of his pursed lips, Danny returns face forward, points up and freezes.

On the thick oak branch above Danny, sitting perfectly still, is a large game bird. Not a western scrub jay or mourning dove. Squatting not perched; a Pheasant. You can't see the bird's legs. Danny's mute. I switch the red-tipped safety lever off, raise Silver's pumped & loaded barrel and take deadly aim. The steel sights are like Pappa's 22 Marlin. The front and rear sights are lined up, I set the bird on top of the front sight, like it's a fence post; breathe in, hold it, and squeeze the trigger.

The bird falls straight down, flapping hard to avoid impact with the ground. The Pheasant flies forward, a foot off the ground. He travels 100' forward along the trail, falls lightly to the earth and dies. Jubilant . . . proud . . . sad.

More Fish Tails

Next spring, Nick Peters invites us to 'Pop's Flop again in Long Barn. I invite a friend, John Velasco. Downhill behind the cabin, at the small creek, using a 12' telescopic tule pole, a 10' piece of 4 pound test line tied to the tip and a dry fly, John hooks and lands a beautiful wild 10" *lunker* rainbow trout.

Later that summer, we returned to Pop's Flop again. This is a family trip, no Nick Peters this time. I'm allowed to bring two friends; Garrett Montaine and John Velasco get the nod. Pinecrest Lake is 10 miles east of Long Barn on Highway 108. John, Garrett and I have one agenda: fish.

Our first drive to the lake is mid-afternoon and the swimming beach. Mom, Pappa and the girls go swimming. Me and the boys walk beyond the buoys and discover a great crappie bite. Ounce for ounce, crappies are the best fighters, and fun to catch on ultra-light tackle. John and I pride ourselves on our fishing prowess; intelligent lure or bait selection, accurate cast, maintained quality tackle, suited for the conditions. Garrett is okay, but he does more snags and tangles, tackle breakdowns, miscasts etc. etc. etc. In an hour the three of us have 60 crappie on the stringer. At dusk we clean em' and fry em', delicious.

The next day, Pappa shocks us with a motorboat rental! The four of us set out from the dock with great excitement and expectation. Pappa too. As the boat cruises to destinations unknown, we tie on double-hook rigs with sliding sinkers. Our bait? Pautzke's Premium Red Label salmon eggs; Pappa stays true to his fishing philosophy, using only a lure. His thing is, " give the fish a sporting chance, whatever you do, give it a sporting chance." The boys want production: three limits, 15 rainbow trout, a full stringer. We do pretty good, we each catch a few, except Pappa. Cast after cast, he flips his Super Duper portside, starboard, fore and aft, at various depths and with varied retrieves. All netting the same result, nothing.

Sunshine reflects up onto swarthy summer faces; conditions are perfect, hope and enthusiasm floats in the boat. It's surreal, the aluminum boat gently rocks and creaks, the salmon eggs are cast on fresh, ultra-light mono-filament lines, making a tiny splash.

A jolt to the boat shatters the quiet, Garrett screams, "Aaaaaagghhhh!!" Wincing in pain, head in hands, Garret turns his head left and right, saying, "no, no." Pappa sits calmly at the stern holding his rod up, ready to cast. His red and chrome lure hangs from the rod tip swinging back and forth. Attached to the lure's hook, also swinging to and fro, is a 2" round afro ball! - Pappa snagged Garrett's hair! - John and I blow up, out loud hysterical. The calm water carries our shameless cackling to every cove on the lake. Garrett is a good sport though, and Pappa caught something after all.

This story is a last second entry. John Velasco and his best friend Devin O'Malley, fish at a spot midway through Niles Canyon on Alameda Creek called, "The Spot," a small campground and diner. To attract business, The Spot routinely stocks their creek frontage with rainbow trout, and when they do the bite is excellent for a few days. Unfortunately, The Spot goes out of business.

I fished The Spot once with Devin and John. The three amigos are doing well, three trout a piece. Pappa got me a 5' ultra-light rod and reel combo for my last birthday. The lightest rod and reel set-up any of us ever saw. Four-pound test line, *ultra*-light, the reel is the size of a spool of thread. I'm breaking it in on Alameda Creek; a 10" rainbow on this ultra-light tackle, fights like a salmon.

The steelhead inhales my Velveeta cheese ball and runs downstream; he never reveals himself. On the bank, the high-pitched scream of the mini-reel alerts John and Devin, they immediately abandon their rods and step near in disbelief. The mighty fish is stripping out the line very fast! The pole tip steadily shakes, the reel's whine is constant. The steelhead doesn't tire or slow during his run downstream.

My head is crammed with <u>Field and Stream</u> fishing stories. Pappa has thick classic books on the living room shelf on fishing, <u>The Fisherman's Bible</u>, and my favorite, <u>The Angler.</u> I've plied their pages and absorbed the gripping stories. Through the written word, I've fished all over the country. I dream at night about catching 50 pound salmon and 12 pound steelhead; I stand on the bank of a wide river and cast to the far side and hook the mighty steelhead, he swims left and right. I wake from these exciting dreams for years.

Is the drag too tight? Too loose? There's nothing else to do but stand, watch and wait and hope the line doesn't snap. 30 seconds of line stripping *rip.* Even if it is new Trilene, how can four-pound test line *hold?* In an exciting fishing story in Florida, I read five times, a guy catches a 100 pound Tarpon on 10 pound-test line! If he can do it, I can do it, right?!?

Shnnaapp! 50 yards downstream the line breaks at the water's surface. Alameda Creek's surface is disturbed for 3 seconds. A mirror smooth ripple spreads five feet across the rushing creek, the line snapped at the ripple's center. From reality I wake.

We love to be at the bank, a fishing pole, bait or lure, that's all we need. A bay pier, ocean surf, a lake, a river bank, a small creek, no matter, and yes, a stringer. In narrow Niles Canyon, Route 84 along Alameda Creek, about three miles in from Mission Boulevard is a picturesque and secluded spot. Not a campsite, not The Spot, just *a* spot. I camped there one night only, with John Velasco and Devin O'Malley.

John and Devin know the location, they'd been there before. Head east, into the heart of the canyon, on the right side, there's a small pull-out and a locked bar-gate. John's mother drives and drops us and our gear off at the gate. John and Devin both can cook, they bring ground beef and a small barbeque, buns, seasonings and condiments. The works. Vegetables may have been involved, though I can't swear to it.

After the drop off, we carry our stuff around the gate and hike east on an old deteriorated road. What makes this spot nice is the wide swath of separation between Route 84 and Alameda Creek, and camping on the south bank places us even further from the road, away from traffic, eyeballs.

This is a first: camping without parental supervision; three compadres roughing it. Only the essentials: ground beef, sleeping bags, drinking water, and fishing gear! John and Devin have been best friends since kindergarten. They're interesting to observe. Their back and forth banter is uninhibited; great senses of humor, with an abundance of mutual teasing. They interact the way I imagine brothers do, acutely aware of each other's foibles. I prefer to avoid the jousting, and just fish.

We catch a couple huge carp and toss them in the bushes for the raccoons. John, our self-appointed camp leader, doles out menial tasks to his minions. I form the ground beef into patties, a first. Mom always forms the hamburger patties at home, before she goes to work. I'm a carp out of water, but I get it done. I don't like grease on my hands. The hamburgers are delicious. The next day at the pre-arranged time, Mrs. Velasco picks us up at the bar-gate. A good trip, another rite of passage entry in Jens' history book.

A young reader reading this today might think, wow, those years were too quiet, boring, depressing even . . . Oh young modern reader; wherever I was, wherever I went, inside, outside, at school (not in the classroom); a raucous, powerful, (tender at times) rock and roll soundtrack plays; from speakers into my ear drum, music plays seven days a week; morning, noon and night. Wherever I go, rock music broadcasts from speakers of various sizes. Every month, sound quality improves, more amps, more wattage, decreasing distortion; I'm an ear-witness to an audio-musical rock revolution. This tuneado spins from varied forms and places; the home stereo in my room, Pappa's old stereo in our living room (less and less), friends' more expensive home systems, the modern car stereos, my word, on and on; from the two local rock radio stations: KOME 98.5 or KSJO 92.3. Jackson Street's album and cassette collections grow in leaps and bounds. We eye-witness the transition from obsolete 8-track, to cassette (thank goodness). Cassettes turn in decks, albums spin on turntables. We don't call them *vinyl*, nobody does. They're records or albums.

And the FM stations . . . wow!

Fremont's rock n roll pathfinder, Darin Vanderberg, leads the way. Two years older, hard working and now a driver's license in his wallet. Darin's first car is a 1968 Buick Skylark Coupe with the vinyl top stripped off. But the stereo in his car is custom all the way. A Pioneer Super-Tuner, a Clarion graphic equalizer (adjusted song by song) and six JBL speakers, two in the doors, and four housed in two custom wood speaker boxes Darin builds himself, in the back on that flat shelf area behind the back seat, at ear level. Whether we're cruising down the road, or gathered around it parked, we're in for a dose of great music that sounds better than we'd *ever heard before. Much* better.

Boring? No. Pandora's box has been opened.

Darin's taste in music doesn't lean toward the hard stuff like Led Zeppelin or Rush, rather, more melodic; Foreigner, Guess Who, Frampton, Toto, Boston . . .Elton John, Robin Trower Live. Darin's personal playlist is endless and never boring. The opposite of boring, fully engaging in every sense. And the sound quality from his car is like nothing Jackson Street has heard before. The *quality and power* are truly remarkable. Darin introduces us to headphones for the first time (home stereo), amazing stereo split sound. But back to his car stereo; when we ride in Darin's car, it's a rolling stoned concert.

The songs are better than our dreams.

The sonic delivery is a separation of sound you can feel, each instrument and vocal is a song within the song, his Clarion equalizer, powerful amplifier and high end tuner create an unforgettable experience for us. Our reaction is physical. Think, Wayne's World Bohemian Rhapsody scene, minus the tongue in cheek. Head swaying left to right, front to back, swinging arms beat tight, convincing air-drums, air guitar of course, in perfect harmony *with the music*. Pot enhances the music, every intricate note is heard. Boys and girls rock out!

Music is a full-time job, there is no Plan B, all in.

At this point of my persuasive argument, best case, I'm positive you're not convinced young reader.

The Darin Vanderberg rock n roll drive experience is more than music and pot, engine and wheels; Darin *drives* better than anyone else. It's uncanny. Darin's driving is so smooth and perfect, always centered in the lane; total driving concentration, razor sharp, never distracted; the Michael Jordan of cruising. The opposite of Pappa's driving. Not to say Darin drives like an old lady. He exhibits at times, but when he does, it's a two hand grip on top of the wheel not one, so he can pull left or right, hard, when needed. One night Darin shows up driving a friend's yellow Plymouth Roadrunner 440, with the raised-hood-scoop and Roadrunner cartoon decal on the tail fin and pulls up in front of Danny's house under the streetlight, "wanna go for a ride?" Danny and I jump in the black leather interior, a joint is lit. Slow up Jackson Street, left on Troyer Avenue, right on Olive Avenue, right on Paseo Padre. "Wow this thing sounds gooooood." I'm nervous; what will Darin do with the excessive horsepower? Right on Washington Boulevard.

Straightaway!

Darin opens it up, foot on the gas, he *slaps* the automatic transmission shifter, gear to gear, bamm! . . . bamm! . . . bamm! From shotgun I watch the speedometer quickly advance to 115 miles per hour. "Woah, ohhh, ohhh!" Too fast. Daaaammmmnnnn! That was scary. "Wheww."

Darin has a sixth-sense for fun. On Friday night, in the fall of 1976, we had a special music moment. It's cold and dark out, the roads are wet, we're driving around, high as a kite with the string cut, Darin Vanderberg behind the wheel, Guy Wellbaum riding shotgun, Danny Wellbaum, and myself in the backseat. We're cruising in Darin's Skylark, listening to Robin Trower Live, loud and crystal clear, when we notice a happening at the Mission San Jose High School parking lot.

We cruise up to the Little Theater, the school parking lot is too dark at night, only two feeble pole lights work, and they're ineffectual. You see the light on, but that's it. Darin parks and we walk toward the action. Evidently a stage performance of, I don't know what, finished and the audience has just cleared out. We poke our heads inside the warm theater, it's bright and busy, people are busy. The stage crew is dismantling stage sets, in front of the stage a 20 foot tall

238

wooden step-ladder is propped up. It feels like we shouldn't be here, but we're not kicked out, the opposite occurs and I soak in the scene.

The stage hands are cleaning up. They slowly come into focus. I know them all; Devin O'Malley, John Velasco, Jim Stanford and others. They're amped up from the night's performance. Jim chirps, "What's up Darin?" "Nothin, what's happenin' Jim?" "Just did a show." "All riiight." Mark Brassi is there too, doing lights. After high school, stage lighting became a career for Mark, and he does well.

Mission San Jose Drama Department, meets Jackson Street. The scene is surreal, and exciting, there's a sense of the unexpected.

There's an Asian guy here, the only unfamiliar face, older, college age, he operates the professional sound system contracted for the show's weekend run. The audio equipment belongs to him and he's about to pack it up. A thin black mustache, affable, chatty, a competent leader, he says to the room, "hey you guys, check this out." The busy group stop their tasks and gather toward the stage. So do we.

The motley crew forms a tight semi-circle around the stranger. From his shirt pocket he produces an unmarked cassette and holds it up for all to see, then turns toward a massive cassette deck and loads it. Like an airline pilot preparing for take-off, he flips on several switches, and lights up serious audio power stacked behind him, on stage left and stage right. The multi-colored stereo lights reflect off the onlookers' eyes. Suddenly a hum and vibration envelopes us like a warm blanket. It feels good because the theater doors are open and I forgot my jacket, I get goosebumps. I look toward the hum source and notice large black speakers that blend into the black stage curtains.

The professional audio equipment transports us from high school theater USA, to a day on the green rock concert, front row. Satisfied with volume, balance, equalizer settings and a myriad of sound adjustments, the music engineer pushes: play. With bated breath we stare at the deck, the cassette is visible behind the clear plastic cover. The two cassette gears turn at different speeds.

The engineer is the only guy in the room who knows what's coming. The acapella is abrupt and we're startled, it's so loud and clear through the 12 speakers:

Carry on my wayward son,

For there'll be peace when you are done

Lay your weary head to rest

Don't you cry no more

(Driving instrumental chorus)

Once I rose above the noise and confusion

Just to get a glimpse beyond the illusion

I was soaring ever higher, but I flew too high

Though my eyes could see I still was a blind man

Though my mind could think I still was a mad man

I hear the voices when I'm dreamin', I can hear them saaay

Carry on my wayward son

For there'll be peace when you are done

Lay your weary head to rest

Don't you cry no more

The song played to the end; five minutes and 26 seconds later we look at each other, jaws dropped. Wow . . . Woahhh! . . . Ha ha ha ha ha . . . alriiight!!

Nobody heard *that* before. Somehow this audio wizard procures a copy and we hear it, before the radio stations get it, and man did we *hear* it! The song releases in days, erupts more like it. A small band from Topeka, Kansas floors everybody. Odds were little to none you'd hear a song before its radio release. You know what? Please stop what you're doing and hear that song. Go to the best equipment you've got and put it to work. Sing along too. Act like you hear it for the first time, like we did.

A great song on a great system. The way classics *should* be heard!

Jack and Inger are great parents and I am fortunate and thankful for their care. While under their roof, in their midst, I live their way, a compliant teenager. Go where they go, friendly visits in San Francisco, Quaker meetings on Sunday morning. The rest of the time I live my life: rock music, pot, bikes, friends, fishing. Killing time in lazy fun ways. Obsessing on girls, but socially stunted and awkward from lack of practice, and my lazy, lousy lifestyle choices. I still enjoy a pick-up game of basketball, but truant daily, my grades plummet.

Day one as a sophomore, two things happen: Three days before school starts, the principal's son burns down the school's Administration Building to its foundation. The arsonist is a senior and a popular creek rat and fortunately for him, a minor. He returns to campus a week later, visibly weak from the stress of crime and punishment. Campus life resumes (minus all student records).

I'm walking to my second class and see a guy I don't know, walking like a penguin (feet pointed out), long wavy dirty-blonde hair, four inches past his shoulders, wearing faded super bell bottom levis with holes in the knees, and a flimsy tye-dye tank-top that reveals a brown hairy chest and underarms. With a wry smile and manufactured low voice the stranger says, "what's going on?" I stop and look at the hippie peering at me through thick glasses . . . Gary Forest?? "Hey man, you don't recognize me?" This guy is scruffy and scraggly, it's only been two years, what happened?!? I want nothing to do with this guy. "Yeah it's me Gary, I moved in with my mom and brother in Niles." Oh, this is not good. For the next five years, I can't shake the guy. Gary Forest is the same guy I hung out with in eighth grade (Great America). Wow! This is like going from freshface 1964 John Lennon, to 1969 John Lennon, but in one year! I haven't heard from Gary in two years, boy, a rough two years. "You look different, I didn't recognize you." "Oh you know, just hangin' out . . . partyn', heh, heh, heh."

When a guy friend moves away, that's pretty much it, you lose touch. The considerable effort to stay in touch: handwritten letters, expensive long-distance phone calls, envelopes and lick-stamps etc. etc. etc. makes it impractical and highly unlikely you'll stay in touch.

Right away, Gary starts trying to bum money and cigarettes, or sell me his lunch tickets. This guy's starving to death. Man can this guy eat, more than me sometimes. Gary is a three-sided person: part leach, part charming and part clown. He gets what he wants, thinks fast, fast on his feet. This isn't clear to me then. He annoys me a lot, but not always.

Like my Sunday friend, Garrett Montaine, Gary is a previous member of the Foster Care system. He's lived through highs and lows, I don't get. Gary lived with a couple great families, the Hoods in Hayward, and a family in Mill Valley. But scary places too, including early turbulent years with his mother and father. Gary's parents split early; his mother wasn't in a position to care for him, so as a young boy, Gary entered the foster system. Prior to our sophomore year, Gary was reunited with his mother and brother in Niles.

The historic town of Niles borders north Fremont along the hills. When Niles' students reach high school age, they attend either Mission San Jose High School or Washington High School. Gary chose Mission San Jose.

Gary talks his way into anything and I'm embarrassed at times, but I have a soft spot for him. Gary endures constant ridicule from peers and everyone we meet; persecution, for his thick glasses. But by a twist of irony, when the glasses are removed, Gary is James Dean, Hollywood handsome. 5'-10", athletic build, good at basketball, spirited rhythm guitar player, fast runner, and to the envy of guys everywhere, full brown facial hair with Elvis grade sideburns, and electric-blue eyes framed in long wavy, dirty blonde hair. Behind the lenses Gary is a real ladies man but sadly, extra-thick eyewear reduces Gary to a jubilant jester. Gary never misses an opportunity to remove his spectacles, and draw sighs from the ladies. These moments of glory are brief however, as Gary is forced to choose between, legally blind ladies man, or sight. The moment the heavy spectacles are returned to Gary's nose, his traffic-stopping looks come to a screeching halt. The world fails to look behind the glasses.

Gary and I are 15 and become good friends again. Gary wins my mother over, again, and spends an inordinate amount of time at our house, enjoying square meals and mom's world-class baking. Our tastes of food differ, Gary likes to eat big, from a kitchen filled with simmering pots and sumptuous smells. Spaghetti with a rich homemade sauce is a Gary Forest specialty. I helped him make spaghetti sauce a couple times. Everything is fresh; herbs and spices, onions, green peppers, garlic, ground beef, tomato sauce, sausage etc. etc. etc.

Gary cooks in the tiny kitchen at his mother's tiny house in Niles. The old, charming, dilapidated, unlevel house is one in a long line of small, old houses along the west side of Mission

Boulevard, opposite the green grass hills of Niles. Behind the houses run several sets of railroad tracks, the old Nile's train yard. Beyond the tracks is the historic town of Niles and Main Street. On Main Street is a pool hall with a pinball machine or two. The pool hall's atmosphere feels shady and dangerous, young and old guys are drinking. Also on Main Street are dusty antique stores I ignore, and Rosie's Cafe. By money earned from pitching quarters, and lawn mowing jobs, Gary introduces me to his favorite thing in the world: breakfast at Rosie's Cafe in Niles.

My first classic American breakfast, served in a restaurant; Gary orders for us: bacon, eggs, sausage, buttered toast with a selection of jam and jelly packets, a stack of pancakes with butter and maple syrup, hash browns, coffee, milk and fresh squeezed orange juice.

Our fast is broken; served with a smile. It is very, very good. Total satiety is very pleasant for two 15 year olds boys.

Gary is a good cook, compared to me, a great cook. I cook next to nothing. Only ultra-basic meals; Inger posts daily dinner instructions for my sisters and I: baked potatoes, hamburger helper, white rice (cooked indian style), bake a premade tuna casserole or bake a whole chicken, mom pre-cuts into pieces. I apply the Shake n Bake coating to the chicken and bake. I mash potatoes. I have zero interest in cooking anything more than kp duty requires. Lunch is usually a tuna fish or peanut butter & jelly sandwich. Or Rye-King crackers smothered with a half dozen different spreads. They're good, and good is good.

John Velasco went to a shopping mall with mom and I. Inger packed tuna fish sandwiches for us. John eats his sandwich but is embarrassed, afraid he might be seen by someone he knows, and teases me about it for months after. He's funny and a friend, so it doesn't bother me.

John Velasco is Basque, and his mother cooks better than anyone I know (sorry Mom). In addition to older brother Don, John has three sisters; Carmen, the firstborn, is an adult, she works and attends college, and two younger sisters, the youngest, a sassy redhead intimidates me, and another daughter two years younger than I. I wonder if either daughter can cook like their Mother? If so, their husband(s) are most fortunate. I've since learned, Basque cuisine is arguably the world's best.

Mrs. Velasco is wonderful.

At Mrs. Velasco's dinner table, I first heard, "tear off a piece of bread with your hands, don't cut." I like the new system, it verifies the sayings, 'breaking bread together,' and 'wash your hands before dinner.'

There are a number of sleepovers at Gary's mother's house. Gary's mother is a lesbian and has a roommate named Rene. Gary hates this, and hates Rene for it. Rene is the heavy, she lays down the rules and her and Gary butt heads. His mother's relationship forms an ever-present toxic cloud in the house and is my first close encounter with a same-sex relationship. I like Rene, she never gives me grief. Gary's mother is an alcoholic. When I sleep over, after dark in the dark living room with a small circle of her adult friends, the drinking starts. Rene doesn't drink and is not there during these times. Sometimes a joint goes around. Gary and I join the circle occasionally and as they drink more, innocent giggles give way to life's hidden afflictions and laments, and eventually loud harassment is hurled at Gary and me.

Gary tells me often, he's an alcoholic.

At his prompting we walk to the local liquor store in Niles. By Gary's solicitation, an adult over 21 is roped in, and does Gary's bidding. We score a six-pack of Schlitz Malt Liquor talls in the blue cans. There's a white bull printed on each shiny blue can. With a brown bag in hand, we hightail it back to the tracks, in between Main Street and Gary's backyard. Long trains of idle box cars sit motionless on the tracks. We pick an open one, climb up and enter. I imagine Gary and I as down on our luck hobos during the great depression huddled around a steel drum fire and ridin' the rails back to fame and fortune. The boxcar is empty, cold and dark.

We pop tops on 2-16 ounce cans of Schlitz Malt Liquor and drink. They taste bad but are fizzy-fun. After one empty can, jokes and pressing matters of recent school days, roll eloquent and enthusiastic off our tongues. Topics of discussion zip along in dramatic fits and starts at elevated volume.

We can yell if we want, in the Niles train cemetery.

After guzzling three 16 ounce cans of malt-liquor in short order, for the first time I am drunk.

Off and on, my head spins uncontrollably. When my head begins to spin, I have to close my eyes and hang on to something so I don't fall. At the historic train yard in Niles, California, I threw up. Gary is hip to this reaction and says, "you'll be okay." After another upchuck, it's getting dark so we go back to the house. Gary's room is a closet, 6 feet deep by 11 feet long. There's enough room for a twin bed and a 10" shelf along the opposing wall supported by cinder blocks. I've never seen a worse sleeping arrangement.

Sleeping on an unlevel, hard plywood floor is no less easy to do drunk than sober, and no less cold. I shiver. The shiver lining is Gary's stereo, turntable and *record collection.*

Gary and I share the same two tastes in music, soft rock and hard rock. The records in Gary's impressive collection are new to me. Late 60's to mid 70's stuff; Bad Company, Lynyrd Skynyrd, Jimi Hendrix, Ted Nugent, Aerosmith and more. We listen to it all at Gary's house, and again at school; Ted Nugent's Cat Scratch Fever erupts from a creek rat's van stereo. The song is engrossing and until it's over, I forget I'm cutting class. This massive rock tsunami overwhelms me, the surge takes me under, spins me round and round. Lynyrd Skynyrd's Free Bird and Fleetwood Mac are common selections of the Irvington poolhall jukebox, listened to while playing pinball or foosball. The music's impact on my formative years is immeasurable. Rock n roll is my refuge, right or wrong. The bedrock to it all is Led Zeppelin, yes I'm a fan. Jim Stanford is a huge fan too. We're into it.

The next morning Gary takes me to Rosie's Cafe on Main Street in Niles. I'm famished and the meal is quite good, it restores my soul and faith in life.

There are five more sleepovers at Gary's mom's place. The encounters are more or less the same, drunk and disorderly, psychologically disturbing. One time there's nothing to eat except a single can of white lima beans. Gary is noticeably upset and embarrassed.

I got my first pair of Levis super-bell bottoms that year. Gary's been wearing them all year and the blue jeans are extremely popular at school. Standard issue in fact. There's only one creek rat, a senior, who wears straight-leg jeans. He's tall and built like a man so no one kids him about it; combined with a red plaid shirt and brown suede boots with red laces, the look is cool, vogue and individual, cleancut suburban lumberjack man stoner. After getting my superbells, the thing to do is wash and line dry them for maximum shrinkage, so they wear skin-tight. I remember wearing them proudly, size 30 - 36. The 30" waist is a tad tight, the 36" length is an inch too long and the Levi's get ragged on the bottom, perfect. I'll be honest, after a wash/dry the 30 inch waist is a little difficult to button up. But my stomach doesn't hang over the belt, even when I lean forward (soon enough, but not today). You notice stuff like that while sitting on a curb at the creek, stoned head down. The pants fit my new lifestyle.

Superbells reflect the way we feel then; hazy, crazy and lazy. Fading, distorted; the constant target of the Soviet Union, nuclear world annihilation 100 times over.

As Soviet nuclear submarines navigate nearby seas and oceans, patrolling to and fro like quiet lions, submerge, rise, periscopes, one thing does not move: the inter-ballistic nuclear warhead missiles they carry, remain *locked* on their USA targets, including Jackson Street and the surrounding San Francisco Bay Area. If the submarine does a 180 degree turn, for example, the missiles do not move with the submarine, they stay locked on target, ready to fire 24\7 right at this 15 year old. I'm aware of this fact 24/7, and of my music 24/7.

A favorite activity for Gary and I, is for 25 cents to hop on an AC Transit bus and ride to the Fremont Hub; Fremont's premiere outside shopping mall, its only mall. Our priority? Meet girls. We always meet girls. We do our best to meet them, but no serious relationships ever come from it. We ride BART to San Francisco a few times. We exit at the Powell Street Station and buzz around; China Town, North Beach, Fisherman's Wharf, Cannery Row, Ghirardelli Chocolate etc. etc. etc.

In San Francisco, gay men hit on us constantly. This aggression by the gay community blind-sides us, freaks us out a bit and pisses me off occasionally. Not to the point of hostility, I just don't like their audacity and rudeness, toward Gary and I. Gary and I are grown enough to brush them aside. I compare their behavior to aggressive panhandlers, but their aim isn't the little money we might have or a cigarette.

My parents have a sweet friend in the city, Mrs. Becky Walton. Aunt Becky is a grand southern lady, 15 years older than my parents. She is white, large and loud with a pleasant Virginian accent, but above all she is *joyous*, even more than Mrs. Starr. Her son is a regular actor on a major TV soap opera and her circle of artistic friends is vast, Jack Moyer included. On one Aunt Becky visit, a talkative lady guest is there, about the same size as Becky but younger, mom's age. She explains to me the art of singing, opera and opera training. She says, proper training is why Luciano Pavarotti sings so well. Out of the blue, she belts out a sustained note, opera style. Her voice hits me like a laser beam! I'll never forget it. Jack knew Mr. and Mrs. Charlie Walton, before their divorce. I only met Charlie once, a nice distinguished guy, a gentleman.

Aunt Becky's home has an ornate, black, wrought-iron balcony outside her 2nd floor bedroom; her home is really cool, unique and artsy, on an over-sized, bushy, treesy, greensy lot. Aunt Becky visits us on several occasions in San Francisco, Palma Ceia and Jackson Street. In Hayward, Aunt Becky joined us kids for a swim in the backyard doughboy pool. She had difficulty navigating the entry and "spilled" out of her swimsuit. Wow, what an eyeful, I quickly turn askance to avoid embarrassment. The Boni's, the Wakefields, the Hatfields and Aunt Becky, make up my parents' inner circle of friendships. Aunt Becky is one of Jack and Inger's dearest friends, and we visit her often.

Distressful news from San Francisco! Aunt Becky and two friends suffer a horrible accident! The three of them stepped out onto the wrought iron balcony to enjoy the view; suddenly the deck gave way! They fall to the concrete below. Becky fractures a leg and the other two suffer similar injuries. Jack looks in on Aunt Becky when he can during her long recuperation.

On one Aunt Becky visit, Gary Forest joins us. The day is sunny and we plan to carry on in Aunt Becky's neighborhood as if we were back home in Fremont or Niles. Our mission cannot be stopped. We're determined to meet pretty and cultured San Francisco lasses. Why not? The time came to come clean and disclose our wily intentions to Jack, Inger and Aunt Becky. Becky retorts with a grin, "Well, I wish you both the best. But I'm afraid you won't have much luck around here! Not in this neighborhood!" Gary and I look at each other, how's that possible? Undeterred, we hit the streets more determined than ever.

We survey the orderly, steep residential street for signs of life. We don't wait long. A tall, thin young white man, well dressed, well groomed and in sunglasses, walks out his front door and opens his car door. Another man dressed in similar fashion, follows close behind. They embrace, kiss and get in the car! Gary starts in with his, "Oh no, Oh no!" The scene repeats over and over. Beaten, we capitulate and return to the Walton house. Becky says, "*well??*" "You were right Aunt Becky, you were right." Aunt Becky lives in the heart of San Francisco's Castro District. Gary and I learned that day what "the Castro" means.

By sophomore year I joined the ranks of smokers. I smoke Marlboro box, Gary smokes Camel Filters soft pack. In addition to smoking, Gary has a beer and wine habit, and I buy a joint whenever expendable money is available.

A few years later I heard a Baptist preacher tell his congregation, "the word *alcoholic* was invented by the Anheuser Busch Company, but Jesus called them *drunks.*"

These stinky unhealthy habits are not free, there is a cost associated with them. Kevin and Kamela Finley are straight. Alex Zolanski is straight. Tivas and Bucky Cortez are straight. Marlo Topper and I are on the same path, stoners who rock, but Marlo lacks musicality that one can see or hear. Darin Vanderberg is a stoner, a talented audiophile who displays intense love and appreciation for music, but like Mark doesn't exhibit his own musicality; he doesn't drink but recently toys with cross-tops or whites, (trucker pills to stay awake) a landscaper, a mechanic and an audio-phile. Darin V. loves to work and accomplish.

Darin Vanderberg and Sherry Tyrell are neck deep in the middle of a five year romance. They are funny to watch, the two of them on the couch (fully dressed) wriggling and giggling for half an hour or more. After a while, it gets old.

Guy, Danny and their youngest brother Curtis Wellbaum are all stoners, Guy and Danny like beer too. Guy the eldest (Darin's age) chases girls constantly and enjoys a great deal of success. He's in good shape, handsome, has the gift of gab and is persistent. Both Danny and Guy speak with a unique gravelly tone, sport good looks (porcelain skin) and possess the gift of humor. They are successful ladies men. Curtis, one year younger than I, seems younger than that. A scrawny runt compared to his older brothers, I avoid conniving Curtis. Curtis has resilience though. Living in the shadow of two dashing, courageous brothers, Curtis develops other skill sets, to offset the hand he's dealt.

John Velasco and I drift apart. John's new best friend, Frank Oleander is very excitable and looks down on me and Jackson Street in general. Partly from affluence and partly from being wound up. His attraction to, and popularity with the opposite sex, is award-winning. For years Frank and John sparkled at every party in town. The two create a party within the party, running at a feverish pitch.

In addition to the ladies, Frank, a year older than John and I, loves to fish. That's where our paths intersect. The banter between Frank and John is hysterical. They're addicted to belly laughs. God help you if you bore them, even for a second and their devil-sharp tongues should point in *your* direction.

When we fish Lake Elizabeth and the bite slows, the hijinks start. Frank spots his latest mark, an elderly Japanese man fishing by himself, quietly amongst the reeds. Frank says, "How's it going today?" 'Any bites? ``How's the fishing?" etc. etc. etc. Perfect strangers are grist for the Frank and John, ha-ha-mill, always at the stranger's expense.

Where is conscience, where is remorse? Same place as mine.

I remember the two magpies cackling over the latest exploit; Frank says, "yeah, I asked this old Japanese man fishing over there, if he'd had any luck? - Frank and John are laughing hysterically, Frank cackling so loud, he can barely retell the story. I've never heard anyone laugh so hard, for so long, at such a high octave - 'The old man says, "oh yes" and lifts his stringer proudly, displaying one average-sized 10" rainbow trout. "I caught this trout." Frank stands there, holding his own fishing pole and tackle-box. With earnest, Frank studies the fish, then looks at the happy gentleman and replies, "I'm pretty sure that's a catfish sir." "Oh no no," said the old man. "This is trout, a rainbow trout." "Sir, I'm positive . . . that's a catfish."

"Young man you are mistaken, this is trout!" As Frank walks away he mutters, "catfish."

Frankie and Johnny are rolling.

Marlo Topper has an older sister Valerie. Valerie is Danny Wellbaum's age, a year ahead of me, Hannah's age. Mr. and Mrs. Topper work outside the home, and the Topper house serves as a daytime devil's den for Jackson Street truants. Every school day, a crowd of five to ten are there.

My Jackson Street contemporaries share a common thread: their relationships are generally long term. They seek a forever soulmate. No quickie fling; which is great. Both Charlene and Paula Lansing have steady-eddy boyfriends, lasting years. Vickie Vanderberg, Sherry Tyrell, long term. Alex Zolanski, Darin Vanderberg and Marlo Topper, long term. Gary Forest and I, the opposite, we don't get serious. We enjoy freedom. We are either too immature, no good, or want something else, without a clue what that something else is, let alone a plan to get there.

Gary introduces me to one of his previous foster families, the Hood's. Mr. Hood and his son (same age and grade as Gary and I) live in the Hayward Hills, up Highland Boulevard off Mission Boulevard. Mr. Hood is a 50 year old fireman captain. He drives a sporty Ford Pinto, goes to Church on Sunday and is in great physical shape. A straight arrow. Gary brags how his Dad can still do 50 push-ups. He's a divorcee and a great cook. He makes homemade lasagna and beer bread that is beyond delicious and we wash it down with an ice-cold Pepsi. So great! This is where Gary learned to cook. The biological son, Bruce, is a loner and not enamored by Gary's charms. Bruce knows Gary too well. Gary, the handsome class-clown athlete, is popular in school, more so than Bruce. Bruce is serious and level-headed. He looks down on Gary, estranged from him by the endless string of disappointments Gary dished out. Think, prodigal son's brother.

Bruce is a champion archer, and has piled up many archery accolades. A successful bowhunter as well. Numerous game mounts adorn their home. I watch Gary play Mr. Hood through praise and brown nose tactics, including belittling the ex-wife and praising Mr. Hood, "All her fault, you did nothing wrong," type stuff. Mr. Hood soaks in Gary's praise.

I begin to understand Gary better. Gary preys on the kindness of others to his benefit. His goals are simple, not bad really: a nice bed to crash in, three square meals, a few beer bucks. He's unabashed in his efforts; the end justifies the means. The bottom line is Gary makes me laugh and feel good about myself. Is he playing me too? Gary Forest is a good friend, and we have a good time together, most of the time.

While ascending another drunken mountain, Gary speaks about a friend of his, from the

Hayward/Hood days. I've witnessed time and time again (especially on Jackson Street) Gary

suffers undeserved persecution, due to his so-thick glasses; his silly nature doesn't help. Gary's

glasses *magnify* his electric blue eyes. Gary's magnified eyes give off a, in your face look, and can

be misconstrued as confrontational, and brings endless grief to Gary.

Hayward High School is no picnic. By luck, I avoided that school. I'm sure it was a great place

in 1949 when Bill Walsh graduated as a Hayward Farmer, but in 1976 not so much. Thank you

mom and pappa for moving from Palma Ceia, to leave it to beaver Fremont. Gary did his freshman

year at Hayward High while living with his foster family, the Hoods. This being a second stint with

the Hoods. During another malt liquor-buzzcapade, Gary tells the story of his near demise at

Hayward High last year.

"Out in the school yard, several older mean kids and their buddies are about to work me over.

I'm surrounded, and a large ring of onlookers encourages my undoing. I prayed to God for help,"

Gary said.

- When I first met Gary in the eighth grade, he told me, "at night, I read my Bible, it makes me

feel better." I've never felt that bad and consider myself fortunate. He showed me his Bible during

the one sleepover at his Aunt and Uncle's house on Paseo Padre Parkway two years earlier. The

Way Bible is a paraphrased version of the Bible, rewritten in modern day vernacular for better

understanding, no thees and thous. - 'Just before the mob does me in, out of nowhere, my guardian

angel arrives. "Leave him alone. You mess with this guy, you mess with me."

Gary's angel is Joey Benecia. Three years older, Joey is strong and brave. The bullies back off.

Joey knows these guys, standard bullies out to impress girls and friends. This freshman kid Gary is okay; he just looks different because of his thick glasses. Gary is gushingly grateful, and Joey has a friend for life. Not a flash in the pan friendship either. For the entire year, Joey protects Gary from coke bottle haters. The way Gary goes on and on, Joey sounds like the greatest guy ever born. A real ladies man, a rock musician, a singer in fact.

Gary plays the guitar and takes the same guitar class I do, but a different period. Like me, Gary always plays at the creek. Our guitar skills are equally mediocre, but enthusiastic and tolerable to kids within earshot.

I finally meet Gary's guardian angel, Joey Benecia. Joey has a car and we putt around Hayward a couple times. Gary is right, Joey's a vocalist, in his Mom's garage on a PeaVey set up, Joey blasts a Freddy Mercury vocal. It sounds excellent with the Queen album accompaniment. This guy *is* cool, and friendly too. Joey Benecia, the Hayward Highlander.

1977 is the year of Gary; chasing girls, drinking, smoking pot, playing guitar. We hitchhike (extinct now, feasible then) with guys and gals, perfect strangers whom mostly smile, pull over and give us rides, within 5 minutes or less they stop and give us a lift. If a City Bus or BART won't get us there, we travel by thumb. Until I drive, hitchhiking is our primary travel option. Though many girls hitchhike, they are wise to avoid it. For me, a thumb is all I need.

Pinecrest Lake

Fishing and the Fifth of July

Ready for more fishy stories? Week in and week out, Lake Elizabeth is our go-to fishing spot. We grow up there, boys to men to boys again. A week hardly passes, where me, Kevin Finley, Guy and Danny Wellbaum, John Velasco, Frank Oleander and many others don't fish. The lake's riches and secrets are important to our teenage years; enriching social development, space to be a kid, and learning to fish. We introduce every bait and lure known to man to the slippery residents, and compete for bragging rights.

The king fisher of Jackson Street is Guy Wellbaum. Far and away the most knowledgeable, accomplished and committed; The compleat angler. Guy's knots and rubber worm double-snagless rigs are *Field and Stream* good. A reservoir of fishing doctrine, taught with patience, awaits anyone remotely interested in the sport. And there's always a new hot spot to talk about.

Guy tells the *best fish-stories*, his tales are exciting because instead of the typical approach of stretching the truth, he lets the truth and his gravelly tone do the talking.

I haven't met a better storyteller than Guy Wellbaum. If Mark Twain and Guy Wellbaum ever meet, they'll hit it off famously, I'm sure of it. When Guy's adventurous tale begins, you can hear the cast splash. With an upbeat tempo, and a mouth full of gravel, Guy's fishy fables are told with sincerity and heart, always worth your time.

Guy befriends a local taxidermist and they produce two beautiful fish mounts. One, a large-mouth bass swimming, the lure dangles from the bottom protruded lip. And my favorite, a pair of trophy blue-gills.

We've all caught bluegills; for many, they're our first fish, the easiest to catch, and ounce for ounce a fun fight. But they're small and consequently, as we get older, we don't bother with them. But Guy's found this "new spot." He alleges this pond holds the biggest, bluest bluegills ever seen; trophy bluegill, 10" long, very wide, and lunkers. A trophy bluegill? That thought never crossed my mind.

A prehistoric genepool?

Not crappies either. Crappies are an inch or two longer than bluegills, good fighters, but pale and nondescript. No, 100 percent blue-gill; before or since, I've *never seen bluegills like these*, so large and so dark blue. Guy's taxidermist is smart, he mounts the two fish together on varnished hardwood, corners cut decoratively, edges routed. The dark walnut stain blends beautifully with the fish's deep blue hue. The trophy bluegills are set in a natural swim appearance. The lure used to catch them, tied to a piece of line mounted near the edge of wood, perfects the realism; in sync, the pair's attention is turned by the lure, eyes fixated on their temptation.

I've seen hundreds of fish mounts; most invoke envy, but Guy's bluegill tandem? It belongs in the home of whoever started Bass Pro Shop, or Mr. Cabala Senior, or a Natural Museum, or the Oval Office. But I hope it hangs in Guy's abode.

America loves the Fourth of July no doubt, but our street *loves* it for two weeks, night and day, loud and wild. A holiday tailor-made for the boys of Jackson Street. We love to strike the match, light the punk, ignite the fuse, the thrill of shhhhhh . . . BOOM!! There aren't enough fuses on earth. The waft of gunpowder in the air and in our fingers, the reports never get old, never enough explosion, I'm not kidding.

When July fourth darkness *finally* arrives, law-abiding families congregate on curbs, - I know them all, in every direction - step onto Jackson Street and ignite their volatile stockpile. Folks with more means, light whole bricks of firecrackers. Pop, pop, pop, bam, bam, Bam, SHBAAAM*BAAAAAMM!!!* What a rush!

There's structure to it; start small, build to a finale. Family's start with sparklers and ground snakes, next, larger safe and sane fireworks: pinwheels, ground blooms etc. and conclude with the best, unsafest, insanest devices from their armory.

After all good people say goodnight and retreat to their humble homes, that's our signal. Time for the *good stuff*. With a little help from Chinatown, we have plenty.

GLORY!!! America!

When it comes to fulfilling our patriotic duty, my friends and I don't disappoint; we love to light a fuse. With lawn-mowing money, we beeline to our neighborhood purveyor of quality stuff: firecrackers, cherry bombs and M-80s; we pool $15 bucks, hop on BART, get off at the Powell Street Station, sprint to Chinatown, score a half-dozen packs of bottle rockets, 12 bottle rockets in a pack, a dollar a pack. Without exception, *every* Asian businessman on every corner of Chinatown has them for sale; immediately if not sooner.

A Fourth of July extra (in my neighborhood), is the morning after, the fifth. I get out of bed early, at first light, hose down three bowls of sugary cold cereal and milk, then, with a like-minded friend or alone, walk the streets. As far as Tim Cucuk's house on Lockwood Avenue and Chadbourne Drive, we sift roads, sidewalks and driveways, for *unspent* fireworks. Unspent firecrackers are the goal (I said we couldn't get enough). Years ago, gleaning was modest, but now, fitted with bag and bike, we clean up.

In my prime, I bag ten pounds of unexpired firecrackers (early bird gets the black cats). Danny and Curtis Wellbaum do well too. On Marion Avenue near Wade Jenning's house, after a good morning effort the three of us relax; laden with impressive hauls and satisfied by the fruits of our labors. We look forward to going out in a blaze of explosive glory, when a scrappy kid pedals up, a gaunt stranger. Friendly, chatty and unassuming, he lulls us into a false sense of security. Two minutes later, the vibe still cordial, *Johnny Lightning rips the sack from my relaxed grip and tears out on his bike!* He's getting away with my record setting, fifth of July firework stash! That SOB! I'm blinking in the bright lights, stunned by his brazen audacity and this kid lights his bike up! I helplessly watch the dastardly getaway: Marion Avenue past Chris Peters house to Troyer Avenue left, poof . . . gunpowder gone! Talk about a major dud. What took three hours to scrounge, took three minutes to steal. Impressive ratios! Well done, dangit, well done. Danny and I can't help but admire the kid's swashbuckle swag.

The last time I did a fifth of July gunpowder glean: I was embarrassingly older, we all were, but old habits die a slow death on Jackson Street. By an evil mysterious force, our maturity is slowed or stunted. Nobody grows up. Curtis Wellbaum, 10 months younger, is around on the "last fifth," we pair up by default.

Down Jackson Street, left on Olive Avenue, right on McKay down that short steep hill, right on Lockwood Avenue to the Cucuks and the Dvoraks on the corner. The firecracker search is half-hearted, our emphasis more on friends along the way and sunshine. However, out of habit, eyes are cast down.

In two hours, the family is scheduled to head across the Bay, for a typical, Moyer San Francisco artist friend visitation. Ascending the rise on Chadbourne Drive to Olive Avenue, something on the ground catches Curtis' hawk eye. He stoops over and produces a good-sized, clean and white roach, (partial joint, saved for later).

In dramatic Curtis fashion, he lifts the tightly rolled roach, to his large nose and "sniff, sniff . . . sniffff." Curtis' big brown eyes grow large and dilate, his eyebrows arch. "Jens, this is crystal," Curtis blurts in a tense hush. Crystal is slang for the drug PCP. They call it gumby too. Somebody under the influence of crystal is described as, "gumbied." Buddy Duke is the only person I know who does that crap. I saw Buddy in the boy's room gumbied one time. Guys standing around him amazed, Buddy on his feet not wobbly, staring intently at nothing, incoherent, unresponsive, mute.

My personal three commandments are: don't go to jail, don't shoot up and don't smoke crystal.

Curtis draws a bic lighter from his super bell-bottom pocket and lights it; puts the crystal roach to his pursed lips, and inhales. He holds his breath keeping the crystal smoke in his lungs as long as possible for maximum effect. He extends the roach in my direction.

Before lighting it, Curt handed me the roach, to smell it and verify his claim. PCP is like nothing else, unlike any pot I smoked before. When the boys gather at Mill Creek along Mill Creek Road, to drink Henry Weinhards in the bottle, crystal is discussed a couple times. Louis Payette said, "it smells like death." Another said, "it smells like burnt rubber bands." I concur with both opinions.

Curtis and I slow our stride, Olive Avenue toward Jackson Street, house by house, lawn by lawn. The roach passed between us six times; I took three hits, Curt took four. We finish the roach three houses down from the Wellbaums, by Steve Rommel's house. Curtis tells no one what he found, he tells everyone. I said, "gotta go Curt," and return home with a pound of pure gunpowder.

Straight to my room, on the edge of a ledge; laying on my bed the PCP's effect holds me still, halfway between, flat on my back, and on my side facing the light of the window.

Frozen motionless, however, every five minutes, my body twitches hard, convulses from head to toe, like a short but violent electric shock. Like those medical dramas on TV (and real life) when they connect the defibrillator wires to a pulseless person's chest and yell, "now!" and the unconscious body rattles and arches from the shock.

I'm awake.

The intermittent body-shocks are the worst of it, fortunately the family doesn't leave for 90 minutes and I'm better by then, however, the unpredictable 'pops' continue. I feel like a guitar string being plucked. They happen when awake and most calm. Though with much less frequency, the jolts never stop completely, even today; when I'm awake but calm, no TV on, not driving, when quiet and still . . . BAMM!

PCP was on the, thou shall never do list for a reason.

Horsepower and Valor

In the 70's, driving a car that looks and runs great is, for the majority, their priority. Fremont's infatuation with the automobile is second to none; between the car manufacturing plants, the racetracks, several well-stocked junkyards and sunny skies year round, anyone who wants a *ride*, gets it done. It's worse than that, a 70's man is measured by his vehicle. You are what you drive. Many cars in town are *breathtaking*. The City of Fremont, is a seven days a week car show/car race - burnouts included.

Every 16 year old's first job is getting their driver's license. Not SATs, not marriage, not fame and fortune, a driver's license. There's not enough drugs or alcohol in the world to stop an American boy or girl from getting their driver's license in the 70's.

You must be 15 to take Driver's Education. If you time it right, schedule it right; pass Driver's Education, complete Driver's Training and pass its test, *and* pass the California Department of Motor Vehicles driving test; by 15 and a half you can get a driver's permit (licensed adult required in car while driving) and finally, six months later, your driver's license.

Plainly put, driver's license = freedom.

Additionally, if you pass the two optional motorcycle tests, written and hands-on, you get a motorcycle permit too. The wonders of the motorcycle permit are many, but most wonderful, unlike the car permit, you can drive . . . by yourself. No parental supervision, freedom, *six months sooner*.

If I've ever had a dream, owning a motorcycle is it.

Oddly, there's not much else I pine for in life; no grand "big picture." A woman's beauty, a hot meal, a hot record, a classic book of fiction. A paycheck? I would not classify these as "dreams." Dreams spurn young men toward noble, meaningful pursuits. However, the open road on two wheels? That's my little dream.

In addition to its lower operating cost, there's something indescribable about a motorcycle. For a 15 year old boy, the appeal is hard to explain. It's that view through the window, beyond that distant view, beyond what you can see. A motorcycle will take me there, to a place I cannot see. Pappa's Vespa is cooler than I know, but not cool enough.

Since the third grade, in class at my desk, I've drawn choppers. Pappa told me, "Jens, before you get married, go around the world on a chopper." Pappa told me this three times. As intended, I took it literally. I love Evel Knievel, love his many accomplishments, and everything he stands for: audacious courage, strength and skill. I like his Elvis-Vegas style, red white and blue leather jumpsuit too. I've spent the last eight years on two wheels, I like it.

For me, the motorcycle is a mythical creature, a fire-breathing dragon or worse. Two wheels, a powerful well tuned engine, teardrop gas tank, thin black seat, sissy bar and lights, raked. As sure as Mr. Ed the horse can talk, this is my aspiration.

On cold and rainy high school mornings, Danny Wellbaum and I shuffle to Chris Peters' house (a year older, Danny's age) on Marion Avenue. You remember Chris Peters, the neighborhood hero, famous for climbing the massive, towering eucalyptus tree at the creek behind Jackson Street, to attach the thickest rope for the best swing known to man? We knock on Chris' door, two wet mooches looking for a ride to school.

Mrs. Peters is sweet and funny, energetic and caring, high strung and worrisome. We always get a ride. Because they went to the same elementary school, Chris' family knows Danny well, but not me. We sit in the warm living room waiting for sleepy Chris to get his act together. Chris' dad, Mr. Peters, is loud and cantankerous. He drives a white contractor's pick-up truck equipped with mounted tool boxes along the sides, and three ladders secured on top of a black steel rack.

When Danny and I show up, Mr. Peters is sitting comfortably in his padded living room chair drinking coffee, about to leave the house for work. To our hilarious amusement, Mr. Peters belittles Chris to death. "Chris, you're such a screw up, you'd f--- up a wet dream!" What's a wet-dream? What's wrong with this guy?! Wow what a mean dad, so funny, but mean too.

Every couple of years, Mrs. Peters gets sad. She gets her old trumpet and plays for hours, all day. I never heard her play, but I heard about it. That's so unusual and very sad to me. Our houses, 450' apart as the crow flies, must be beyond a trumpets range. She died a few years later to much grief and sadness throughout the neighborhood. Mrs. Peters is very special.

Chris Peters and John Velasco are good friends, so there's a pinch of overlap. Once on one of their many trips to Playland in Milpitas - a popular pinball and video game arcade and miniature-golf place along Interstate 680 at Jacklyn Road - I came along. Chris hangs out with John Velasco and Frank Oleander; they share the same quick wit and creative humor.

For infinite reasons, we all want to drive: independence, mobility, pride . . . a place to party, a ride to a party, improve social life, girls etc. etc. etc. To be a man, you must drive.

My birthday falls in mid-August making me a younger one, and delays my quest for a driver's license. I should complete Driver's Education, Driver's Training, and the State Driving test in my junior year. By New Years 1978, I should have two driving permits: car and motorcycle. My New Year's resolution is: living the American dream . . . *from the driver's seat.*

In between dreams, I convince Valerie Topper to get the spare key to her dad's old green Dodge pick-up truck and I drive a vehicle with four wheels for the first time. Manual-transmission? No biggie, I'll figure it out. Granny gear? No problem. Shurky-jurky a few blocks, then wow, I'm rolling! This is *unbelievable.*

Danny Wellbaum and I attempt to build a mini-bike out of loose parts; another time, we got a long since retired Husquarvana dirt bike running for 15 minutes. The mini-bike, almost decent, actually makes it around the block several times. With the left hand on the grip, while driving, reach down with the right hand and manipulate the carburetor linkage. Our hands smell of gas, but it does a respectable 30 miles per hour on a flat. It held together for a fun-filled week.

I got my motorcycle permit and regularly ask Pappa and Mom for their permission to ride the red Vespa scooter, or the yellow Vespa Ciao moped. Exciting days under California sunshine.

On a cold Christmas season night, mom lets me take her moped out. I bee-line it to John Velasco's house, in the very nice Gomes neighborhood near Lake Elizabeth. A hilarious sight; the two of us zipping around, struggling for maximum speed, dirty blonde and brown black hair blowing around, overgrown, hanging off a little moped. John sits on the cold, metal rack behind the single seat and doesn't complain. John's neighborhood is decked out for the Holidays, festive multi-colored festoon lighting highlights roof lines and garage door frames. What a sight we were; Santa and his elf minus the sacks or reindeer. We find ourselves on Washington Boulevard approaching Mission Boulevard near the old Spanish Mission San Jose. The left turn traffic light onto Mission Boulevard is red, but there's no cross traffic, it's clear, so I proceed left onto Mission

Boulevard. John and I look ridiculous, unzipped jackets flapping, runny noses, we're freezing. The flashing red lights in my side-mirror are *not* Christmas lights unfortunately, it's the police! I got my first traffic violations: running a red light, and driving without a license, a two for one. At least no speeding citation.

Mission San Jose High School has a big parking lot. And it's full of cars, many modest but a lot of them fixed up, All-American muscle car classics. Chrome mag wheels, chrome exhaust pipes, custom candy paint jobs, pumped-up V-8 engines with huge carburetors. One or two even have wheelie bars in the back, like a dragster or funny car do. These are street legal?? Sweet. If you put a foot into it, you literally see the gas gauge needle *move* toward empty. Eight miles a gallon? 50 cents a gallon gas, no problemo.

Many classmates are resolute, patient, *ambitious* and fix up their cars to eye-popping perfection. A pretty girl adorns their passenger seat.

The first time I rode in a hot-rod, Danny Wellbaum the savvy handsome sophomore and me the lanky green freshman are walking home from school. Danny's wearing his new cool, dark blue Levi corduroy pants, leather belt and a nice long sleeve button up shirt with a pattern. I had a jean vest on, otherwise nondescript. We're struttin' on Palm Avenue, a sunny day, thumbs out. One of the Twins pulls over in her custom white, 1966 Chevelle Super-Sport. I don't remember her name, we call them both the Twins. Straight, long blonde hair, pretty and tough. Ultra cool people, super nice seniors, identical twins, full grown women, erect posture, knockouts, *intimidating*. She pulls over, Danny knows her (I don't) and jumps in the back seat, so I follow him. "Hey! Do I look like a damn chauffeur?" Danny whispers, "get in front," I feel like an ass. Four on the floor, she eases it onto Palm Avenue - Black Sabbath and Ozzy Osbourne bang away on the 8-Track Stereo - shifts gears pops the clutch and punches it, the acceleration pushes me back hard, into the black leather bucket seat, the tires spin and squeal. What control, so great! She lights up a joint. One click closer to becoming a man, many strange curvy roads ahead.

During my 10 years in Fremont, not a single day passes, where revved engines aren't heard, two cars don't race, tires don't spin and smoke. Not one day! There are *so many* young people, and everyone drives. The princes and princesses of Fremont, the nobility, the V-8 royalty that rule by day and by night; an aristocracy of internal combustion, gas, oil and rubber.

Dorothy, Sherry, and Glenda Tyrell live next door; their Oklahomans. A neighbor's origin never matters then. Their family histories don't interest me. My thoughts are simple, shallow and self-serving.

During hot summer, after dinner when it's cooler, friends engage in a spirited game of hide-n-go-seek, or freeze-tag. This is usually a co-ed activity. Hannah, Marja and Tessa never participate. All of us, more or less, have entered puberty, we're interested in the opposite sex. The games are a fun way to get to know each other, the games provide an objective framework, a social icebreaker. Between the boys however, competition is fierce.

Teenagers play hide-n-go-seek; hiders race the seeker back to home-base; home-base being the spot the seeker started from. The seeker, eyes closed, counts to the agreed upon number while hiders hide, then seeks out the hiders (everyone else). Hiding strategies can be duplistic, I try to hide with Glenda when possible. Sherry hitched her wagon to Darin Vanderberg a couple years before and Dorothy is too far along the road of womanhood. Glenda still likes to squirm and laugh. Mr. and Mrs. Tyrell are both high-spirited, sweet people. Mr. Tyrell is unique, he gets in your face quick, but always with best intentions. He's big hearted and looks out for us. A good friend of

Kenny Starr, Jim Tyrell hangs out there on weekdays after work and weekends, sippin' a beer or two, and is generous with fatherly advice for us and auto-repair advice for Kenny.

Kenny Starr landed, fought and survived on the shore of Omaha Beach in World War II, the D-Day Invasion (opening scene of Saving Private Ryan). Mr. Tyrell fought in two wars, the Korean War and the Vietnam War; wounded by enemy fire three separate times, including shot in the leg mid-air, while parachuting down. These facts were unknown to me through the 70's. They didn't talk about it. I learned about Mr Starr and Mr. Tyrell's military service and gallantry later, in the 80s. I was so proud of them after that, and so ashamed of me. Ashamed for not knowing and appreciating their bravery and service to our country earlier on. And for the scoff and scorn I dished out, we all did; I mistook Mr. Tyrell's spirited, all-heart approach, for Okie foolishness. I made a gross error in judgment, committed a disservice to him and other Veterans, and to myself. I'm surrounded by real-life heroes and don't know it?!? Once, Alex Zolanski referred to Kenny Starr as the king of Jackson Street. I didn't get why then; I do now.

The Tyrell's are a horse family, a fun but foreign aspect to me. Sherry is best friends with Rose Pimentel, my first kiss in the fifth grade. Rose lives at the Tyrell's during high school. Sherry and Rose are like sisters, I imagine they still are. Rose's family is well known and highly regarded throughout the area for her father's, Pimentel Farm, located along Mission Boulevard at Driscoll Road, on the east hillside

Throughout the 10 years on Jackson Street, Rose always had an encouraging or kind word. She never turns against me, even when given cause.

A blue horse trailer is parked out front and Glenda and her father travel the country to compete in big time rodeos.

Glenda Tyrell wins the National Barrel Racing Championship! All-heart, like Pop.

Recently, a strange phenomenon (thank goodness short lived) infiltrates the neighborhood, CB Radio. The Tyrell horses are boarded on Osgood Road; horses are boarded up and down Osgood Road. No commuter traffic, just stables, corrals and horse manure. You can't go near the Tyrells or their CB associates without hearing, "Breaker, breaker, Jack Slack, this is Lady Lulu. Jack Slack, do you copy? Over." I know they understand each other, but the language is too cryptic. I have no clue what they're babbling about. CBrs have a blast with it for sure. Darin, Sherry and her sisters are all over it. A private language, so curious. CB radio is a big deal for the inclined. I have zero inclination for CB Radio.

I float stoned, and flutter from guitar class to the creek, to the Topper house, loitering in front of The Wellbaums and Cortezes, daytime, night time; morning, afternoon stoned, fun-filled evenings drinking and smoking with Gary drunk and stoned, barfing out of train cars, zipping up skin tight bell-bottoms, riding in cars familiar and unfamiliar, sticking my thumb out, never a bad experience. Always rock music. House parties Friday and Saturday nights with live bands, the musicians, schoolmates. Shoot a basket here and there, Quaker Church on Sunday morning, one day to the next. Nothing stands out, or lends itself to conversation. Nothing to brag about. Nothing to feel great about, except, feeling good. I know this much, I don't want to go to jail and I don't want to shoot-up. And I don't want to freak out from drugs, go insane or see visions, go Jim Morrison. I see that happening all over the place, I know it's real. Keep my brain intact. No blackouts. No insanity!

Summer of 1977, time to be a junior; let's get it on.

Wait, wait, time out. One more thing. Way back in 1972, I promised you a future Mark Munster encounter. You remember Mark Munster, consummate jock, tall, an inch taller than me, stronger now, a class-clown with a mean streak. Athletic and entitled. Butterfingers, hang onto that lateral pass! Mark's father, Mr. Munster, is everywhere, including assistant varsity basketball coach. Mr. Munster, a man's man; barrel-chested, brash and bold, loud and proud. He pushes Mark every step of the way. Well off, nice house, Cadillacs and Lincolns etc. etc. etc.

You remember Mark on the BART field trip in 1972, getting the entire sixth grade's attention by staging a "stumble" on the station platform next to the BART tracks and dropping his brown-bag lunch onto the tracks? Anything for attention this guy. And the sixth grade flag-football championship game? Making my big debut at backup quarterback; I lateral back to Mark, and he *drops it* (Mark's fumble nefariously similar to dropped lunch at BART) What a turd.

Mark disliked me then, in fifth and sixth grade, me and my long hair, insulated in the MGM class. Mark wants to show me up, hard. Beside the fumbled lateral, Mark never got that opportunity, until now that is.

They say, 'everything comes to those that wait?' Today has come at last, Mark Munster gets his big chance to squash me like a bug, in Coach Ruiz's, PE wrestling class.

Coach Ruiz is arguably the most popular Mission San Jose High teacher ever born and absolutely the most popular Mission coach of all time. Back in the day, coach Ruiz came within a whisker of making the Olympic Wrestling Team. He drives an amazing 1959 red and white Corvette convertible everyday. White teeth, dark Polynesian skin, Hollywood good looks, when Coach Ruiz crosses the street, traffic stops. Women young and old love him, and oh yeah, he's the head coach of Mission San Jose's reigning State Champion wrestling team. A real stud! 19 years later, his daughter, Dina Ruiz, a popular local television weather lady . . . marries Clint Eastwood!

After separating fact from fiction, the story goes: Miss Ruiz and Mr. Eastwood are to be married in a beautiful intimate ceremony, in a quaint wedding chapel, located on the Pebble Beach Golf Course in Monterey, California. The holy moment finally arrives and the wedding music begins. It's time for the father of the bride to walk his beautiful daughter down the aisle, to marry the famous (and much older) Clint Eastwood . . . but Father Ruiz is missing. Where in the world is coach?? You can cut the tension with a knife.

Tiger Ruiz is stroking Pebble Beach! Slicing and dicing the famous 9th Hole! With a dazzling smile and Churchillian timing, Coach Ruiz drives up to the ceremony, parks his golf cart, and enters the chapel. Uhh, did coach upstage Clint? Awkward.

With Mission Warrior pride and not skipping a beat, Coach Ruiz walks his beautiful daughter Dina (four years younger than Marja, two years older than Tessa and her friend) down the aisle, his thick, gelled, curly mane rocking. Father and daughter beam dazzling the guests, their reactions are audible, salutary.

Arm in arm, the king and princess sweep elegantly past friends, family, dignitaries and celebrities packed in the ornate chapel. The blooming bride, beset in rich shades of white, her broad-shouldered father, clad in glamorous golfy glitz, and . . . ramrod straight, thin as a rake, but a bit pale, the exceedingly handsome Clint Eastwood stands patiently at the altar, grinning. The happening approaches Elvis & Priscilla fervor.

But that's not all.

The Parson says, "with the power vested in me, I now pronounce you, man and wife. You may kiss the Bride." Clint and Dina embrace and kiss. The chapel erupts with clap n'cheer. Afterwards, father kisses daughter tenderly on the cheek, a pause and says, "I love you sweetheart," and walks out, jumps in the golf cart . . . and *plays the back nine!* Did the coach just leave his daughter's wedding . . . to Clint Eastwood . . . to finish his golf game? Yes, he did. Preposterous, audacious, outrageous! Badass coach.

This is the same Coach Ruiz (minus 19 years) who is teaching the PE wrestling class that I did not sign up for, yet find myself in nevertheless. It's the first day of wrestling class, I'm stoned and stumble in, back against the wall. Since junior high, in PE boys wear a reversible blue and yellow T-Shirt (Swedish Flag colors) to create opposing teams that are easy to identify. Now, ostracized by students and teachers alike and shunned by jocks, I walk into mandatory PE class, blue side out. I look better in blue.

We aren't supposed to repeat a PE sport. If I've already taken swimming for example, I can't take swimming again. The PE Department wants us to be rounded, do different sports. I would never choose wrestling and frankly, don't understand how I wound up here, but here we go, wrestling class, and the mighty Coach Ruiz is my teacher. Oh and look who else is here, Mark Munster. There's no salutation between us, a grunt maybe. We've attended the same schools since fifth grade, but this is our first class together.

I get a bad feeling. Smiling Coach Ruiz says with intense understated authority, "Okay, let's get going, two-minute matches. First up: Jens and Mark."

Earlier that year, I had Mr. Ruiz for Basic Geometry, the class filled with average, fun-loving students. I appreciate very much that Coach Ruiz pronounces my name right, in geometry *and* in wrestling class.

Every year since kindergarten, every new teacher on the first and second day of school at roll-call, pronounces my name wrong. They say, "Jens" with a j-sound. The correct pronunciation is yence, sounds like fence, sense, or dense, but with a y-sound in the beginning. Ughh.

It's not their fault, even so, I tire of making the correction, over and over, every damn year, for every teacher, every new friend and acquaintance. But I won't give up on you!

Swedes are stubborn.

There is one exception to this annoyance: meeting a girl, then I don't mind correcting the pronunciation, and explaining the name's origins. It's an icebreaker, like a puppy or a baby.

Big Mark Munster is no baby; 20 pounds heavier than I, all muscle, two inches taller, and barrel chested. Tree trunk legs, like his father now. Mark towers over me. What does this guy eat? We take our spots on the professional wrestling mat, inside the dedicated wrestling gym, and face off. The majority of the 30 classmates/spectators present are Mark supporters, his personal cheering section. "Go Mark, you got this!" "Easy pin Mark!" "Crush him Mark!" Mark Munster is very well liked. No one roots me on. Lack of popularity is hard to wrestle with.

Apparently this is not only Mark's day of reckoning, but others present as well. Guys who watch me throw my life and so-called friendships away, the rejected. Familiar faces from basketball, football, academics, the Quad. Everything the screaming, torch and pitch-fork wielding villagers held dear, I rejected, and they despise me for it. Jeering hyenas lick their chops. Jens gets his comeuppance, *finally*, today. The tribe has spoken. Vicariously, through Mark, they all intend to drill me to the mat, make it hurt, make me pay.

Crucify him.

Oh man, I don't wrestle, I've never wrestled. Mark's on the wrestling team. I'm clueless, but I do know this much, this is going to hurt.

Coach Ruiz has us start from a standing position, facing each other. Mark's head begins to rock side to side, to a beat in his head. I hear his thoughts, "go time baby, go time baby, lets go go baby!" Dang. Mark's going to kill me!

Coach Ruiz says, "GO!"

Munster wastes no time, he stops rocking, leans forward, drops his head slightly and marches the four steps. Goliath approaches.

While I'm strumming my six string and getting loaded, Mark's working out, training, developing himself, pushed hard by his father to excel. Naturally strong, now with training, Mark's a rippled beast.

Mark knows he'll win, he's already won.

Mark's forward momentum continues with force. He positions two palms squarely on my shoulders and pushes me back. There's no stopping it. Futile to try.

I stand there and face the music.

Mark's apparent goals: drive me straight back, flat on my back, crush me straight through the floor and bury me, inflict injury, deliver justice and get the win-pin. Like a spider rolls a fly in his web, Mark's long fingers wrap my shoulders. I'm knocked off-balance and begin to fall backward. His heavier weight is squarely in my face. There's no bail-out option available. I'm forced to accept the law of physics, a backward freefall. Damnit, Mark is going to flatten me like a pancake, pop me like a balloon, there's no escape!

At 60 degrees, there's no time to waste. I grab Mark, pull him in *tight*. My right hand goes behind his neck and I pull his neck and head toward me, with my left hand I clamp Mark's right wrist, a Viking vise-grip, locked.

Backward free fall continues, now 45 degrees, the two of us, now as one, one second till impact. Mark's commitment is 100% and like me, he's falling. But he's on top, chest down and I'm down chest up. I'm scheduled to hit the floor first.

Mark's off balance too.

We need to switch places. His palms are open on my shoulders, a shove not a hold. My grip is good, I've got Mark real close. Had I three seconds not one, I'd say, "let's dance," instead I twist my body hard left, like a batter swinging for the fence. Mark's upper body is close and secure, as I twist left, Mark twists also. Bamm, Mark lands square on his back! Me square on top, that fast.

Had it been a judo match, that would be the win, an ippon! But this is not judo, it's wrestling; I get two points for the takedown

This ain't over, we've only begun, and the bear is awake!

Coach Ruiz booms, "HEEEEYYYY!!" Distracted for a moment, I get back to work. In judo, an ippon can also be achieved on the mat, by securing your opponent on his back for 20 seconds. In judo, both shoulders are *not* required to touch the mat, just control your opponent on his back.

I'm not concerned with the "pin," only to maintain control. Do what I know, don't overthink, just go. I'm wrestling a lion, big, quick and strong! On his back, Mark convulses to get away. I shoot out my legs and body, lying on my right side, perpendicular to Mark. My right arm slides further around Mark's lovely neck, until my inside elbow centers under his neck, *pull* my right arm in as hard as possible, *pull* Mark's right cheek into my right chest and lock, I can smell Mark's hair (Prell Classic). Losing control of Mark's right wrist, I move my left hand grip to under Mark's right tricep, grab his right arm and *pull*! My right arm around and under his neck, my left arm under his right arm, both my arms pull up and secure Mark's head and right arm.

The rest of Mark flails about, a wild animal, a demon!

The screaming crowd runs onto the mat and tightens around Mark and I. Coach Ruiz rushes in, spreads his arms and shouts, "back off!"

I *do* have support!

Amidst the yelling mob, my head goes quiet; if Mark throws his legs toward me, I scoot my legs clockwise away. If Mark throws himself the other way, I scoot my legs counterclockwise away. If Mark snags my legs with his, I'm done. Mark explodes left . . . explodes right. It's all I can do to keep my legs away from him. The match won't be won this way. I don't care. I'm not letting go. Mark should arch his back up, high off the mat to create space, then twist around fast, his stomach to the mat, but I guess Mark doesn't know that.

My hold is sound but weakening fast. Mark the strong man, in front of a mighty cloud of witnesses, will break free then hurt me. Don't let him go! Mark's body, below his arms, is free to move. Too much free Mark! My grip is about to fail and Mark can sense it; he goes berserk.

I switch it up. The time gap between my holds will be Mark's golden opportunity. But what choice do I have?? I have to be *fast*.

Three moves as one: (1) Twist the entire length of my body a quarter turn, from right side, to face down. My chest down, over and across Mark's middle core. I'm still 90 degrees to Mark. (2)

Shoot left hand and arm under his neck. My left inside elbow under Mark's neck, *pull tight*. (3) Pull right arm out from under Mark's neck, and jam it between Mark's upper legs, slide my right arm through until my right inside elbow is under Mark's left hamstring, then cinch my right arm up, *pull tight*.

I secure Mark's left leg with my right arm, his neck and head with my left arm and his core with my upper torso weight. This hold uses my body weight centered on Mark, to help secure him. Like Pappa says, "whatever you do, give it a sporting chance." This hold gives *me* a sporting chance.

Here's a simple way to picture the holds: From a bird's-eye view; the first hold-down position resembles the letter L, the second hold-down position resembles the letter T.

Picture Mark on his back and my chest face down at a 90 degree angle to Mark. My upper chest centered over Mark's lower chest area. Mark's left arm is free to grab, push or pull, and his right leg is free to push himself off and around the mat. I shift my torso weight toward the problem area, to keep Junior on his back.

I won the match by the takedown points, not by pin, because while the two judo mat-holds are effective means to keep the opponent on his back or side and win a judo match, they don't effectively pin both shoulders to the mat long enough for a wrestling pin.

I don't want to mislead the reader to think; I crafted these two great moves on my own, on-the-fly. Nothing could be further from the truth. The two holds I used on Mark Munster, are both basic judo mat holds, ingrained in me from years of judo instruction.

The two holds are called: Kesa-Gatame and Yoko-Shiho-Gatame.

After doing judo for a while, these basic mat holds become instinctive. The only reason Mark landed on his back instead of me, and I could control someone much stronger for two minutes, (the longest two minutes of my life) is because Pappa dragged his boy to the dojo for five years.

Those two minutes were a big deal for me, in front of Coach Ruiz, in front of vindictive jocks, but it ended there, on the mat in PE class. I do not heed Coach Ruiz's advice to pursue wrestling. However, I don't think Mark, his buddies, or Coach Ruiz forgot *that* match.

Viking Song

Do you mind if I rewind? I forgot something important.

At Hopkins Junior High, the school counselor made a loud-speaker announcement to all classrooms, "I have a litter of Maltese Terrier puppies to give away. If anyone is interested, stop by my office today. Thank you."

My own dog! Sounds great. After school, I get the pick of the litter. I give the pup a ride home on my white Schwinn stingray. Mom says, "I'll have to talk to your father about it."

Jack and Inger say, "okay!"

I name him Joey. He's scruffy and loveable, a true companion. The counselor's claim that the pups are Maltese Terriers proves to be false advertising, loveable-mutts, more accurate.

Alright, back to high school. Mom noticed the help-wanted-sign in the window and mentioned it. Bim's Ice Cream & Donut Shop is a Mission San Jose staple. Located in the same strip mall as Charley's Market. Bim's sweet delights are very popular. Big Bim: tall, white, older, large and balding, wears a white paper hat (fast food style) and a white cloth apron. I apply and snag the job. A Swedish teenager, surrounded by *vast* amounts of ice cream, in a dozen flavors and an impressive variety of *fresh baked* donuts. Wahoooo! Also available for human consumption are microwaved hamburgers and hot-dogs. Oh boy, jeez.

Wow, a microwave.

I fulfilled my two day, server apprenticeship under a journeyman server. Like Bim, we both wear white folded paper hats and white cloth aprons. My boss is two years older than me. He surprises me with a friendly ice-breaker question, "what kind of music do you like?" I hesitate to answer. I don't want him to freakout, or his face to melt off. "Oh, everything on the radio pretty much . . . rock, Motown, Barry Manilow. How about you?" Blah, blah, blah. Blah blah blah, blah blah blah. Chatty-cathy, a nice guy, with integrity.

After the initial two days, I run the place on my own (big mistake Bim). The baker comes in at 4:00 am to fry doughnuts. I arrive at 7:00am, when they open for business. One afternoon, Bim stops by to check on things. I give him a glowing report, satisfied, Bim grabs a couple doughnuts and takes a bite, conducting the daily quality control. Unannounced, Mrs. Bim pulls up out front in her nice car. Startled, Bim springs to life, "oh, shoot, umph, uhh, ohh." With cat-like reflexes Bim jams the circular pastries into the large apron pocket. "Emm, huh, ha, 'hello dear, how are yuuu?" Well done Bim. Inside, I'm craaacking up like Frank Oleander.

In recent days, the DJs on my radio stations have started rumors. "They're coming to town. Day on the Green Six, two shows, two days. Saturday and Sunday at the Oakland Coliseum, July 23rd and 24th," [1977].

Weeks later, the donut shop is empty, there's nobody here but me. It's 9:00 in the morning. Outside it's sunny and hot already. On a wall shelf behind me, a cheap radio plays loudly. I'm tuned in, listening, finger on the pulse, head in the game.

Then it happens.

The DJ says, "Led Zeppelin, Day on the Green Six tickets go on sale today at 10:00 am at Ticketron Outlets everywhere."

Breathe Jens . . . think . . . *think* . . . got it, okay . . . *go!*

I open the cash till and withdraw $12 dollars, not a penny more. While removing the hat and apron I walk to the back room, calmly; roll my dark blue, Schwinn Varsity ten-speed through the donut shop toward the front glass door. In the store-front window, I flip the OPEN sign to CLOSED, confirm the shop keys are in my pocket, and step outside. I veil my excitement from passersby, invisible. I lock Bim's Ice Cream and Donut Shop.

A blink, a deep breath, I lock in the route, a second deep breath. Head on a swivel, I cover the three miles in record time; Paseo Padre Parkway west past Driscoll Road, over the two sets of tracks, past Hobo Jungle and Lake Elizabeth, past Stevenson Boulevard, the Library and Police Station. Run all red lights. Phoo phoo shoo phoo - mphm mphm mphm, left on Mowry Avenue, past Fremont Boulevard, past Blacow Road, to Tower Records.

The line is already formed outside the record store, around two sides of the building! I lock up the Schwinn and immediately take my place in line. Like headwaters of a large river, people funnel in from all directions and get behind me. At 10:00 am the door opens. 30 minutes later, inside a clean white envelope, the golden ticket is in hand. I secure the ticket and speed back to Bim's. The ride takes 12 minutes there and 15 minutes back. Bim's is back open for business before 11:00 am.

I'm beyond excited. I'm going to see Led Zeppelin! The greatest rock band of all time. Rick Derringer is going to play too. I love Rick's music. I play his hit, *Rock N Roll, Hoochie Koo* on my git-fiddle everyday. The concert opener, Judas Priest, is an unknown. They sound weird but hey, they're just the opening act. Oh man my first concert, and my favorite band of all time. Perfect! This is everything I'm about. I need to craft a perfect, get-high/stay-high strategy, for the big day.

Two shows are scheduled: Saturday, July 23rd and Sunday the 24th. My ticket's for Saturday. My first concert and first Day on the Green! Days on the Green were just that, all day concerts conducted on professional sports fields. The Oakland A's and the Oakland Raiders play here. I haven't been to the Oakland Coliseum in eight years, since Pappa took me to my first NFL game; the Oakland Raiders versus the Denver Broncos in 1969.

I wasn't sure if I'd get the chance to see them live. The moment is not wasted on me. The world's greatest band: Robert Plant the strident-bluesy vocalist, Jimmy Page the greatest guitarist (scary good), awe inspiring John Bonham, best drummer in the business, John Paul Jones the famous dark horse, the understated bassist and keyboard hero and band's musical baserock . . . *LIVE*! Careening through a sea of like-minded young people, kindred spirits who share my rockin' n' rollin' passion. Unified!

In 1977, Led Zeppelin was still red-hot, Robert Plant only 29 years old! Far from stagnant, the Presence album was released a year ago and In Through the Out Door, two years out.

Two years ago, in the summer of 75, our Swedish grandmother, Dagga Bergstrom came for a visit. At 76, granny Daga flew from Stockholm to San Francisco. On my 14th birthday Daga hands me a wrapped gift: Led Zeppelin's sixth album, <u>Physical Graffiti</u>. A double album! The thoughtful gift filled a large hole in my Zep collection.

Led Zeppelin's concert movie and accompanying live album soundtrack: <u>The Song Remains the Same</u>, was released nine months ago in October of 1976. I bought the double album and wore it out; I saw the movie with friends in a theater, a midnight showing; Gary Forest was there. The movie and soundtrack album are from two concerts at Madison Square Garden in 1973. The well-timed, movie & album double-punch, reignites the band's popularity and cranks upcoming Day on the Green Six, to a feverish pitch.

Stealing $12 from Bim and closing his Doughnut & Ice Cream shop for 75 minutes was wrong;

Nobody's Fault but Mine.

Concert seating is general, if you want to kick back in stadium seats and relax, you can. However, any fan worth their salt, presses ahead, toward the source, the stage.

I take BART to Day on the Green Six, alone, but not for long. Bart is standing room only, the pedestrian bridge over the railroad tracks, from the BART Station to the Coliseum is crammed fan tight. The line starts on the pedestrian bridge. I go early, 9 am. But many, many fans spent the night there; the zealots.

115,000 thousand fans attend the two days. Unbeknownst to me, Led Zeppelin previously canceled a 1975 show here, and at the show's start, Robert Plant apologizes for their extended absence. Instead of Day on the Green, Bill Graham might have called it: Smoke in the Stadium. The pot smoke is thick, smelt and seen everywhere.

Where there's smoke, there's fire.

In 1976, Jerry Brown, the Governor of California signed a new law, reducing the penalty for marijuana possession, from felony to misdemeanor, but then, news travels slowly. For myself and others not interested in the news, news is received word of mouth. Our level of legislative ignorance is like us, high. Our fear of the police is based on yesterday. I remember the black and white TV commercials repeated everyday: inside his prison cell, a close-up of the prisoner's ankles, clasped in chains, gazing wantonly through the black prison bars; on the screen a dire warning, "penalty for marijuana possession: *FIVE YEARS.*" That daily warning etched fear into our hearts.

Smoke a joint, risk arrest.

Day on the Greens and other legit rock shows provide a free-space, free from being arrested for smoking pot, underage drinking etc etc etc.

In 1977, dazed on the greens were crazy crowded, yet peaceful gatherings. People still maintained (though stepping on another's fingers was frowned upon). Deep within the claustrophobe crowds, a few drugged-out kooks dance out their drug trips. Within 100' feet of the stage, you're pressed hard by an oscillating undertow of human flesh. Rockers are there to have a good time. Anything snuck past the anemic security, accentuates the party.

My friends and I love the music we live, it defines us.

Popular bumper stickers read; "Sex, Drugs and Rock n Roll." I'd read those cliches for years, but I'm aware hedonistic living is nothing new; as old as time. I lack self-control and self-respect, not enough dignity. I lack wise judgment and commitment to anything decent or selfless. However, I do *not* lack an ear for good music or an appreciation for good humor; my quarterback arm still throws passes made to catch, and my jumpers and set-shots still ring true.

I love riding on two-wheels. I need two wheels (with a little horsepower) and a sweet girlfriend.

Sweet 16?!

I'm strangely unaware of Hannah, Marja and Tessa, their interests, friends; forget about their hopes and dreams and issues. We don't communicate.

Sisters, did you give up on me too?

I know Hannah is serious, a hard worker, studious, completes her assignments and soldiers on. I know Marja is smart and funny, popular and loved by people I don't know. Tessa, mmm, not sure. She joined a gymnastic club in town, maybe that came later. I'm starting my junior year, the year to get serious (I find out years too late). Tessa is starting the sixth grade, kiddy stuff.

The adolescent joys and trials of my three sisters were lost on me. These permanent familial omissions are hard to face and this writing is fast becoming an affliction I don't want.

Captive, chained by powerful vices; I drift further and further from Port Reality, closer to the edge. Swept by an invisible/invinsible force (stronger than Mark Munster and Ray Weisbrod put together) to nowhere, into darkness. Belly deep in quicksand, lacking the sense and strength to dig myself out. No compass for direction, no introspection, no governor to check my speed.

Three weeks after Zeppelin, I celebrated my 16th birthday. The day's festivities, I don't recall. Mom makes a birthday cake, she always makes a delicious cake for my birthday, for Pappa's and sister's too. Yellow cake with chocolate butter frosting, from scratch. "Another piece please, bigger?" Thanks Mom.

I got driver permits, they're in the wallet. One for four wheels, and one for two. Pappa lets me drive the 1972 white Ford Ranch Wagon here and there. Most Sundays I drive the family to the Hayward Quaker meetings. Even today, when I sense my driving is off: too fast, not tight enough, sloppy; to reset driving back to perfect, I reflect on those Sunday morning drives, family in the station wagon, driving to the Quaker meeting; during the driver permit stage, my driving was never better. I strove for perfection, considerate for my passenger's comfort and well-being. My family is in the car, I have to drive the best that I can.

Any serious girlfriend Jens? No. I want to hang with my buds and run the town. I'm not interested in serious, long-term relationships and I avoid them like the plague. I try it once, for a few days. She had some words for me, well deserved no doubt. She was ready for a five child, Jackson Street family style relationship. At 16, I want to smoke, drink, kiss pretty girls, play guitar, rock out, and *fiisssh*.

Junior year is almost here.

The 1977 Oakland Led Zeppelin concert; what a huge musical step for Bay Arean mankind. A daytime concert lacks that advantage of intense, indoor stage lighting seen in the Song Remains the Same concert movie. The light of day tempers the band's rock assault. The contrasting darkness and multi-colored lights of an inside show intensifies the performance and enhances the fans' experience. Daylight dilutes the band's impact and the audience's focus toward the stage. Acoustics are worse outside, but not terrible. Whether inside or outside, one fact remains the same, the closer you get to the stage, the better.

The Jimmy Page signature move: Jimmy smacks his guitar strings with a violin bow, then points the bow toward the audience left, in time with the echo; repeat, to the right. Like a magic wand, BUH-*BUH*! . . . BUH-*BUH*! This powerful gimmick galvanizes the stoned masses; awaken the dazed and focus the confused. Yeeaaaaaaahh!

Six weeks later, school starts up, "did you go?" "Yes." "So good!" Most everyone I knew went Saturday. I should have gone to both shows, but Bim may have noticed $24 missing from the till. Some conscience intact. Good, and good is good right?

The Quad is where the heart of the student body lives. Only when absolutely necessary, do I walk through the Quad, the epicenter of good student life. It is loud here. The students are collectively loud. There's more spirit and vitality here, more joy, than the creek. By junior year, I'm invisible on the Quad. Invisible to my clear-eyed contemporaries.

My tailor-made cloak of invisibility has attained full power.

The decision to walk away from sports, education and teachers, to embrace music and creek rats and its trappings, within a couple years, morphs into an exile. In exchange for good friends, golden opportunities and a future? A reputation.

I'm not certain *what* I'm missing, but whatever it is, I *am* missing it.

Barred and shackled deep in the dungeon I built; if there's a tunnel back to the light, a solution, I can't see it. I get a glimpse of what they're doing, the kids who remain true to themselves and their parent's expectations. These kids, young men and women, stay away from the creek and the bozos and the sin.

The excitement, the joy . . . the comradery! Everyone has a role, their own place within the school's identity and social structure. Smart, strong, supportive, loyal. Humorous all, covered in happiness, the byproduct of living right. Their wit and physical strength fortify the Quad's buttress of protection: moral walls thick and tall, surround and protect the quad from the creek, separate the good from the bad. Pretty, proud, some loud, some quiet but all showing up; unity and . . .

friendship. Learning, growing, ultra-competitive . . . great hair. Loving, sweet, bold. Scary tuff.
Young men and women, where awkward kids once stood.

Bonded. So great, so great.

Don't live all at once, pace themselves, do good for themselves, respect teachers and parents.
Eat sensibly. Survive disappointments, initial heartbreak. Return quickly to a healthy lane, make
sense. *Active* participants, civic *pride*.

Train.

Study.

Learn.

Grow.

I saw the right, but ran. Duck and run. Oh the misery and regret! Do it wrong deliberately. Is
this look in the mirror over!? I see Gary Plummer walking around. A senior like Hannah. The
broadest shoulders, head up laughing, eyes ahead, confident, capable.

Friends, once respectful, disdain subtly. Amongst classmen, is mutual respect. Not so for creek
rats. Why should there be? Cut class, smoke pot everyday?! Loiter, carouse, skirt responsibility?
You don't work, try anything worthwhile. Respect? Get outta here loser! This isn't spoken, but
heard loud and clear by body language and facial expressions. The rejection I initiated has become
mutual.

The good girls are almost neutral I hope. They're still sweet on me, but not willing to risk
alienation from peers, by investing their heart in a rat. What alienation? Oh, that alienation. Good
call ladies, right call; you're not to blame.

Pappa saw the writing on the wall; the road I was on. He wasn't stupid. I was, but he wasn't. His patience is long suffering. Before class registration, Pappa suggests I sign up for an ROP class, specifically ROP Printing. Pappa can sell a good idea. The Regional Occupation Program are classes designed to teach students a vocation, a trade. If Jens has steered away from college and a professional career, let him learn a trade. Smart. If Jens missed the good ship *Professional*, he needs to board that other boat, the last boat, still moored in the harbor, the banged up skiff, however unbecoming, and set sail!

I signed up. ROP Printing is in a portable classroom, removed from Mission's campus, on the fringe of Kennedy High School's campus, four miles from Mission. Three times a week I ride a yellow school bus from Mission to Kennedy and back again. Stoned windshield time, sweet. The portable classroom has everything, printing presses, ink, desks etc. etc. etc.

Mr. East, our teacher, is tall with long thick wavy red hair, and a big bushy strawberry-blonde beard, a viking! His cute assistant, Jenny, has straight platinum blonde hair, 36ish, short and cute. Red Beard's shield maiden. Hot class.

Red Beard is tough, he embarrasses me in front of the class once, "you act dumb, but you're not." I don't like that, regardless of the positive spin. I hate public humiliation . . . I won't tolerate it.

There are high school students and adult students enrolled. Half over 18, half under 18. The adults average 19-28 years of age. There are two levels: ROP Printing 1, and ROP Printing 2.

Robert Sparrow is one of the adult students. The Sparrows live close by, in Irvington. Robert's younger brother, Jeff, is two years younger than I. I met Jeff the following year; funny and endearing personality. To the envy of all, Jeff has Robert Plant hair, same color, texture and length, striking and impressive. Jeff's good nature shines through, he's a sharp wit, fast on his feet, able to

diffuse a tense scenario with humor and panache, and will only fight as a last resort to maintain

self-respect and family honor. Robert Sparrow, my classmate, is cool as well. 19 years old, Robert

is a good example, keeps quiet and works. A valuable life lesson for me. I like Robert Sparrow and

he likes me.

The adults are paid minimum wage and I'm jealous, but with the paycheck comes

responsibility: stricter attendance and punctuation requirements, and a full-time 40 hour week.

There's a melancholy associated with full time employment that's hard to define.

The work ethic is a good thing for a 16 year old kid to see, good people. I think Pappa had this

in mind, for me to see firsthand, men and women at work. Education is where you find it.

In subtle ways Pappa taught me ethic stuff too. In his studio Pappa asked me for a screwdriver,

I handed him the blade end. Pappa stopped and said, "Jens, whenever you hand someone a tool,

give them the handle end." Years later it dawned on me what Pappa meant: Don't screw people

over.

There's an adult student, a long-haired white guy, who gives off a creep-vibe. Studious, quiet

and menacing.

Jenny is cute, so I flirt with her whenever possible. Jenny is nice but too old for me. Her deep

alto voice makes her older too. I'm attracted to nice girls from ages 16 to 40 give or take. An older

woman's voice is a little deeper, but they both look great.

Gary Forest and I found ourselves in Berkeley one sunny afternoon with Mom. Now, in those

situations with a friend and a parent, once an agreed time & place to meet is established, we cut

loose. Gary and I are hip to a well known fact, unique to Berzerkeley; Berkeley is the place to find acid. I've been hearing about acid and want to give it a go go. I've heard some acid trip stories around.

We hit downtown and in no time find a source. The drug comes in the form of a little perforated piece of paper, business card thick paper. The squares are small, ½" x ½," torn along perforated lines from a sheet of identical squares, each square with an identical printed cartoon graphic. Gary and I get a square. Apprehensive of the acid's powerful effect, we split the hit. Gary's tried it once or twice before. With cartoons on our tongues we keep moving. The high was weak but positive. Not bad. We giggle a bit, that's it. Maybe we bought a bad cartoon?

Junior year 1977, wow, here we go again. I've been on the lookout for an old friend for a week, a kid from the neighborhood.

Outside, I'm whisked along a crowded thoroughfare between classroom buildings, shoulder to shoulder with fellow students, all in a rush to get to the next class. 40 yards ahead where the Quad opens up, I spot Kevin Finley.

Kevin stands out, tall, thin, and fast, poised for success; pertinent school books and materials held smartly under his right arm. Like a samurai sword, Kevin slices his way through the chaotic student swirl.

Samurai!

Fluid, graceful and long legged, (37" inseam) Kevin has all the right stuff; competence and energy combined with a sense of urgency and purpose. Ingrained confidence and the will to succeed burns bright. Comparable to Chadbourne's groomed MGMrs, Kevin is a sight to behold! In a flash, he's gone.

Kevin at the creek?? He'll have a *great time*.

Valerie Topper starts a serious relationship with a good looking drifter from Reno. A clean-cut, reserved, short white man. He looks like a college student, or a pharmacist, but he's from Reno. Valerie winds up having his baby and Reno winds up abandoning them both, leaving Valerie to raise the boy alone. The little boy follows Valerie everywhere and wears prescription glasses, through which he observes Jackson Street in sharp focus.

Alfred Butkowski (goes by Al Butko), has raven black hair and is a greasy, menacing drug dealer, with a confusing streak of easy going, good-natured generosity. Al lives on Denise Street with his parents and younger brother, between Mission Valley Elementary and Driscoll Road. Al, two years older than I (a year older than Hannah and Valerie), practically lives at the Toppers. Al and Valerie are unceremoniously crowned king and queen of the Topper house, at least while Mr. and Mrs. Topper are at work. Although Marlo puts up a valiant fight for control, the royals trump Marlo in the important decisions. Before selling pot full-time, Al Butko had a good job, as a clerk at a large grocery store in downtown Fremont. He gave up corralling shopping carts, to be his own boss and operate a thriving marijuana business.

Cordial to my friends and I, Al Butko cuts a dashing movie star figure (the bad guy) and is generous with his pot. Swarthy and slow to speak, with a thug attitude and a keen sense for business, Al does Jackson Street right. Due to a slight speech-impediment, Butko slurs a little. We address him as, "Bucko." Did I already mention Al's generosity?

Wherever I am, pot is there. A joint burns, a pipe bowl glows red, white smoke races through a glass bong, red eyes look at me, and Cheshire cat's grin at me; smoke is my best friend.

Tom Petty and Eddie Money's first albums boom from Marlo's room; his single window frame rattles when the volume is cranked. I hear it from Danny's house across the street; I hear it from my house! On most days, Danny, Guy and Curtis, Darin Vanderberg, Marlo and Al are smoking a bone in Marlo's room. Sometimes all at the same time. I can take a half dozen drags, not much more. By now, pot's strength seems unreal, approaching hallucinogenic levels, and the neighborhood's prodigious consumption approaches dangerous levels. If you don't believe being stoned 12 hours a day is possible, guess again. We are smoking Butko's pot 80% of the time. "Bucko, what's goin on?" "Heyyyy mann, what's happenin?"

A sad scheme is hatched, a Pied Piper tragedy; Darin V. has an epiphany and alters the educational course of Jackson Street's *male* population. Darin V. discovers an easier path to graduation day; *purposely* bombing out of Mission San Jose High School and sent packing to the district's continuation school, Williamson. Williamson Continuation School accepts *not only* Mission San Jose High students, but Irvington High students *as well* (remember this*)*.

The elders lead the way: Darin Vanderberg, Guy Wellbaum, Al Butko, Valerie Topper and Danny Wellbaum. Then my age group: Marlo Topper, Alex Zolanski and Curtis Wellbaum.

Jackson Street's mass exodus from Mission (sad), causes an unexpected *side-effect* (sadder still) to Jackson Street: like-minded contemporaries from Irvington High School invade *our* neighborhood.

Stoners from both schools cross-pollinate at Williamson and *combine forces* to create an artesian well of drugs on Jackson Street.

This association of cast-aways, organize and operate on Jackson Street.

Jackson Street becomes the head and the heart of Fremont's immense drug problem. Fremont is drug central for the East Bay, Jackson Street its epicenter; scary to say.

I have no idea how involved it really is. I cruise the fringe. I stay away from the hard stuff and big money. People die etc. etc. etc. Meth-amphetamines, random home robberies. Loose cash, jewelry, handguns.

Good news! I don't purposely flunk out of Mission San Jose, and run to easy street Williamson. Yay? Honestly I don't need help flunking out, I'm far along that path on my own.

I never see a needle used, they are used. By the skin of my teeth, I escape shooting up. But I'm way beyond socially acceptable, I don't limit pot to recreational use, aka, in front of a TV after work, or, at a party with friends. There is no wrong time or place to get stoned: before school, on break, lunchtime at the creek with 100 different people, at the Topper house, in any of Darin V's cars borrowed or owned, cut class, wind up at the Irvington Pool Hall. Pinball lends itself to being stoned. I go home stoned, maybe Visine, Tic Tacs, or nothing, hide in my room etc. etc. etc. I'm broken but not burned-out beyond recognition, I haven't blacked-out, forgotten where my bike is the next day. This stuff happens weekly on Jackson Street.

I'm still frisky. Girls, music, pot and driving, fishing, in no particular order. When driving the family car, I'm straight. Pappa lets me drive his pride and joy, the red 180cc Vespa Rally, once in a blue moon, if all the planets are aligned, caught up on chores, the sun is shining and hearts are merry (twice), I'm allowed to take Jack's Italian scooter for a ride.

This was one of those days and is on par with a birthday or Christmas morning.

"Be back in an hour Jens." In 1977, California had no helmet law. When Pappa rides to work, to Cal-State Hayward, he wears a white full-face helmet and a thick black leather jacket with a very large Vespa Patch sewed on the back. Pappa insists I wear his helmet.

Even for one hour, freedom is magic. I love life and driving Pappa's Vespa. It looks cool too. Not Kawasaki Mach 4, 500cc 2-stroke cool, or Honda CB750F insanely cool. Absolutely not Camaro Z-28 or Trans-Am cool. But cool. *Artist-cool*. Not, I'm faster than you cool, but, I'm slower than you and good with it, because I'm happier than you are and don't need to be faster or richer than you to be happy, but if necessary, I can and will throw a football farther than you cool and punch you out cool. I feel this way all the time.

My plan is to ride up Mill Creek Road, and enter the wild Ohlone Wilderness. The Wellbaum cousins, the Aubreys, live there: David, Peewee, Gary and their parents. Mrs. Aubrey and Mrs. Wellbaum are sisters.

Mr. Aubrey is a long-distance trucker and not home all the time. The Aubrey boys are unique; born 100 years too late; wild as Indians, excellent hunters with bow and arrow, and rifle.

Fighters.

The oldest son, David (Guy's age) is feared by all, except Guy and Darin Vanderberg. His face is noble and swarthy, his romantic exploits legendary.

Mill Creek Road, the 4.7 mile, uphill, single lane road my friends and I worked hard to summit a couple years ago, the same road where Kevin Finley, riding a demon-possessed bike crashed, now effortlessly up I careen, amongst its majestic oak trees and long green-grass slopes. With a twist of the throttle, I glide along the ancient Indian path and pass 19th century homes; the Chadbourne Estate and others. The drive up Mill Creek Road is splendid, the weather not hot or cold, perfect. Graceful corner-leans, the 180cc, 2-stroke engine sounds good and pushes strong. Caution on blind corners, timely gear changes maintain a healthy rpm, I'm in no hurry, it's not a race up, rather, I'm enjoying it.

I lean into a well engineered right turn and climb the long straight-away section; the same spot where Kevin Finley lost control of his bike and suffered a bloody high-speed wreck. I remember the beautiful long distance southern views here, toward Mission Peak. The hills were summertime brown then, but after recent rains, wow so green, Ireland, so beautiful. To take a good look at Mission Peak, I center in the lane and reduce my speed, to avoid becoming *part of the scenery*. To my right, immediately next to and following the road is Mill Creek, beyond the creek green grassy hills gradually ascend for a mile and eventually reach Mission Peak.

Suddenly, across the creek on the grass, 20 yards away, a young man and woman stand side by side, staring at me. I let off the throttle and coast. Sharp in appearance and older than me, 25? Hard to say, make-up? They look pale. Rockstar thin and dapperly dressed, the two of them are *very* out of place, like transported from a formal party in the 1700s, to the grassy spot; erect and statue still, both smile and stare directly at me.

From the first startling moment I see them, until the last when I have to turn away, were seven very long seconds (count seven alligator to sense duration). The couple's position, stance and smiling countenances, never flinch. Not a blink. Their eyes are trained on mine, and *follow* me. There's no parked car, no trail, only two well-dressed figures standing in knee-high green grass. Smiling, staring and still. Though it's late morning, sunny and warm, a chill runs up my spine to the top of my head, then tingles my neck, ears and face.

I look forward, (avoiding a second glance) away from the couple across the creek. I'm gripped with confusion and fear. I continue to the top of Mill Creek Road and take a short break. Disturbed by the pale pair, smiling in the grass, but not joyous, I cut the break short and split, back to Jackson Street.

Their presence is unsettling, I don't like it. A stain etched in my mindseye. Her long straight

hair and long dress, his shaped black facial hair, dressed in a dark blue black fitted jacket,

button-up solid color shirt, standing there, haunts me.

Don't look back Jens! Okay!

1978 is a very, very big year for new music, the kind I like. Tom Petty, Journey (with the Steve

Perry sound), Van Halen, Eddie Money, Styx, AC DC with Bon Scott and more. It's a red-hot,

melodic mushroom cloud of new rock n roll! I love it all while enjoying the classic bedrock bands

as well.

John Matthews, Chadbourne's sixth grade starting quarterback, now in high school, excels as a

lead and rhythm guitarist. John Matthews becomes Fremont's #1 guitar hero.

Friday and Saturday night house parties are the place to go, year round and John Matthews

Band gets top draw. John's fluent, virtuoso guitar is faithfully played with joy, and easily wins over

the party crowds. *Everyone* loves John's guitar solos. The ladies love his cascading, wavy, dirty

blonde mane and stoned grin. I like his effortless, smooth lead guitar. Great chops, a product of

hard work.

For a few bucks you can sidle up to a keg of beer and drink until the room spins. Invariably,

fragile neighbors eventually call the cops to bust up the fun. For this reason most drink sooner than

later, to get an adequate return on their investment.

Without wheels, party attendance requires friendly support. Many nights I'm happy to hang out

in front of the Wellbaums house and laugh at Tivas Cortez's jokes. Seven days and nights a week,

crowds come and go here. The telephone pole/street light between the Wellbaum and Cortez houses is the *hot spot*. The spot to score pot, or find a friend with pot. Half the town's ornery

youth pay homage to Jackson Street. I can be as popular as I want.

In my parents bathroom on the counter next to the sink, Pappa keeps a large plastic container of

the chewable antacid reliever, <u>Tums</u>. Mom tells me Pappa suffers from acid-reflux via a leaky

valve at the top of his esophagus tube. Mom says,"half the time, Pappa has trouble keeping his

dinner down." Pappa is 52 now, Mom 47. In their 40's, Mom and Pappa both get full sets of

dentures, top and bottom, additionally, Pappa's arthritis is so bad the leaky esophagus revelation is

taken in stride.

Two healthy pursuits happened in my junior year. Pappa convinced me to join another judo

dojo, at Chabot Junior College in Hayward. It's been three years since I bellowed a ten count in

Japanese: "Ichi, Ni, San, Shi, Go, Roku, Shichi, Hachi, Kyuu, Juu!" Ahh, the game of throwns or

be thrown. No license yet, so Pappa drives me. Here we go again.

The 49 year old black mustached Filipino sensei is in great shape. Stern and no-nonsense he

runs a tight ship. There are three other boys my age. Like before, every session ends with one on

one matches for all, against those similar in size and equal or better in skill.

I attended the Chabot dojo for nine months. We meet once a week, so it's not *too* much. This

memory is positive and constructive, in stark contrast to the rest of the week.

The other occurrence is an offshoot from the aforementioned judo class. Chabot judo student,

Daniel (greenbelt), invites me on an all-day bicycle road ride. My longest ride to date had been

Mill Creek Road a few years back, that's it. Armed with an old Schwinn Varsity, I don't know if I

can do it; in blind faith I accept. Bike loaded in the station wagon, Pappa drives me. At 6am first

light, we meet Daniel and his father at the old Mission San Jose.

We ride south on Mission Boulevard, past Ohlone College and under Interstate 680. Left on

Warm Springs Boulevard south. Warm Springs Boulevard changes to Milpitas Boulevard in

Milpitas. Right on North Abel Street, continue on South Abel Street, continue on Old Oakland

Road. *Tired yet?* I feel better than I thought. Mostly flat, continue south on Old Oakland Road,

right on Fernando Street past San Jose State College, left on 4th Street along the west perimeter of

the college. Right on San Carlos Street, continue onto Stevens Creek Boulevard under Highway

17. After a few hours of pedaling, I enter a semi-hypnotic state. Continue on Stevens Creek

Boulevard, left on Saratoga Avenue. Saratoga Avenue under Interstate 280 Freeway south to the

town of Saratoga.

Saratoga is a charming town. Main Street is lined with attractive shops and people. Daniel

informs me the hill before us is affectionately nicknamed, "The Ballbuster." Ballbuster is a

seven-mile climb up Highway 9. At the top, Skyline Boulevard 35 intersects Highway 9, and

forms the boundary between Santa Clara County and Santa Cruz County. Daniel mentions each

challenge, as it comes. He knows this is my first long road ride, and doesn't want my head to

explode.

We labor up the mountain enjoying fabulous local views of the Santa Cruz Mountain terrain. So

grand compared to the burned out, drug infested, suburb back home. At last we approach the

summit called Four Corners, the county line. The third county in one day, wow! *Snap,* my chain

breaks! Ahh! Daniel's experienced cool head prevails. "Lets coast back to Saratoga, we'll go to the

bike shop there and repair the chain." "Okay" (Thanks Daniel, for not leaving me to die).

I wonder what Daniel's plan would have been, had my chain not broken: onward to the Pacific

Ocean? For the cost of a masterlink: 25 cents, the damaged chain is repaired. We pedal home on the same route, in reverse. I make it home by dinner time. What a ride! I had no idea everyday people rode bicycles that far. 70 miles round trip, 2,800 feet of elevation gain! What an eye-opener, what a person is capable of, the possibilities.

Back to the never-ending lava flow of hot music (to overstate is to understate). The new bands and sounds slowly steer me somewhere other than Led Zeppelin, which needs to happen. The band Yes, is another guilty pleasure in need of weaning. Too much of a good thing ruins it? Ha ha yeah right!

Gary Forest and his mother argue frequently, a meltdown every other day. Something has to give. In 1978 halfway through junior year, a social worker moves Gary to the Buenas Vidas Youth Ranch in Livermore, California. The ranch is located on Arroyo Road, just past the Veteran's Hospital and the painted bridge, before the Del Valle Reservoir Dam. What beautiful countryside; open rolling countryside, vineyards, flowing creeks, Del Valle Lake, and pretty girls.

I visit Gary's new home for incorrigible youth in Livermore, whenever I can. A significant 17 mile trip one way by thumb. It's very different there.

The ranch is peaceful and serene on the outside, but within, it's a simmering cauldron of emotion. Good people live here, young people under 18. Emotionally vulnerable, but genuine people, all in. Most of them are manipulative, street-smart con jobs like Gary, wary to some degree. Untrusting but looking for something or someone to cling to.

The residents consist of young men and women from seventh to 12th grade. The Buenas Vidas Youth Ranch group home is run by a married couple, Directors Butch and Ruth Fitzpatrick. Ruth won Mother of the Year for the City of Livermore, the framed certificate mounted high on the living room wall. I remember the Fitzpatrick family very well.

Ruth is in her mid forties, Butch mid fifties. Ruth has two sons and a daughter from a previous marriage, the two younger, Ben and Leah live there; Leah, one year older than me, very nice and tough like her Mother, compassionate toward hurting youth; Ben is two years older and stuck on the edge of manhood. The eldest son is grown-up and moved away, his framed picture hangs proudly on the dining area wall, a cowboy riding a busting bronc in the Livermore Rodeo. Leah rides horses too, but not Ben that I see.

There's a black boy living there my age, Wes. Wes is from Oakland, cool, mellow and fearless, thin but scrappy. Not one to back down from a fight, but fortunately Wes prefers peaceful solutions. About five guys and five gals live there. The Fitzpatricks have a son together, a six year-old toe-head named Casey, everyone called him Case. I remember Saturday mornings, Butch and Case sprawled out on the floor, lying on huge pillows, watching cartoons together. Short, bearded and Irish, Butch is a straight shooter and a hard worker. If one resident makes a derogatory comment about another resident, kid or adult, who isn't there at the time, Butch says, "let's not talk about so and so, they're not here to defend themselves." I like that, we all do; wisdom and fairness.

The Buenas Vidas Youth Ranch brims with life, desperation, hurt, and love. Past and present childhood pains, harbored, too numerous to count. Homelife pain, abandonment pain; all real, is in concentrated form here, beyond understanding.

Three dynamic forces make the home special, make it work: the need to be loved, tough love, unconditional love.

Everyone is kept busy, given chores to do. Some act grown up, like adults. The women are mature, domesticated already, they help Ruth with the running of the house, the inside chores.

Good Samaritans donate their time. A big, gregarious, athletic, vocal white guy helps out at the boxing gym up the hill on the ranch property. A chip-seal road winds through the property linking long since abandoned, tuberculosis sanitarium buildings together, most of the windows are busted out.

A smaller sanitarium building was converted into a boxing gym, run by an older local boxer. Free boxing lessons are available, three times a week. Gary Forest is into it; I haven't tried.

There are at least four, part-time adult counselors who work at the house. These volunteers *want* to be here, to help troubled youth. They cover for the Fitzpatricks when they go to their weekend house in Clear Lake of Lake County. During Mr. and Mrs. Fitzpatrick's absence, we fool around a lot more.

Gary Forest and the other Buenas Vidas residents, attend Livermore's continuation high school. I'm not sure why, Gary's smart. I don't know whether continuation school is part of the deal living at the Ranch? Probably because the stay is temporary. Either way my life is on Jackson Street.

Bicycles and Bad Trips

The Rop Printing Class level 1, taught by Mr. East and his lovely assistant Jenny, proceeds well. The class is attended by students my age, and earn-while-you-learn working adult students. Pappa takes an interest in the class; Jack knows printing and graphic design experience is valuable toward art education and or a vocation for his son.

A very nice family with two young boys, begin attending our Quaker Meeting, Mr. and Mrs. Doug Cannon. Pappa and Doug hit it off. Mrs. Cannon is the director of child nutrition for the New Haven Unified School District, in next-door Union City. Pappa asks me, "How would you like to design the cover of the New Haven Unified School District's quarterly magazine?" Gulp, "yes."

Mr. East allows the project to count as a class project. Two birds with one stone. I work on the cover art in class. The necessary verbiage with a forgettable metallic silver background and a large blue feather. The magazine is published with my abstract cover.

Speaking of forgettable, remember the benign acid trip Gary Forest and I experienced on the streets of Berkeley? Acid in the form of tiny paper squares, each square with an identical cartoon, each square perforated and attached to a larger sheet of thick paper? The creepish, dirty blonde, long-haired adult man working in my printing class shows me a similar acid sheet in his possession. "You want to buy a hit?" "Hey, I know a lot of kids at my other school, who would buy that, you want me to sell it for you?" I'd already sold some pot for him, nothing big, one zip-lock sandwich baggy, full of $2 sinsemilla joints. Back at the creek, I sold-out in one day; selling is fun, handling the green.

Greasy long-hair cautiously agrees and hands me a sheet of acid, 40 hits. I sell them all before the next printing class two days later. For high school students, ROP classes are three days a week. The adults go five days a week, eight hours a day and are paid minimum wage. I do not take any hits myself. I receive a percentage of the profit. The career is short-lived, one sheet. I'm not comfortable with it or Mr. long-hair.

Recently, at the Topper drug scene house, a new white kid starts hanging around. A straight, clean cut kid from Mission. I met him in school recently, level headed calm, normal. He went crazy with the acid, got it from somewhere (not me). He takes acid 30 days in a row and his stomach turns *green*! He starts selling it around Jackson Street and elsewhere. I bought a hit from green-belly; who'd changed from a fresh-faced, articulate, enthusiastic young man . . . to a slow speaking, slow moving, burn-out, in two months! His rapid transformation from good to bad, handsome to ugly isn't wasted on me; the awful change is fast, too fast.

His transformation came in a pill.

I took half a hit while waiting for the yellow bus at Kennedy High School, to return to Mission. Back in the safe arms of the creek, I feel nothing. I'm half relieved, because I'm nervous about the "bad trips" I've heard about and think, "*another* benign acid experience?" So I take the other half. 30 minutes later I have to leave school, get away from any supervised, structured activity, now.

I'm getting very high.

I catch a ride to Jackson Street, bypassing my house straight to the Topper's Wildlife Refuge. Once inside, no amount of card playing, seed spitting, pot or beer calms me. I want *me* back but that's *not* happening. People's faces and hands become distorted. I *feel* weird and that's okay. But things *look* weird, not okay. Alex Zolanski, making an unusual appearance, senses my fear and agitation, I can tell by the look of concern on his face. Every tick of the clock intensifies the drug's effect. Music booms from Marlo's room, the party within the party. In the living room, Valerie, Butko, Alex Z, Tivas Cortez and a half dozen others, all at once, see me. "I gotta go."

I have no place to go!

I walk up Jackson Street toward my house, past the nursery school, the Zolanski's and Lansing's on the left, the Cortez's, Cardoso's and the Starr's on my right. In crisis, I float up our walkway and spot it, the blue Schwinn Varsity 10-speed next to the porch. I grip the turned down handlebars wrapped in the stock, cheap, blue vinyl tape. Something firm, non-distortable. Confused and paranoid, anxious to hide, I turn the bike around, point toward the street, mount and coast. Beginning my hopeless journey back to normal, I roll down Jackson Street slowly, careful not to accelerate, I roll past the Topper's house. I strain to maintain sanity. It's hot, the street is devoid of people, everyone's inside, there's hot air on my face, hesitant to breathe.

Self-awareness is excruciating; it's a bad trip and I know it, I'm *scared*.

There's no end in sight, the intense feeling ebbs and flows like waves crashing in my head. I roll down Jackson Street slow, modulate the brake. I have no intention of leaving this familiar feeling: balanced on two wheels. I seek quiet streets. A guilty fugitive running from myself. An impossible conversation.

I ride a tight-rope in hell? Slow left onto Olive Avenue, crazy slow right on Mckay Street, just fast enough to keep my feet on the pedals, past Ron Mudder's house on the left, down the short steep drop. I look up for two seconds, Mission Valley Elementary and the American Flag atop its pole is before me. The flag limp. The school I was too smart for? A critical decision; right on Lockwood Avenue, or left on Denise Avenue?

Ohh.

Ron Mudder's family moved in last year. Ron, my grade, is mouthy, rude and contentious. Well built, a bigger chest than mine which doesn't say much, being myself narrow chested, round shouldered and round backed, a notoriously bad posture, well suited to loiter and lurk. Proportionally similar, both Ron and I have short legs and a long torso, however, overall Ron is very short, almost dwarf. Rude but funny, crude but charming, smart and persuasive, we do not run together. We aren't friends yet.

I'd break a leg to feel normal. But then I couldn't ride, scratch that deal.

Left on Denise Street, leaving the elementary school I didn't attend, but friends did. Every turn is life or death. I choose roads graded down I can coast on, to avoid a blown head-gasket. I constantly brake to: stay connected to reality (cause and effect), the illusion of control (slow my speed), and to avoid a fall and death. A right on Erma Avenue past Jerry Cranks house and the house of Bailey: the Twins Creg and Dave, and big brother Kent.

Yesterday Dave the twin told me, after he and his twin brother Creg got their licenses recently (few months older than me), and that Creg, while driving his parent's large car down their street, Erma Avenue, misjudged the width of the large car and side-swiped two parked cars in a row belonging to nextdoor neighbors! Even today, when I'm driving on a narrow suburban street jammed with parked cars, I recall Creg's Folly.

Creg's shabby depth perception should've produced a 20 second belly laugh, but no.

Deep in hostile territory I turn right on Plumleigh Drive and another immediate right on Joyce Avenue, then left on Dorne Place. I don't like what's happening, I can't take it. I stare down, 2-3' in front of the bike, scanning and surveying right to left. I'm seeing *too much* minute detail; the asphalt's different shades and textures, obviously the stripes and markings; the yellow crosswalks, white bike lane striping on Paseo Padre Parkway (I just turned right onto), the wheel and hubcap designs of parked cars, the tires: tread depth and configuration, the brand, the size. Only when absolutely necessary do I look up and peer forward.

Too hot to handle!

The slight downgrades that required little to no effort, only balance, now are flat and slightly up. I maintain an even pace, the same speed as those electric battery toy cars, rich kids get on their birthday or Christmas, about three miles per hour. Faster than a tricycle, slower than a big-wheel. Being a rich kid probably isn't all it's cracked up to be, but I'm not 100% convinced.

To this point, life has been a natural progression of movement and self. Laws of nature say, "go go go, be active or be calm," or "run run run, feel tired, eat, drink, rest." Sit still, lay down, stand, sleep, walk or run. Do what you choose when fitting. Freedom of choice, risk versus reward, balance.

Not this time.

I capitulate to a small pill, wielding great power and influence; like a great ship's rudder, though comparatively small, has authority over the great ship; this tiny pill says, "Jens, you *will* ride this way, slowly. It doesn't make sense, too bad. Do it!"

Pill slave.

I turn south and begin the long slow pedal up Chadbourne Drive, past Doug Carlson's house. Voted: Most Musical, by the MSJ yearbook staff, Doug Carlson (my age) reads music, plays drums, teaches drums and leads a rock band, then and now. Doug then, a popular leader of a high octane, high school band with Joey Amarillo on bass, and John Velasco's cousin Ron on guitar, I enjoy watching them play at 50 garage parties.

Doug's older brother Richard Carlson, six years older, very long medium brown hair to the middle of his back, is technically the best guitar player I know, better than Buddy Duke, and better than John Matthews, the best in Fremont, a wunderkind. I took two guitar lessons from Richard in the Carlson home. He showed me the harmonic intro to; Ain't Talkin Bout Love from Van Halen's first album and while I'm working on that riff, Richard, his unplugged Fender Strat on his leg, withdraws to a different place, and a volcano of scales and biting lead guitar erupts. Richard ping pongs easily from guitar teacher, to rock concert performance.

Richard joins the rock band, Aldo Nova.

At a snail's pace, up Chadbourne Drive past Prince Hokulani's house - Prince, my tall, curly brown-black hair, very popular and chatty Hawaiian schoolmate - to cross street, Lockwood Avenue where Tim Cucuk lives on the northwest corner, the Bostok twins, Martin and Dennis live on the northeast corner. Brothers, Doug (my age) and Charlie Allen (Hannah's age) live on the southeast corner.

Chewy, Martin and Dennis are all two years younger than me, and I have no dealings with them. I know Dennis Bostok is a lively, talented drummer and plays with John Matthew's Band: the most popular band in the Mission San Jose area. Twin brother Martin plays electric and acoustic guitar wherever he is and wears a portable guitar amplifier on his belt, pretty cool. Mrs. Bostok grew up singing in a popular family vocal group in France, and a young Mr. Bostok and his brother were horseback-trick riders in a French circus. The twins' older sister is a world class ballerina in Europe.

It lowers my blood pressure and anxiety to mention affable friends while reliving this experience.

Bracing myself, I pedal up the Chadbourne Avenue incline, turn right on Olive Avenue and finally left on Jackson Street, to our house.

The one and a half mile trip takes two hours.

The yellow Ciao moped is out front; Mom is home.

The drug effect peaks. I force myself inside, walk through the living room, I can't feel the floor, jerk the reins right, shoulders bump the walls, down the dark hallway to my dark room. Though my room is the first door off the hall, it is *too* far. Three steps closer, but three steps from my bedroom door, I hear footsteps. From the other direction, Inger rounds the hallway corner. Two steps from my bedroom door, (correct, too far) our paths collide. During the fraught faceoff I blurt, "I have poison oak real bad!" Mom says, "okay, okay." I avoid eye contact, turn right, push open my bedroom door, walk in and close it. I don't suffer a mind-blowing interrogation from Inger. I lay on my bed and stare at the window. The window has an opaque, translucent, green cloth curtain I can see through, but only large shapes. Outside my window, the roof extends over and shades the porch walkway to the garage door, keeping the view cool and darkened; easy on my eyes. The bedroom window faces north toward Jackson Street and the Lansings and Schultzes across the street.

I shut my eyes but it doesn't matter, they still see; there's no escape, no place to hide, no *anecdote*. Fetal position, eyes closed, I shake for three hours.

A few long weeks later, I tried it again. Maybe *this* time will be good? Hit a euphoric sweet spot? The results are the same, bad. Minus the bike ride, it ends the same, my bed, fetal position, eyes closed, shaking for three hours, unable to turn it off. Nowhere to go, another bad trip.

Alcohol is predictable, strong pot less so. But LSD?

We're not doin' that.

Empty

After initial resistance, I convince Kevin to try the creek, to check it out. I sell it; fine girls, cars, music, fun and "freedom" etc. etc. etc. Once Kevin nails down day to day campus navigation, a routine, he explores the creek.

Kevin realizes this place is the shizel-stick. I make the necessary intros and we smoke a cigarette.

Not to stray, but my sweet job at Bim's Ice Cream Shop? Over. I was dismissed, fired, let go, smoked, 86'd etc. etc. etc. Feeding friends free food was seriously frowned upon and led to my demise. After violating a verbal warning, Bim's patience ran out, I got canned.

Next day, at the creek, Kevin Finley in tow, I buy a thai-stick joint. $5 bucks for one joint. I did well pitching quarters this morning. Several guys pitch quarters daily, against the cement planters on south campus next to the Little Theater. Kevin and I smoked the thai-stick joint, 15 minutes before the end of lunch, all of it. The actual thai-stick, is an 1/8" x 5" long wood dowel, wrapped with sensemilla along its length, held securely with thin organic twine. Then dipped in hash oil, I think? I'm not an authority on hash oil, thai-sticks, or any expensive exotics.

After we smoke it to ash, Kevin and I are as stoned as the earth permits. Salmon egg eyes, Cheshire cat grins, distorted vision, an audible buzz in our ears. Unsaved by the bell, an endless slew of retarded giggles ensue. Class after lunch? Out of the question. We hang out at the creek for another hour or so, killing time with fellow truants.

For the remainder of the day, Kevin and I cut class, bee-lining it to that oasis of licentiousness, the Toppers. The home, void of daytime adult supervision, gyrates with like-minded youthful occupants. The Topper latchkey oasis never fails to provide moral support and munchies for Jackson Street truants.

There's no turning back for Kevin; he rockets past the point of no return in record time. I don't know it, but that day marks the beginning of the end for him.

Three months *after* Kevin starts smoking pot and committing rampant truancy, a drastic personality change takes place. In a 24 hour period, Kevin's attitude completely changes for the worse; light to dark, smiling to solemn and cynical, tender hearted to stone. I try everything to make Kevin crack a smile, to laugh again, like every day for the last six years. Nothing, nothing, ever again.

What happened, where did Kevin go?!? This permanent Dr. Jekyll-Mr. Hyde transformation isn't against any specific person, It's against everyone! Unlimited contempt and scorn for all. He never passes an opportunity to expose someone for the fool they are, and there's no shortage of that on Jackson Street. Happy Kevin is gone for good? I hope not!

Woah, too fast, let's back up the bus.

The next three months were packed with shenanigans and antics; an endless cycle of pot smoking, class cutting (50% truancy rate) and fruitless endeavor.

Kevin and I find ourselves at his home alone. We snoop through the humble Finley liquor cabinet, ornamental really. Why is there liquor here, if Mr. Finley and alcohol don't mix? Be that as it may, a sealed quart of vodka stares us in the face. Do you think we should? I don't know. Kevin grabs it and heads to the backyard. Gulp, gulp, burn, *wooshahh*! Gulp, gulp, burn, *woww! Yowww!!* Gulp, burn, gulp. Chug, burn, chug, *whooahh, yeOww! Woooooooo!!*

"Kevin, I'm *feeellinn' itt!*" "*Mee tooo!*"

After initial burns, the quart goes down easily, shared equally and amiably between two 6' 3"
red-blooded young American men. A pint each, 16 ounces of straight vodka, each! Sober to drunk
inside of nine minutes.

The bottle was freaking empty. EMPTY! *Noo waaay! Yessh waaay!* Kevin sent the empty bottle
soaring into the creek behind the back fence. Clank, thud. *Wee gotta gohhh!* Let's get *outta herrre*!
Let's *go! Okaayy*!!

Crazy drunk, Kevin and I stagger across Jackson Street to the Schultz, Lansing, Zolanski,
Topper side of the street, we bob and weave west on the sidewalk.

The Schultzes moved in four years ago, next door to the Lansings, into the Farmer house,
directly across the street from our house and the Tyrell house. The Schultz family are a fun bunch,
horse people. Ray Schultz is a deer hunter, super-cop; undercover narcotic division. Ray looks like
a Hell's Angel. 6' 4", white, large, broad shouldered, long dirty blonde hair, well past the
shoulders, a thick walrus mustache and full brown beard hides the neck, scruffy and scary. Ray
infiltrates Fremont's underbelly, and becomes one of them, living in their circle. He gets high with
them too. Some weekends at Starr parties, John steals away by himself, into the middle of Kenny
Starr's huge garden and crouches by himself, trying to clear his head and reconcile his career
choice. I relate Ray!

We plow crooked furrows past the Wellbaums and Cortezes; we're too energized! No one's
around; zig-zag down Jackson Street to Olive Avenue, drunker than drunk, Mr. Topper drunk, but
without his iron-legs and experience to cope. Weaving left and right, we need the whole sidewalk
to stay upright.

Kevin and I stay the course: headlong to nowhere; in drunken synchronicity, right on Olive Avenue, "hang on Kevin, look both ways," left, cross Olive Avenue on Chadbourne Drive. Impossible to continue, the plane is out of fuel, one engine dead already, going to crash land! A cross street, Lockwood Avenue. A small group of animated, semi-familiar kids Kevin's age, are surprised to see us.

Tim Cucuk on a skateboard, I don't know, his little sister Denica, their next door neighbor Pete Winger (two years younger) and his older sister Linda Winger, a brunette a year younger and pretty, but a bit dark, melancholy.

Across the street from Cucuk's on the southwest corner of Lockwood Avenue, there's a 12' wide strip of luxurious cool green grass, between the side yard fence and sidewalk. A six foot tall dark green hedge runs the entire length against the fence. Kevin and I crashland on this unblemished oasis (no weeds), catch our breath and establish nothing.

Kevin retches, collapses prone and passes out.

Blackout!

Thankfully, an ambulance is called. Minutes later paramedics raise Kevin onto a gurney and slide him in the ambulance.

Damnit. Damnit. *DAMNIT!*

I lay low, and desperately fish for a Kevin update.

Kevin's okay!

Medical personnel pumped his stomach; Kevin got home later. I sober up and hope all is forgiven.

Punishments are doled out by the strong to the weak, to what degree I don't recall.

Life resumes, the party restarts, the spin-cycle fires back up. Stoned, cut class etc. etc. etc.

For reasons unknown, hope stubbornly clings. Walking home from school with Kevin one afternoon I say, "Kevin, there's nothing I can't do. I can do anything." Kevin must have thought, what an idiot. Occasionally, I truly do feel that way and for two seconds, believe it. I can always make Kevin laugh. He has a great sense of humor. Only a little cynical, but so funny, so much fun we had. From 1972 till 1978 it was this way. Then one day, it wasn't.

I'm confused, I want an answer. Why is Kevin so uptight and hard now, why? Jackson Street wants to know what happened, not just me. We will find out, we have to.

Kevin gets bit by a werewolf.

He walks into his house, before dinner time, like nothing is wrong. He's immediately confronted by Mr. and Mrs. Finley, each holding a bundle of typical letters; tardy and cut notices shipped in a box from Mission San Jose High School addressed to Kevin's parents delivered by the mailman.

Kevin is cunning, and turns flippant rejoiners into an art form. Wickedly witty like his father, Kevin can make you feel stupid anytime, but keeps it in check. He's comfortable with his parents, the family is close knit and have fun together, they enjoy verbal jousting. The Finley's possess a strong vocabulary, and are capable debaters. Rather than bite his tongue in humility and face the music quietly, Kevin *talks back*. I don't do that well; I'm no good at it. In Kevin's defense, sass is celebrated at home; it's graded. As long as the target is not family, (certainly not Father or Mother), the better the tease, the bigger the laugh. Today Kevin's timing is way, waay off. He goes too far, crosses that line, and forces Mr. Finley, the tiger, into a corner. Kevin picks the worst time to talk snash to his dad.

He makes the worst comment possible, with awful effect.

"Kevin, what are *these*??" holding up two handfuls of truancy notices. 'These say you cut class, a lot. [Possibly a rude response from Kevin?] "What do you have to say for yourself??" [unsubstantiated tension building, possibly another curt response?] The story goes, Mr. Finley said something to the effect, You're grounded you mouthy son of a bitch, go to your room! The "mouthy" reference is why I think Kevin *may* have been rude moments ago. But I don't know.

Kevin . . . stop . . . think . . . *don't say it.*

Kevin's five word rebuke: "don't call Mom a bitch."

The moral unwritten principles that guide his heart and direct his path, the values ingrained into Keith Finley's psyche, instilled by a tough, South Dakota no nonsense, tough upbringing; each hallowed military code, learned the hard way, in War, the unconditional love and redemptive goodness given to him, by God's grace in the form of his wife, Mrs. Finley, her love and sacrifice for him and his family; his entire world, in five words, was trampled on by his only son.

Kevin, who stayed thus far, on the right side of the paternal line, by speaking five words, declares rebellion against his father. A challenge of the highest order. The young male lion challenges the Pride's undisputed king. The young, ambitious Indian Brave, attempts to be Chief, Absalom rebels against his father King David for Israel's throne.

A challenge, Kevin is ill-prepared and unqualified to win.

Kevin pays dearly; Mr. Finley's discipline is immediate, up and down the hallway, up and down his room. The specifics are unknown, and I apologize for errors in this account, but when Mr. Finley is done, Kevin lay shaken, his heart permanently hard.

Why did Kevin cross the line? Was it an error in judgment, or inevitable? I don't pretend to understand. What I do know is Kevin's demeanor changed drastically that day. Straight and narrow, joyous before, no more. Happy Kevin died.

In the heat of the moment, Kevin mistakes parental concern for a word game; Kevin takes his father's angry words, you're grounded you mouthy son of a bitch, go to your room! - Mr. and Mrs. Finley are beside themselves because of Kevin's documented truancy; Kevin's callous responses fan the flames - and rearranges them to create a slanderous and mean accusation. Rather than admit his mistakes and repent, Kevin flips his dad's words, *accusing his dad* of calling his mother a bad name (his wife) as if Kevin is defending his mother from her husband, (don't call mom a bitch) obviously *not* Mr. Finley's meaning at all.

Kevin pushed his dad too far; Mr. Finley's response is a lightning bolt. Kevin doesn't know what hit him.

Was this a rite of passage for Kevin? My good natured, agreeable young friend is gone forever. Adios to the restraint every sharp tongue needs, the intangibles that maintain family order, adios to social order, law and order.

Lithe, tall, athletic. Friendly, funny, brilliant and compliant. A pit-bull who's tasted blood; hard, ornery, ready for a fight, to instigate a fight. Before, exhibiting restraint and respect, now, hell no. Kevin spews razor sharp criticisms, with justice and cruelty for all, without bias. Bold and mean, but logical, not without his form of justice. My friend Kevin is too damn mean now; his new outlook chills our friendship. We aren't close anymore. Graceful Kevin died. Merciless Kevin took his place. Our relationship is there, the history, we just don't like each other much anymore. Kevin makes new friends with similar interests. We drift apart, but remain cordial. We party together on and off for the next four years.

Trauma *can* change people permanently, and I see the world differently.

I sold debauchery to a best friend and helped shatter the fragile balance of a family I love. I was either the catalyst or the cause. For that I'm truly sorry.

Greatness in the Garage

Pappa loves art, *being* an artist. He's committed, does the work, fueled by passion. Pappa loves creating in his studio, the garage. From the street, a typical two-car garage with a typical spring-loaded heavy swing-up plywood door. But inside, no parked car, or typical garage mess.

Pappa dedicated the years after WWII, while working as a butcher, to art education and developing his own artistic voice, a long-term, beautiful, inspiring effort.

The studio's west wall is 20 feet of pegboard for hand tools; a vast assortment of woodworking instruments hang here. A long workbench and a Danish furniture making table line the entire wall.

A Danish furniture making table has two large vises built-in to the top, the vises are at right angles to each other. The vise's gripping surfaces are wood, lined with textured rubber, so wood pieces aren't marred. Vise handles and tightening augers are hardwood too.

A large wood lathe, a black dial wall phone, and a stand-up drill-press fill the south wall, opposite the big door.

Finished and unfinished paintings, stacked on edge like books, lean against the east wall, a table-saw with no safety guard stands next to the stack. There are no law books in the antique, glass-door lawyer bookshelf; rather, it is full of art supplies and stands next to the big door. Near the studio entrance door there's a large square table covered with a dusty assortment of miscellaneous supplies and tools; stored below the table: 15-1 gallon cans of Ditzler automobile lacquer, a gallon for each color of the rainbow.

A dusky wood smell permeates the space. Above the rafters are loaded down with planks of unique hardwoods and more art material, and a heavy green canvas WWII tent collects dust.

Two large, solid and heavy, rectangular tables with an aisle in between, fill out the studio's center. The wood crate sides from Italy for the Vespa Scooter and Moped, form roman roads throughout Jack's empire, providing hours of standing comfort. An antique, black-iron kerosene heater keeps Pappa warm and productive in winter; the warmth softens his thick arthritic fingers just enough to push, ply, pour, drill, turn, carve, saw, pound, glue and cut.

You enter Pappa's shop from outside, under a covered porch. From the porch you notice the large Harley Davidson Motorcycle decal on the garage window, a gift from Jack's friend, Big Dave Wakefield in Colma. - Big Dave's driveway is where I learned to balance on two wheels, with Little Dave's encouragement - halfway to the shop door, you pass by my bedroom window.

Entering the Jack Zone, you step down three concrete steps to the shop floor. Before descending the steps, you reach to the right and turn on two light switches, "click, click." The shop flickers to life as many chain hung, fluorescent light fixtures fire up simultaneously.

Inside, Pappa's life is seen and smelt. The pungent aroma of wood, toxic lacquers and stains fill the air. The outside observer stops on the steps, blinking eyes wander, taking in prolific amounts of art, eventually resting on a specific piece that tickles their curiosity, sparks imagination, or bewilders.

In the studio is just a normal day for me, but for my friends? A trek through an enchanted psychedelic forest. Occasionally, I catch them humbled or vulnerable, their mouths hung open.

Pappa's art is the bedrock of our family pride.

Christmas 1977 is the best. Typically, the bigger or heavier the gift, the better the gift and there is a *big one* under the tree with my name on it. And if that wasn't enough anticipatory joy, it's from Santa. The package smells of chocolate and reindeer.

Santa Claus rules Jackson Street with utmost magnanimity and benevolence.

The Christmas gift to end all Christmas gifts; an AFX slot car track. Not just any track, no figure-8 stuff. This racetrack is *colossal in scope*! Like Mr. Zolanski's Winnebago Commander, this track is the *biggest* they make.

Up and over (Mount) Olive Avenue, down Washington Boulevard, over two sets of tracks into Irvington, past the head shop, in the same strip mall as the pool hall and the nudie bar, by the car wash with the famous trained parrots perched out front, is the establishment that epitomizes everything great in life; The Irvington Slot Car Track. The track is full-size, not small HO scale stuff. The track fills the large room. The cars are big, 10" long. Father and son bring custom slot-cars and controllers to the pay-to-play track and race. What a blast to watch! I want to race a slot car on the Irvington Track, more than anything. More than basketball, football, more than fishing, maybe more than girls not quite sure there. But it was not meant to be. Like Tiny Tim limping through the snow, staring through the frosted bakery windows; for five years I wish for one hour at the Irvington big boy track.

During Santa's finest hour, I unwrap.

Beneath the torn holiday paper is a man-size box, with three letters: AFX.

All three genie in a bottle wishes, have been granted.

Dreams do come true!

AFX and Tyco make the small slot cars and tracks, H.O. Scale. AFX is the best. The track is *more* than I hoped for. The Indy 500 AFX track is long and intricate, *three-levels*. Pappa and Mom, thank you, thank you, thank you, for letting Santa know what's up.

Santa Claus, from the bottom of *my heart*, thank you; you're the best alright.

Pappa, ahead of time, had taken a 4' by 8' sheet of plywood *and* a 4' by 4' sheet of plywood, wave-nailed them together, and attached a 2" x 2" frame piece all the way around the bottom sides and one across the middle to stiffen the large platform; rounded the corners, and varnished it with clearcoat. The finished size is 4' x 12'. Massive!

The custom track base is already set on Pappa's black work table, nearest the west wall, waiting for the track to be built. Pappa and I put the track together, together. On the side closest to the west wall, the driver's area, a straightaway runs the full 12'! At the end of the 12' straightaway, to our right, a high banked 180 degree turn rises two feet off the base! The radically banked turn is vertical in the middle. You hit the bank turn at *full speed.*

Jens' Raceway is open for business. The good times surrounding that slot car track signify a high point of my youth. I've never seen a better home track.

Jackson Street friends are raceway regulars, but once, four familiar older boys drift in. They show us advanced slot car tricks, for example: two drops of liquid bleach on the track, set the car's rear tires on the bleach and punch it, producing a glorious white-smoke burn-out in H.O. scale.

It didn't cross my mind then, but the 4' x 12' track and the associated hootin' and hollerin' teen-age boys, took a big bite out of Pop's valuable creative time and work space. Now I see the sacrifice it was. Thank you Pappa.

1978 heats up and Pappa starts new types of art projects: Carving intricate canes and decorative headstones from wood. A dark turn. To decorate these projects, Jack learns a new technique called chip-carving.

Pappa teaches Jackson Street how to chip-carve.

Armed with a small assortment of tiny hand chisels and the chip-carving technique, attractive, three-dimensional kaleidoscopic decorations are cut into the wood's surface.

Pappa does a very cool thing that summer. He opens the big shop door, and welcomes the neighborhood in; Jackson Street's young and old, male and female, stoned and straight, to come inside and learn how to chip-carve. He embraces the *entire* neighborhood.

Pappa's nightly chip-carving classes go for three weeks! Suddenly, it's cool to hang out with Pappa. Pappa looks like an artist too, dressed in a pin-striped Ben Davis shirt and black felt euro beret.

For each student's initial lesson, Pappa makes available a set of 12 small, wood-handled chisels, in a clear plastic sheath with a fold-over, snap-button flap . The cost to each student for the chisel set? One dollar. "Pay when you can."

Darin Vanderberg, Alex Zolanski, Kenny Zolanski, Mr. Zolanski, Guy Wellbaum, Danny Wellbaum, Curtis Wellbaum, Kevin Finley, Marlo Topper and me. Jimmy Lansing, Dean Lansing, Jeff Cardoso, Bucky Cortez, Tivas Cortez and Gary Forest. Paula and Charlene Lansing and the four Schultz kids; Sheri, Kari, David, and John Michael. Kenny and Olney Starr, Norma and Donnie Croh. Dorothy, Sherry, Glenda and Mr. Tyrell, all wield their own set of sharp chisels. Pappa supplies small chunks of quality hardwood for carving. What a sight!

For a few short weeks it was super-cool to hang out with my Pappa, the artist and teacher. Many work on their chip carving projects at home and excel. Not me. After lesson one, I'm done. As quick as it started, the red-hot interest wanes, dies. But for a moment, Jackson Street shone bright, a unified creative light. An exchange of mutual love and admiration I didn't know existed before.

Pumpkins and Hearts in Livermore

The Comprehensive Employment and Training Act, the CETA Program, offers minimum-wage summer jobs for low-income students.

Danny and Guy Wellbaum worked CETA summer jobs in Fremont a couple summers already. It's impressive how Guy and Danny hand their paychecks directly to their single mother, Christine, to help with family finances. Every autumn, Mrs. Wellbaum gives each of the three boys and daughter Julie, a nice chunk of money for new school clothes. The Wellbaum kids dress sharper than me and I'm jealous. Work for it Jens!

Gary Forest gives me a heads up; this summer the Youth Ranch in Livermore will host a CETA work-program. Gary signs up for it along with all the resident youth. Gary encourages me to go. The work program isn't only for ranch residents, but for all qualifying, low-income high schoolers willing to work.

One logistic problem: I'd have to *live* at the ranch Monday through Friday. I need both parental permission and the Fitzpatrick's approval to work and live at the ranch for incorrigible youth. A wide river to ford. Lo and behold, permission is granted by all liable parties!

I fill out the CETA application, send it in, and am accepted. The plan: save wages and buy a motorcycle before the end of summer, by my 17th birthday, and before senior year starts.

"Go around the world on a chopper, Jens."

Gary Forest and Danny Wellbaum have similar plans. Guy wants a car. Danny and Guy work a CETA job in Fremont. Jack and Inger aren't blind to their son's wild living and likely figure, hard work is part of the cure.

My commute plan from Livermore to Fremont and back for eight weeks are thus: on Friday after work, I catch a three mile ride to the corner of Wetmore Road and Vallecitos Road Route 84 from whoever's available at the ranch, or thumb; typically Ruth, Butch or Leah Fitzpatrick, or an adult counselor drives me. I cautiously cross Vallecitos Road Route 84 (a very busy two-lane highway), to its west direction and stick my thumb out; get picked up within five minutes and get a non-stop ride to the Interstate 680, Washington Boulevard off-ramp. The plan works well, sometimes good samaritans drive me to my front door. When they drop me off on Washington Boulevard, I thank the driver for the ride, drop into the creek, hop the back fence, done. Joey greets me in the backyard. Ahh, home sweet home.

From Fremont to Livermore, I'll do the same thing in reverse; after Sunday Supper (light till 8:30 pm) jump the back fence, cross the creek, walk up the trail to Washington Boulevard and cross, walk left to the Interstate 680, northbound on-ramp entrance, and stick my thumb out. In minutes, a car pulls over, the passenger window goes down, "where you going?" "Livermore." "Okay, hop in" etc. etc. etc. I never wait long, or experience a bad trip.

One Friday, rather than go home solo to Fremont, Gary and I hitchhike to Niles together, to visit his mother and brother, and spend the night. Two *very fast* motorcycles pull over, crotch rockets, with young drivers, three years older than us. We get on and fly through Niles Canyon. I don't remember Gary's ride, but I got on a Kawasaki 2-stroke 750 Mach 4.

Faster and more fearsome, there is not. Nobody wears a helmet.

It's a thrill ride and I'm loving it! My driver commands his Kawasaki well and I do my best to lean correctly.

When the road straightens out, two miles from Mission Boulevard, my Kawi Mach-4 *gets on it*!
We launch and I hold on for dear life. Looking ahead, my eyes flutter so violently, I see only a
shapeless colored mirage. High Voltage!

Work at the ranch is outside and Livermore summers are hot. I work shirtless and get dark. In
between the fence line along Arroyo Road and the main house, the youthful crew tills the hard soil
with hand picks, to sow a large pumpkin patch.

10 workers are ranch residents, another 20 come from the surrounding Livermore area. There
are six black workers, some related, all friends, they hang together. Ruth Fitzpatrick's son Ben
works too. Ben is smart, he has a critical tongue like Kevin Finley, and an outlaw's heart. Gary
looks up to Ben a lot, and sings his praises to foster an alliance. After work, Ben likes to read the
local newspaper, he reads the latest crimes out loud, critiquing the crime and criminal, expounding
on their lack of intelligence, and why they're caught. I keep my distance, preferring the company of
kids my age, especially the pretty girls. There are two that catch my eye, Delilah and Maryanne.

Delilah is pretty and nice and later that summer, she works at the Donut Wheel in downtown
Livermore. Gary and I visited her there once. There at the Doughnut Wheel, Delilah serves me my
first cup of coffee. I drink two cups but have to stir in a lot of sugar to get the nasty beverage
down.

Throughout the day while working in the patch, I sing rock n' roll songs in Delilah's direction.
I bellow from the far side of the field as loud as I can and still stay on key, swinging around my air
guitar, "feel like making love! Ba! Bada, Ba! Bada, Ba!, feel like making love! Ba! Bada, Ba!
Bada, Ba! Feel like making love to you!" A Bad Company classic. Oddly, I never feel

embarrassed, nor does Delilah. From across the tilled dirt patch, not as loud, she sings the same song back to me! One line or so. I never ask Delilah why she lives there.

The CETA workers are familiar with each other from school. I'm the lone wolf, the traveler. One worker, a nice guy our age, commutes to work on a miniature motorcycle, a teeny-weeny street legal Honda CB100; his short, very long-haired brother, Kenny, rides on back. This hilarious sight; the toy-Honda overloaded with the brothers, buzzing in at 6:50 in the morning, kicks off the daily circus atmosphere at work. Gary, Ben and I, ride the CB100 every chance we get, zipping along the ranch's narrow road (once the Tuberculosis Sanitarium service road), a racetrack to us. The bike, though small and slow, is plenty fun and perfectly suited for the ranch, not too fast. Gary and I have a blast riding it.

Another guy: tall and lanky, white, greasy long black hair, black framed glasses, sweaty and nondescript, married and a father, is older, 19 or 20, and commutes to the job in a Chevy Vega with his wife. Once he lets me drive the Vega at the ranch. I've heard around the Chevy Vega is an unreliable dog, prone to breakdown. I gun it and the engine blows up. Vega dies right there in front of the deserted 4-story sanitarium building with most of the windows broken out! I feel awful, but only 3% as sorry as I should. The incident proves the vicious Vega rumors true.

Del Valle Creek runs along Arroyo Road in front of the ranch. There is an excellent swimming hole 300' east of the ranch gate. I hang out there once; many older kids congregate there, feet in the creek and party up.

The best part of work is lunchtime, the job includes free lunch! A small carton of milk, a sandwich, some chips etc etc etc. A warm entree wrapped in foil half the time, nice. If we can get a hold of two lunches, twice as nice. They come in open cardboard boxes, hence a box lunch. We get 30 minutes for lunch.

We work hard or hardly work, cultivating the largest pumpkin patch I ever saw. I wonder now, did families go there and pick a Halloween pumpkin to carve a jack o lantern, and roast the seeds? I don't know. That question *never entered my mind.* I never heard of a harvest pumpkin patch growing up. I had bigger fish to fry.

If anyone picked a pumpkin from that patch in 1978 or after, please let me know. Thank you in advance.

I stayed a couple weekends at the ranch. Ranch antics ramp up on the weekend, we look for trouble. On the weekends, Butch, Ruth, Leah and Case high-tail it to their Clear Lake house, for fun & relaxation etc. etc. etc. During Fitzpatrick's absence, those at the ranch attempted the same. The lone adult ranch counselor, supervising ten young adults, is outgunned and outmanned. The counselor sleeps in the master bedroom off the living room. The segregated boy's and girl's bedrooms share a common wall. The minors use a cryptic form of communication (hormones) and rendezvous are inevitable. Delilah and I make out once, nothing more.

The Fitzpatricks and adult counselors are good to me. Dispensing patience and grit, wisdom and paternal tough love to kids who need it, me included. I remember them with fondness.

One afternoon a popular woman counselor, the wise owl, very nice, a wife and mother, gave us kids a heart to heart. She is soft-spoken and maternal, respected and liked by the kids. Wrapping up a spirited group conversation about life, she says to us, "We all have problems. You, me, everybody." Offended, I arrogantly replied, "I don't." What an idiotic thing to say. Without guile she gently says, "I think you might." I say, "what do you mean?" "When you look at people, you look at them with distrust." "What? ah c'mon, no" . . . hmmm.

Me and Mom at Hannah's High School Graduation, 1978

Wheel of Life

Finished with work and love in Livermore, I amassed a small fortune: $400 bucks!

Now I need to find the purrfect motorcycle.

I accompanied Danny Wellbaum to check out a 1969 Honda CB350 for sale, in beautiful shape. Danny negotiates, pays $300 bucks and drives away. Danny's first wheels! It's a fine motorcycle; custom brown painted gas tank, matching brown side covers and a strong, dependable Honda drivetrain, clean. A great fit for Danny; Danny beams, he is proud of it, me too.

Next door to the Schultz's, east, live a white, born-again Christian family, the Raeders. Most residents of Jackson Street are Catholic and if I had to choose a Christian affiliation, it would be Catholic. Crossing the hand on the chest, that's cool. Confession seems good too, but scary and I don't try that.

The Raeder family is different and we poke fun at them a little. The youngest daughter Alicia, is a very sweet girl, a year younger than Tessa. She's super nice. Alicia's father, Mr. Raeder is a mountain of a man, 300 plus pounds. He rides a beautiful new Honda Goldwing. But tucked out of sight under the dark recess of their carport, hidden under a disheveled blue plastic tarp, is a dusty blue, 1975 Honda CB360. I've never seen it driven.

I take a chance. "Mr. Raeder, would you sell your blue Honda motorcycle?" *Long pause . . .* 'yes.' *Medium pause . . .* "For how much?" *Long pause . . .* 'for a Moyer? $300.' *No pause,* "I'll take it. Thank you very much Mr. Raeder." Unbeknownst to me, Mr. Raeder respects Pappa, though I never saw a conversation between them.

Jack and Inger let me buy it! They know I'm in the market for a bike. It's a good deal, only 4,000 miles on it. The Honda belongs to Mr. Raeder's grown son. He's in the military and prefers a car.

A 1975 Honda CB 360 looks good, and has six gears, not five like most motorcycles. My first gas-powered chariot, a life reformation. I pay cash for it, and do the required paperwork for a legal transfer: handwritten bill of sale, signed pink slip etc. etc. etc.

The black and blue pony is really mine! As powerful as Pappa's 180cc Vespa scooter, *times two*.

Time for the maiden drive: up Jackson Street, left on Barbary Street, right on Olive Avenue, right on Paseo Padre Parkway and open it up. For some reason, it isn't very fast and doesn't sound good, too throaty. Right on Washington Boulevard, I open it up again hoping the engine's cold, again slow top-end speed. I only get to third or fourth gear, underwhelming.

I know what to do, go see Davey. This will be my first solo "Davey experience."

I went to Davey's shop once, with Danny. That's how I know about Davey. He's a genius, which is rare. The story goes, Davey has too much of a certain naturally occurring chemical in his body, an imbalance. The way I heard it, this chemical imbalance causes a reaction comparable to a 24-7 acid trip. Davey has suffered mental breakdowns in the past, but feels better now. Davey converted half of his parent's garage on Denise Street between Mission Valley Elementary School and Driscoll Road, into a mechanic's dream-shop. Two-wheel riders, near and far, flock to Davey for help. His shop, though small, has it all.

It seems therapeutic for Davey to fix things, to troubleshoot. He's one of the smartest people I've been lucky enough to meet. I wonder how he's feeling and doing?

The last time I rode past Davey's shop, I was on my ten-speed coasting, careful not to exceed five miles per hour. My new Honda isn't doing much better, so I go to Davey.

I park on the street next to his driveway and idle. He strolls through the shop door to identify the strange engine, "Hello Davey." 'New bike?' "Yea." 'Good bike, Honda makes the best disposable bike.' "Thanks." 'How's it run?' "Slow." Davey's long, straight, dark red hair goes to the middle of his back, held in one long ponytail by three evenly spaced, black elastic, inconspicuous hairbands; whenever he leaves the house on his dark green Honda CB500, he wears a black hat, like Fidel Castro's. In Davey's shop, a radio station plays good music, but at a strangely calm, low volume. I'm able to converse and hear myself think.

The man of few words says, "pull it into the driveway." Buh buh buh, up the driveway deploy kickstand, get off, buh buh buh. One at a time Davey reaches down to the end of the two separate exhaust pipes and holds his hand over each one, feeling the exhaust pressure. The CB360 has a twin cylinder engine; each cylinder has its own exhaust pipe. "It's only firing on one cylinder, turn it off." Davey gets a spark plug socket wrench and removes the spark plug from the cylinder that isn't firing. He checks the spark plug's gap with a feeler gauge, and bends it to the correct spec. "The plug is dirty." He screws the spark plug into a small plastic machine. "It's a battery powered, spark plug sandblaster for cleaning the tip." I'm blown away, and haven't seen one since. Davey reinstalls the spark plug and for good measure, cleans and sets the other spark plug gap. Davey is short, about 5'7". "Start it up." With bated breath I push the electric start button . . . brghrghrghrghrghrghrghrghg, listening with intense understanding, Davey takes the throttle and twists it a few times, whuummbb!, whuummmmbb!!, WHUUMMMBBBB!! Wow, what a difference! Davey's built a rocketship!

I thank Davey very much and give him five dollars. Wearing tennis shoes, a colored t-shirt with a cool graphic, cheap jeans and ear to ear grin, I sit on the untorn black, firmly cushioned seat, the engine idles purrfectly. We're firing on *both cylinders now*! With respect and right hand and fear, I grip the throttle, left grip left hand, roll backward across Petey's driveway; using legs and feet, I push the bike forward, aiming it down the driveway.

I wave goodbye to Davey who waves back and peeps through wire framed spectacles. From a dead stop I begin coasting . . . past the cactus garden in Davey's parent's front yard - Davey's good natured father, also has dark auburn hair, though balding and wears silver framed glasses too - right foot up on right footpeg, right toes positioned over the back brake pedal, right index finger on the front brake lever but not squeezing it. Left foot up and resting on left footpeg, toes feel for the delicate gear-shift lever, there.

Coasting, left hand pulls the clutch lever in, left toe gently pushes shift-lever down, just enough to feel the "click" into first gear. A quick glance right, clear, then left the way I intend to go, clear. Unsure of the engine's response but ready, I give it some gas and fly off the curb onto the street, shift to second, then third. What a feeling. Power! Adrenaline, wind in my hair, freedom! I can go *anywhere!*

Straight to Driscoll Road right, open it up, wind up the RPMs, test the engine. Driscoll Road past Paseo Padre Parkway, past Hopkins Junior High, straight to Mission Boulevard. I want to exceed the speed limit, break the law, but refrain. A left turn onto Mission Boulevard, open it up more, more upshifts, to fifth gear.

Wow, wow, wow, my bike really *goes! Thanks* Davey!

A right turn onto Niles Canyon Route 84, head east, zip through the curvy canyon and familiarize myself with the bike's handling. New internal emotions electrify my whole person, impossible to convey. A physical, head to toe tingle sensation, magnified by the wind is part of it. Euphoria mixes with hot summer air. My travel range along the earth's surface, my capability to go, increases dramatically, with no end in sight. The tank holds 3.5 gallons of premium leaded, "purple" gas. A fill-up in 1978? Cheap. For two bucks, I go where I have or haven't been, anytime, fast.

Before Davey cleaned the spark plugs, my life circle was defined by how far I would hitch-hike alone, (up to that point, Livermore) or BART to San Francisco; After Davey the circle expands from a 35 mile radius, to North and South America's farthest drivable points.

The advice Pappa gave to me as a boy, "Jens, before you get married, go around the world on a chopper," is now within reach.

From Sunol, California, Interstate 680 south, to the Washington Boulevard off ramp (don't plum me Kevin) then home.

The maiden voyage (firing on all cylinders) concludes with a glorious paradial procession up Jackson Street. Jens' blue steel reveal; slow motion past the Wellbaum's, the Cortez's and the Topper's; big smiles and shouts ring out, I stop for a minute. The Wellbaum brothers, Tivas and Bucky Cortez and their young sister are there. I show off the blue and black, let it idle. Everyone loves it, two-wheel glory, happy day, *independence day*.

In Niles, Gary Forest buys a Honda CB200 motorcycle from his mother's partner Renee. Similar to my CB360 in design, but gold and black and smaller, the bike is in like-new shape, reliable and freeway legal. A sensible choice.

Back at the ranch, before the summer job ends, Ben Fitzpatrick purchases an older, late 60's Honda 350, like Danny Wellbaum's. Not waiting for work to end, Ben sets out on the open road to discover America and himself. With nothing but a bed-roll and small sack of clothes secured to the handlebar, a full tank of gas and a paycheck, in the early morning fog Ben Fitzpatrick pulls away from the ranch. We all stop, wave, hoot and holler, a jolly good send off. Ben paints an adventurous picture, inspiring, a vivid symbol of daring and freedom, especially to the field hands leaning on their shovels and rakes.

Still 16, still summer and 17 a week away, I own a reliable and handsome motorcycle. Life buds with promise. My senior year starts in three weeks. No serious girlfriend, burned out and crispy around the edges, but lean and strong.

On top of my senior schedule; Advanced ROP Printing with Mr. East and his pretty assistant Jenny. And happy to say, no glaring issues at home. Pappa isn't feeling so hot, there's his daily stomach upset and nausea, but he never talks about it and there's no concern. Occasionally I faintly hear him retching from his bathroom after dinner, but this has been the norm for years, nothing new. Jack still does his art everyday. He went to Kaiser in Hayward and they burned gnarly red lines on his chest, like hieroglyphics or an antiquated roadmap. Radiation treatment for something. Other than that, everything is good. And good is good, right?

Life changes, I drive the Honda everywhere. I spend more time with other riders. Since Danny has a motorcycle too, we hang more, cruising around town. Older Jackson Street guys like Dean

Lansing (Honda 500), Mark Brown (Kawasaki 500 Mach III 2-stroke) and Darin Vanderberg

(Kawasaki 900) also ride. Jimmy Lansing prefers his old truck and dog. After Sonya passed away,

Jimmy gets a hound dog and wherever Jimmy and his truck go, the obedient and loyal, 90 pound

hound dog is visible riding in the bed. Jimmy is an exceptional mechanic and keeps his classic

truck running good.

The older guys plan a day trip with their girlfriends, to San Gregorio Beach on the coast. Danny

invites himself and I tag along. For Danny and I, this is our farthest ride yet: across town, through

Newark to the Dumbarton Bridge, across the Bay to Highway 101, north to Woodside Road Route

84 west through Redwood City and over the peninsula hills, all the way to the coast.

Mark Brown, five years older, rides solo like Danny and I. Mark lives on Marion Avenue in his

parents house, next to Wade Jennings. Their Father, Mr. Brown is a mathematical genius and very

strict with the boys. Before we moved in, Mark's older brother committed suicide in his bedroom;

a shotgun to the head. Mark found his brother right after. I heard that Mark is slightly slow, but I

don't see it. He's a successful house painter and very funny, a quick wit.

Dean Lansing drives his gold Honda 500cc four cylinder, and is a crack-up. Dean's bike has a

cruise-control feature (novel for the time). I'd never seen cruise-control in a car, let alone a

motorcycle, but yes, super-cool Dean Lansing has it. Riding on the Dumbarton Bridge with his

bleach-blonde girlfriend on the back, Dean's cruise-control is set to 55 miles per hour and to our

horror, Dean takes *both* hands off the handlebars and acts like he's paddling a canoe! Alternating

strokes on the left then right side. His antics have us in stitches (bad pun). His girlfriend's reaction

is mixed, she is *not* laughing. Danny looks up to Dean. Darin Vanderberg's new girlfriend Leslie, is on the back of his black and gold, 900 Kawasaki. This is my only ride with the older Jackson Street guys. The trip is well-organized and pleasant.

Around Denise Street there's a group of more experienced riders. I see them, but don't hang with them. There are two guys in particular, Tony Francois and George Kesselring. Both are three years older than me, and both drive Honda XL350's. A very cool motorcycle, the XLs are dirt and street capable. More ground-clearance, lighter, moto-cross handlebars, plastic fenders and at the heart of it, a powerful single-cylinder, 350cc four-stroke engine. We call them "Thumpers." They look like dirt only, but are street legal, equipped with front and rear lights, turn signals and a license plate.

Davey has worked on all their bikes. A signature Davey modification is to remove the four, 6" long, blinker-lite extension tubes (the wiring chase), and cut them short; just long enough to clamp on the lite and frame bracket. So the blinker lite is tight against the frame, leaning out the bike's look. Davey did this blinker mod for me and Danny's bike too; a Davey standard of excellence.

The XLs are super cool looking. The single tailpipe is custom fitted on the end with a sound-trap device, enhancing sound and performance, and they do sound good. The light XL enables Tony and George, more so Tony, to ride long wheelies on the street. They shift gears while riding wheelies! This amazes Danny and I and all onlookers.

It looks fun, we want to ride on the hind wheel too.

Danny and I shadow these guys around, partying with them a little. These guys are party-pros, with an outstanding capacity for beer. A smelly, soggy, depressing scene really. Like medieval peasants, they drink their gallon of beer every day. Pot is toked with alarming regularity as well, but my my how the beer flows.

Social patterns are altered.

We meet day or night, pool resources and buy either a twelve pack or a six-pack of beer, whatever we can afford, and as a pack, drive to one of several iconic spots in the Fremont countryside, or in front of the Wellbaum house, and drink a few, smoke one; joke and laugh, come up with a crazy idea, a place to go, and go.

When we ride, day or night, Tony rides wheelies; solo or with a capable passenger. We all want him to, he's so impressive. Even with a passenger, Tony rides wheelies! He's the best rider we know. On Mill Creek Road, downhill, *downshifting* on the back wheel! He's the Motorcycle's answer to Darin Vandeberg's car driving.

Life is a circus.

Tony's trusting passengers are TT'd (Tony-Trained) in wheelie safety basics; dominant hand grips under the side of the seat in front of them, and their other hand grips behind them on the frame bar. The fore and aft cinch grip stabilizes passengers to the seat, and to my knowledge, Tony's never flipped it, or dropped one. Traveling to the agreed party spot, a lot of us carry friends on the back. Since the beginning of time, friendly passengers have offset party and fuel costs. Marlo Topper rides with Danny a lot. And Marlo always, always has pot (not bingo, *Butko!*). Passengers bring the party and no, it's not optional.

There's a terrific spot off Mill Creek Road, a favorite haunt, a mile past the Aubrey house (Wellbaum cousins). We pull off the road, drop 15 feet down the packed dirt trail into dry Mill Creek, turn left and go 50 yards on a trail along the creek bed. A perfect Indian brave gathering spot; spacious, suitable for 10 street bikes, out of sight from unfriendlies, where underage boys can converse, solve the world's problems, drink beer and smoke pot, undisturbed. Our world.

Tony Francois explains to Danny and I in explicit detail how to set up our bikes, to make them more fun to ride, capable of light dirt riding and street wheelies. We soak it up, Danny and I waste no time installing the Tony mods. We start with dirt-style handlebars and an air-fork kit.

An air-fork kit consists of a blue metal braided cross tube to connect the two fork tubes. There's a single schrader air-valve in the middle of the cross tube. The tube connects to kit replacement nuts for the top of each fork tube. It's an easy swap, just remove the stock cap-seal nut at the top of each fork, and replace with the kit nuts. Install the cross-tube to the kit nuts, drive to the closest gas station and pressurize your forks to 15 lbs or so. The compressed air makes the forks extend a couple inches, improves ground clearance and firms up the front suspension, all for $15 bucks! The raked angle looks aggressive too.

Tony mods 101: replace the stock clutch-plates and clutch-springs, with a Barnett racing-clutch and four racing clutch-springs. The springs are harder to compress and engage the clutch *quicker* off the hand lever. The Barnett clutch plates have four groove cuts in the surface material as opposed to 30 grooves on the stock plates (minute marks on a clock face). The Barnett clutch plate surface has only four grooves, (12, 3, 6, and 9 o'clock). In summary the Barnett clutch plates *grab* more, and the racing clutch springs engage engine to wheel *quicker*. And guess why we want that? Danny and I drive heavy street bikes, not light, XL dirt/street bikes. With ease, the high-performance clutch action yanks the heavy street bike front end up off the ground. Wheelie time!

With practice, we can pop up our front ends and ride on the hind wheel, soon shifting from first to second gear. We have the energy, desire and daring. Now, thanks to Tony, we have racing clutches.

The result of the aforementioned cross-pollination of Mission San Jose High and Irvington High students merging together at Williamson Continuation School is: guys from Irvington befriend guys from Jackson Street, and they all hang on Jackson Street. Al Butko's flourishing pot trade also attracts numerous additional outsiders: Lee Hill and best friend Tony Souza, Tim Cucuk and his friend Billy Coe and many, many others, too numerous to count, become familiar sights on Jackson Street. Regulars.

I live here.

Lee Hill is two years younger, gifted in mechanics and smart. Lee motors up Jackson Street daily on an older red and white Honda CB 175. He lives with his older brother Manny Hill, in a 2nd story apartment on High Street in Irvington, just the two of them. He has an older sister on her own, whom I met once. Lee's enrolled at Williamson Continuation School. That's how Danny met Lee and I met Lee through Danny.

No mother or father at home, just Manny and Lee! Manny is 21 or so. Lee is short, about 5'-7", dark black hair, white fair complexion and stocky solid build. Manny is the same but 5' 10", brickyard stocky, Robert Plant hair and scary, but always cool with everybody. Manny is the strong silent type, the type you absolutely know in your heart, not to cross or challenge. There can be no upside to upsetting him. Though Manny might share a joint with Lee and I, I keep contact with Manny to a minimum.

Lee Hill is a good fit and soon Jackson Street becomes Lee's home away from home. Gary Forest lives and attends school in Livermore, so we seldom hang out. Lee's older brother Manny, owns both the Honda CB175 and a larger, heavier, red 1972 Honda SL 450, a four cylinder beast with a double overhead cam. On rare occasions, Lee negotiates and drives the 450, but ninety nine times out of a hundred, Lee rides the 175.

When Lee comes around, which is daily, he stubbornly attempts to get the heavy Honda 175 on its hind wheel. Lee's efforts are noble, but the under-powered, high geared Honda can't keep the heavy front end up for more than a few seconds. Lee's bulldog tenacity reveals the high caliber of his character. Never sad, always upbeat and encouraging, Lee Hill is different from anyone I'd met before. Humble in social settings but a clever wit, Lee holds his own in conversation, never short of homespun logic. Lee is wise.

The Hill patriarchs own and operate a successful family business: D. Hill Trucking. Lee doesn't share private information, and I never ask, but sometimes when he and I are partying, he tells me this or that about his Uncle's trucking business.

Lee's father and uncle started the company together, in California's Central Valley, in the small town of Keyes. Before I met Lee, the Uncle bought out Lee's Dad. That's all Lee shared about the family business history. Lee and Manny are actively involved with the business, more so Manny. Lee and Manny often refer to; "the yard," "I'm going to the yard," or, "I went to the yard." Always, "the yard."

Finally I go with Lee to "the yard." In Fremont off Durham Road west on Abelyn Street, the D. Hill Trucking yard is ten acres of flat, hard packed dirt, concrete pads with garages and covered truck-ports. The Company's rolling stock is kept and maintained here. The trucking business is foreign to me. Harsh, dirty, heavy and greasy.

Manny becomes a top-flight diesel mechanic at age 19. Lee wrenches too, part-time. Manny is a senior diesel mechanic for D. Hill Trucking.

With tools for toys, Manny and Lee turn a wrench before they learn to read.

Privacy impressed early, neither brother pops off about the family business. Even when partying, young Lee never brags or throws the family name around, never mentions it, ever. I haven't met Lee's Dad. The only comment Lee ever made regarding his Dad was, "He's not afraid to throw anyone down the stairs." Lee's dad lives in California's famous Central Valley, somewhere on the 500 mile stretch, between Redding and Bakersfield.

Lee and Manny live in a second floor apartment, in a pink, four-plex on High Street in Irvington. A long, narrow black metal stairway leads up along the outside of the building, from the asphalt parking area to their front door. Often I drive to High Street to see if Lee is home. I pull up on the 360 and let it idle out front. If Lee is home, within 15 seconds he slides open a little aluminum-framed window, no screen; Lee sticks out his white face, wavy black hair and beaming smile, his head just fits through. "Hey Jens, I'll be right out!" One time he says "want some lunch? C'mon up, I'm going to make a sandwich." I go upstairs, Manny's there, "hey Jens," "hey Manny" and passes me a lit joint. I watch Lee make a cold cheese on white-bread sandwich. "You want one Jens?" "Yes please." I think, wow, so simple. Lee pulls out four pieces of white bread, some mayonnaise from the fridge, puts a little on all four slices and two slices of American Cheese in each sandwich and we eat. I'm not sure what to expect. Lee's cheese sandwich tastes good, I enjoy it. I have a newfound appreciation for Lee's culinary ability. We're off for a long day of fun: wheelies, pot, friends, girls, and beer, drenched in rock n roll sunshine.

Darin Vanderberg buys a black 1970 Chevy fleetside short-bed pick up from his dad. A classic? Not yet, but almost. Darin trades the truck to Manny Hill for a very nice motorcycle, a magnificent black and gold 900cc Kawasaki four cylinder, four stroke street bike, what a beauty! Manny knows *exactly* what he has. He removes the truck's back bumper for that look, and drives it everywhere. The 1970 Chevy truck is Manny's pride and joy, and if Manny's alive and I hope he is, he must still have it, or his kids have it.

A whole lotta life is happening on Jackson Street. Alex Zolanski has a steady Mexican girlfriend who moves in. Previously, she lived around the corner, on Marion Avenue with her parents. Maybe behind Alex's house. She is a very nice girl, funny, cute, friendly and feisty. They marry and have a son together. Paula and Charlene Lansing have steady, serious boyfriends. Guy Wellbaum has a serious girlfriend, Cathy, and one child together. The timeline gets hazy. In my defense the numerous relationships are difficult to track. I fiercely guard my independence, not allowing anyone close.

Tivas' brother, Bucky Cortez (my age) and I rarely cross paths. Once in junior high, we hung out for a minute. His family is large, come to think of it, the same size as ours and the same child sex and age distribution: Mr. and Mrs. Cortez, Rhoda the oldest, Bucky, Tivas, and Lupe the youngest. Rhoda is grown up, and married with one child. Mr. Cortez is down on his luck, unemployed since Pacific States Steel on Mission Boulevard in Union City, shut down that year in 1978. Mr. Duarte appears close to retirement age. The Cortez's are a very close, loving family, but Bucky does have one complaint against his father. Every Sunday, Mr. Cortez goes to the horse track. What upsets Bucky is, no matter what's going on at home, on Sunday his Dad goes to the track. Birthdays, someone sick, he still goes. That's how Bucky sees it. The Cortez children love their parents. Everyone likes the Cortezes, a great family.

Bucky is extremely good-natured and charismatic. With a booming voice, he always has an uplifting thing to say, supportive, and funny, never boring. A straight shooter. One night I am stoned hard in the back of a parked car and Bucky gets in front. It may have been Bucky's car, I don't recall, but I *do* recall what Bucky said to me, "look at yourself, you're ruining your life. What are you doing?! Straighten up Jens." I'll never forget Bucky's reproof, spoken in love. Bucky is beloved at Mission San Jose High School. A volunteer on the football team, everybody loves Bucky, he's a good guy. Family oriented and a stand-up guy.

Senior Year!

By the start of senior year, my Honda is set up. Cycle Salvage in Centerville is our go-to for new and used parts. The manager is fun to deal with, long dirty blonde hair and two different colored eyes, blue and brown like David Bowie. Funny fact; in addition to my scruffy, lovable dog Joey, we have a white female cat. Her name is . . . White Cat. White Cat also has one blue eye and one brown eye, an Odd-eyed White is the breed's name. I wonder if the world looks different, through different colored eyes? It looks very different through red eyes.

I installed a used, two-in-one, chrome header exhaust pipe. It sounds good, *snarly*, and very cool. The Barnett racing clutch comes with a "Barnett" decal. It looks perfect on the black chainguard, and the ultra-sweet, "Santa Cruz" decal, on the right side of the buffed, blue gas tank, makes it. The bike looks and sounds hot, rocknroll. The creek is mine for the taking. Gone are the hardcores. The Buddy Dukes, the Twins, Jim Stanford. Gone were the Brassi's, the older Clayton's, Mark Bailey.

I feel prominent and strong, with something to prove.

I cruise the parking lot with discretion. An occasional wheelie, leave em' wanting more. On the super-social-stage of high school, a clean ride makes a *big* difference in how you're perceived. My Honda 360, diminutive, doesn't stack up against the student body's Mach 4 Kawasakis or new Honda 750F rockets, the Vettes, the Camaros, obviously not the Trans-ams.

I don't care, I love my Honda. It looks classy, and sounds sassy.

The hot new thing that year is the "mini-truck." Initially, the compact Japanese pick-ups were ridiculous to me. However, if you drive one of these mini-trucks, the girls line up for a ride (think, end of *Back to the Future*).

Another major benefit of owning a motorcycle is cruising the Fremont strip. Friday and Saturday nights, Fremont Boulevard between Mowry Avenue and Peralta Boulevard, is packed with drivers young and old, but mostly young. A car show every weekend; glossy muscle cars that cruise and park, are stunning under the streetlights. The cliques gathered round the best cars are impenetrable, hot-rod nobility. I'm on the outside looking in, but used to it, content. I know my place within my hometown, the fringe. We all do, but enjoy the show just as much. The lookers and lookees are equally important, both play a part. It's here I see my first 4-wheel-drive mini-truck. Danny and I know the skinny white kid driving it. "Heyy, Haaay!" Two blond haired gals are in the cramped cab with him. What a great problem to have! The timing of his truck purchase is perfect. We pull up behind the mini-truck at a stoplight, when the light turns green, one of the cute gals in the cramped cab, the taller one looks back and gives me a wink. Yes!

Friday and Saturday nights on the strip, a happening; a concentrated social and mechanical showcase of custom engineering and paint; against a stunning backdrop of lights, smoke, music and roaring engines . . . engines scream, tires squeal, white noxious smoke chokes. Yes an eco-social pecking order exists, at the top, the regal Trans-Am; eagles wings cover the hood, at the bottom, a Japanese Honda CB360. The economic divisions don't dent our excitement or fun. I'm just happy to be here. No ride, big deal. Pal up with friends who do. He can always use gas or beer money, smoke and a joke.

Next year, police shut down cruising Fremont Boulevard forever. No doubt in response to outcry from residents and businesses.

The end of an era.

In defense of my humble Honda, there's a group of six guys - popular on the strip - cruising every weekend. A bike club of custom Honda CB360s. There are blue ones like mine and hot red ones. The gas tanks are stock colors, the engines are hopped up with 400cc piston-kits. Stock handlebars, chrome fenders and exhaust, all gone. Instead: cafe-style race bars, two-in-one header black, side covers black. Cafe-style red or blue plastic fenders (chopped short) to match the tank, beefed up front ends with an anti-sway air-shock. High performance tires. An impressive group to behold, the 360 gang thunder past, making my night. The bikes sound quick, very loud as a group, the riders look great, long hair flowing (still no helmet law), The 360-club leader looks Swedish or German, a shock of short blonde hair, his taut face a solid nerve ending. The bike mods take the 360 as far as possible. I always get a nod of respect from them, and they likewise from me.

October in the Bay Area can be hot, called indian summer for some reason. I'm a senior now, my Honda runs purrfectly, campus life is surreal. Something new; kids look up to me. Even better; younger girls look my way, they like me, think I'm cool. I think they're cool too, their attention feels great. I can do no wrong, and what's wrong with that? The wheels help; the ride appeal. My 360 always has room for a lady. I like when they hang on while we ride, the sun's out, the intimacy. Goosebumps every time, every time goosebumps.

Advanced ROP Printing is the only class I attend regularly, it's a smart move, tolerable. I even take adult lady students for rides. I stay good for that class, the vocation/artistic emphasis suits me. Pappa likes it too and that's cool. Class schedule wise, I don't recall what else I take.

I party every chance I get, with anyone who wants to get high. If the vibe gets negative, I don't

stay. The motorcycle gives me this freedom, in and out. I stay in contact with Gary Forest in

Livermore. He has his motorcycle too, so I might go to the Youth Ranch on Friday or Saturday and

visit.

Gary and I take a ride into downtown Livermore, I forget why. I do remember the ride back to

the ranch. On Arroyo Road at night, Gary and I drive up on a fresh motorcycle accident. A young

guy and gal, a year or two older, stand on the dirt shoulder, banged up and bruised; a motorcycle

lays on its side. His date said, "we hit some gravel and the motorcycle went down and we rolled

against the barbed-wire fence." The accident just happened; a dust cloud illuminated by our

headlights. Road-rash was the worst of their injuries. The two are understandably shaken up, and

Gary and I offer to help. The lady makes it clear, she's not going home on "his bike." I say to the

gal, "can I give you a ride home?" She nods hesitantly, "okay." She gets on and I slowly drive her

back to town, to the front of her place. She gets off my bike and under the streetlight I get a look at

her parked white mustang, a nice car. "Thank you very much," she gives me a kiss on the cheek.

She is nice looking and appreciative. "Goodbye." I drive to the ranch. I never got her name.

At the ranch last summer, after work before dinner, a loud skid and *Bang, Bang, Bang, is heard*

from the direction of Arroyo Road and startles everyone. Butch Fitzpatrick and a counselor, b-line

out the door.

The Painted Bridge is an old white concrete bridge, straddling Del Valle Creek on Arroyo Road,

next to the ranch, south of the Veteran's Hospital and a mile from the back of the Lake Del Valle

Dam. The Painted Bridge is covered with trippy colored murals; a green one-dollar bill, George

Washington clearly depicted, the Zig-Zag Man, Ziggy and many more. These images that cover the landmark bridge are now long gone, forgotten.

The rest of us steel ourselves and make our way to the Painted Bridge five minutes behind Butch. Six adults stand next to the bridge, looking into the dense bushes along the creek. A motorcycle, a chopper, lays on its side in the dirt. Quietly I move in behind the first responders, and peer into the bushes. I see a young man in his late twenties, on his side on the ground not moving. A mustache and goatee, wearing a white T-shirt, blue jeans and a black leather belt and black leather buckled boots. His clothes are torn, and his hair dirty and disheveled from the fall. He groans in a slow rhythm for five minutes, and takes his last breath.

He hit the curve too fast and crashed. He died on the ground under some bushes, on the side of Arroyo Road at the Painted Bridge.

A soon to be rider, I take the accident to heart. Our generation suffers from an endless cycle of two and four wheel tragedies; not far off on the evening news, but close, down the street. We're eyewitnesses, pallbearers; friends, schoolmates, killed, maimed, many sad accidents sting our hearts.

A new goofy white kid I'd seen at school, trying to impress, drove his car 110 miles per hour on Driscoll Road, past Hopkins Junior High School. He lost control and killed the faithful crossing-guard, a sweet elderly woman. So tragic. We mourn and struggle to learn life's lessons from the many senseless losses.

I met a girl at the creek, Nicole. She appears out of nowhere, I didn't notice her before. I know her brother (my age), he's a drummer, smart, funny and respectable. I forgot his name. She's spirited and looks like a dancer, a ballerina. Nicole likes to sing out loud. She likes me too and enjoys zipping around town on the back of my bike, and I like her. She lives in Niles with her mother, brother and younger sister who is also pleasant. Nicole's Mother manages a trucking business. Trucking is big in Fremont. Their house is outstanding. Literally standing out in a field by itself. A Victorian on a large lot on Mission Boulevard. We ride to Niles Park together off Route 84, near Mission Boulevard. There's always a party going on there. Nicole likes to smoke pot, but in moderation, not ridiculous amounts. At their house her brother says to me, "you're probably the nicest guy she's brought home." I thank him for the compliment and feel accepted by her family. Over the next two weeks, our relationship grew slowly. I went to her house a couple times and got cozy once or twice, nothing more. Our courtship ends abruptly.

Jose Maria Montealegre Fernandez

On Halloween morning, I wake up at 8:30 am, frisky; get dressed, hose some cereal and start the Honda, let it warm up until the idle gets steady; bu bu, ba ba ba ba, 1,000 RPM on the tach. I throw my leg over the seat and relax, no hurry, look around, cruise down Jackson Street, downshift rrrooommmbbbaaaa left on Olive Avenue uphill, wind up to 3rd gear, downshift to the stop sign at the top of Mount Olive, stop. Merge onto Washington Boulevard downhill past Driscoll Road, rrrooommmbbb over two sets of railroad tracks, a right on Union Street for a short way, left on High Street to Lee and Manny's pink apartment on the left. I pull up, let it idle, no revving, bububububu, the second floor window slides open, Lee's head and neck lean out and look down, white teeth and a grin he says with enthusiasm, "hey Jens. I'll be right down." "Okay" and turn it off. A few minutes later Lee appears outside, "Hey Jens, I've got Manny's 450 today, you want to ride, get some beer?" The Honda SL450 is a big deal, a serious upgrade from the lowly 175. "Yeaah." Off to Charley's Market. We sped off, Union Street to Grimmer Boulevard right, to Paseo Padre Parkway right, past Driscoll Road, left into Charley's parking lot, the 450 is impressive and I study it, VRRROOOMMM! Within 10 minutes we obtain a 12-pack of Budweiser cans, in a red box, ice-cold.

Aimless, we drive away relaxed and happy. Lee's got the 12-pack on the seat in front of him between his upper legs. Everything is still new; the motorcycle, the joy, freedom.

Still sharp, still fresh, still strong, still young.

We're out of every kind of smoke. Lee doesn't smoke cigarettes, never has, which impresses me. I'm a Marlboro man, we both love pot.

Charley's Market's in the rear view mirror, we ride to the end of Paseo Padre Parkway and head east on Washington Boulevard, toward the green foothills looking forward to a brew.

We stop at the red light at Mission Boulevard. Lee and I don't discuss route or direction out loud, no plan other than a cool one cruising down our bods, destination: all over.

Impulse defines our guiding light. The two bikes idle side by side and sound terrific in the crisp fall air. The two engine harmony gives our excitement a voice the world can hear. We glance north toward Mill Creek Road, a favorite spot for a cool one. After a moment of mute conversation, we look south; the southern sun warms our faces, it feels good and we rumble off. Musical gear shifts at the correct rpm, firrrstt, seeecconnd, thirrrrrddddd, fourth; speed limit cruise, responsible, restrained, check your speed.

Unlike mine, Lee's mind is logical, mechanical. One time, riding through downtown Fremont, on the strip, I started driving fast, screwin' around and Lee said, "Jens, that's crazy, speeding in town. There's too many cops downtown. That's the best way to get a ticket, speeding downtown." He spoke as a man with experience, so I incorporate that nugget of wisdom into my own head. Today when driving downtown, I hear Lee's wise words.

Shiny and new Ohlone College appears on our left; countless college students, drive in, bike in, busloads coming and going; so many bright futures, and it disturbs me. Next, also on the east side, the beautiful and majestic Weibel Winery. In seasons past, Weibel Winery employed many of my friends, many creek rats, including Danny and Guy Wellbaum, John Velasco, Devin O'Malley, Jim Stanford, and Mark Brassi (technically not a friend) and countless others. Weibel hires them to, "picka da grapes, picka da grapes! You! Picka da grapes, okay?!" commands the Italian foreman.

Lee does a double take to the right; something caught his attention. Along this rural stretch of Mission Boulevard, green grass hills rise and fall beautifully. Above the engine's din, Lee yells, "hey Jens! Let's go back there and check that place out!" I missed whatever Lee's yelling about. Confused, I nod. We slow down and turn right onto Durham Road, swing a U-ee and stop at the stop sign. All clear, make a left back onto Mission Boulevard, back the other way north. I don't know what Lee wants to check out or when he'll stop, so I lag behind a bit.

Lee's left-turn blinker begins to flash, he downshifts and crosses the double-yellow line across the oncoming lane and parks on the southbound shoulder. Nobody drives toward us, so I follow Lee and park next to Manny's 450 on the extra wide dirt shoulder. The 1972 SL450 is big and heavy, 450 lbs.; significantly more than my CB360 weighing 375 lbs. A considerably faster top-end speed too, the CB450 is capable of 104 miles per hour, given enough time.

What caught Lee's eye on the west side of the road is a very, very old, almost hidden, narrow concrete staircase, rising up sharply from the shoulder, to a hilltop. An ancient gateway to the past, easily overlooked by 20th Century motorists zipping by at 50 miles per hour. I've never noticed it. A portal to Fremont past, rediscovered by two adventurous young men, abreast their mechanical steeds, searching high and low for lost and ancient civilizations.

A much steeper angle than a modern staircase, the steps rise almost straight up, like the Mayan Temple of Kukulkan. At the top of the stairs, a weather beaten, black-iron sign secured to the dark concrete retaining walls, arches over all who enter. Barely legible, we ascend a few more steps and read: "Saint Joseph Cemetery."

We look at each other, clear eyed, bodies rested, minds lucid, "Woahh!" In hushed reverence Lee says,"Let's check it out." We trudge step by step to the top, the red 12-pack under Lee's short, stout arm. The tall concrete side-walls, combine with the encroaching hillsides to form a tall, narrow tunnel with a sun-roof.

Lee and I step out of the dark into the light, winded. We scan left and right, catching our breath. From our new vantage point (30' above our bikes) you see the entire cemetery, 100% hidden from Mission Boulevard. It's intimate and congested. The stone epitaphs teeter left and right like a horror movie scene at night, but it's day. Lee's voice is low but deliberate, "Jens, there's a couple guys sitting over there" . . . "where?" ``There, they're smoking a joint, c'mon." The on-shore breeze proves Lee correct; the scent of skunkweed wafts in our direction.

Lee and I walk toward the graveyard's center. A low, ancient concrete wall, 30 inches high, encircles a small, dedicated burial area, 25 feet by 15 feet; two young men hunched over, sit side by side on the wall, facing our direction. They're looking down at the marked grave stone in front of them, then look up, peering at us through their long hair. Lee walks right up and in his congenial way says, "hey, how's it going? Wanna' beer? Mind if we sit down?" One makes an arm gesture, signaling to sit. Lee hands them each a can of Budweiser. Lee and I grab a beer and sit on the wall, not too close to the long-hairs. "Pop-a-top" in stereo, pshhh, echos from one side of the graveyard to the other. Lee and I tilt the cold cans back, inline with our necks, the cool suds cruise down our bods.

The two men sitting on the wall never change position, never stand or speak. They have identical builds and height, a thin 5' 8", fraternal twins? Skin and bone, like shirts on a hanger, nondescript facial features, gaunt. I don't stare, question or embarass them. Their hair lengths are similar, very long. Their hair droops close to the middle of their backs. One has dirty blonde hair, the other, brown, both wavy straight.

Lee's acute sense of smell from the top of the cemetery steps is confirmed, they pass us a joint -
a third gone - to Lee and I. The joint gets to us thrice. I don't remember the skinny long-hairs
drinking their beers. The pot is strong and tastes good. Our beer goes down the hatch fast.

A minute later we say, "thanks for the pot,' and, 'take care," no reply, and walk away. In the
world of pot, quiet stoners aren't out of the question. The graveyard party *was* weird, I thought.

Relieved to leave, we weave past the spooky monuments, not pausing to read chiseled
inscriptions and exit the cemetery that time forgot; pass under the black-iron sign, and descend the
steep concrete steps. No handrail. Escape from hell, impossible!

We're satisfied with our 18th Century anthropological discovery, but anxious to return to the
1970s. Lee and I mount our bikes, turn our respective keys one click; green neutral lights light up.
With right thumbs we push our respective electric-start buttons and fire up the willing engines. Lee
secures the remaining eight beers in the red box, on the tank, between his legs and away we go.
Lee is a safe rider, a good rider, we're comfortable riding alongside each other, we'd ridden
together for months. We cross the south bound lane, turn left and head toward familiarity.

I pace Lee 50 yards back, going north on Mission Boulevard. We pass Weibel Winery again,
then approach and pass Ohlone College on the right. These landmarks look different, brighter with
the sun behind us. I look around and enjoy the day. It's close to noon, but I'm not hungry. Almost
past Ohlone College I hear Lee let off the gas and downshift one gear, his right turn-signal blinks. I
know where he's going. I slow, downshift to fourth, wmbaaahhhh, third, wmmbaaaahhh, right
turn-signal on, second gear, wmbaaahh, Lee turns right, onto Witherly Lane.

Witherly Lane is a familiar road. It forms the north border of Ohlone College. Unique among
roads, Witherly Lane is a gentle, consistent upgrade its entire length, no undulation; its entire

length is drag-strip straight, and no cross-streets, only a couple driveways to the left at the end of the road.

For me, Witherly Lane *is* Fremont drag strip.

Lee just putt-putts up the road, looking left then right, like a sightseer taking in the emerald hills and stately Mission Peak for the first time. I like that about Lee, he's observant and nature pleases him. I immediately pass him, open it up, go as fast as my bike will go, winding out 2nd, 3rd, 4th and 5th gear (not enough distance to hit 6th). At 75 miles per hour I recall a pretty young lady I went to school with, Carol Acevedo.

You remember Carol from the freshman pool party a few years back; the day she snubbed Johnny Leon's crass advances, in his tracks. Carol in her black bikini, is still crystal clear in my mind. Carol lives on her family's sprawling estate, at the end of . . . Witherly Lane. I'm on Carol's road, right now!

I wonder . . . is Carol home?

I'm racing alongside the Acevedo Estate. I know because I recognize the red brick blur to my immediate left. To my right lay the Ohlone College Campus in full view.

I am close to Carol's gated entry. The questions are; at 75 mph, *can I slow in time* to make the left turn through Carol's gate? And is her gate open? The feat demands exemplary braking. Why slow down? Two reasons; see if the black wrought iron gate is open and two, *if* the gate *is* open, go slow enough to *make* the left turn through the black gate into the Acevedo Estate, and respectfully, approach her front door and knock. She might be home; I'll surprise her by calling on her. I conceive and hatch the spawn-taneous plan in two seconds.

Is this romantic, or too forward, smart or dumb? We don't hang out or anything. We haven't spoken in over three years and Carol is not a creek rat. My optimism is based solely on unfounded hope.

I'm going for it.

I shift my hips back, step hard on the back brake pedal, as hard as I can and not skid, and squeeze the front brake lever tight. The gate is open.

I roll only fast enough to keep both feet on the footpegs, three miles an hour. I have good balance. Awesome, turn left and enter Carol's Gate. I feel great and think, "wow Jens, you're brave and romantic; Rombravo, bravantic!"

I turn left.

I face Carol's driveway, seated calmly and excited on my blue Honda, mustering courage as I go, perpendicular to Witherly Lane, dead center..

Lee screams, "JEEEENNS!!!" from the left peripheral, a front tire, red and black blur, Lee's short stubby white outstretched arms, hands clutch chrome handlebars, white face, black hair blown-back, Manny's 450 at full throttle . . . at *meeeee* **Lightning Bolt T-BONE!!**

An unsolved mystery baffles to this day; my missing Honda and the eight cans of beer.

Carol

From Lee's perspective, the accident is dead ahead, unavoidable, unbelievable, spectacular. Lee's life flashes before his eyes. Lee flashes before mine. His front tire hits my left side low and square, centered, a perfect tee shot. Perpendicular to each other, Lee hammers me with tremendous force, to maximum effect. The 625 pound red cannonball obliterates its blue bullseye, God only knows how fast he was going: 80, 90 miles per hour.

I smash the asphalt at the point of impact. The 450 punches my bike out and away. In less than a blink, I pivot from upright to horizontal, lying on my left side, head cradled on left bicep (thank you God). I appear to be taking a nap on a bed of pavement.

I'm conscious.

With the peripheral vision Coach Brown and Coach Anderson worked hard to develop, I watch Lee and the accident continue. From ground level, facing Carol's open gate, and an adrenaline surge similar to Alex Zolanski when lifting the car off his crushed father, I watch Lee and the 450, roll over and over and over, through bushes and dirt along the estate's red brick wall, a foot clear of the wall, east of the gate. Lee barely missed the brick wall corner on the far side of the driveway, dodging a dirt nap. Lee and the 450, three times his weight, hit open space. Cartwheels, rolls and a slide-stop 150 feet later; bike and rider come to a dust-choked halt, next to Carol's city wall.

Lee groans, "Jens . . . we wrecked. Jens . . . jens." His plaintive cries grow faint, unintelligible. Too weak to speak, Lee focuses on breathing.

Alone inside my painado.

Without a goodbye my Honda left. I was told it lay in the grassy field between Witherly Lane and the newer Anza-Pine Road, part of the new Ohlone College Campus; where contemporaries crack books, attend class and follow instruction.

My Honda shot 100' through the air and lies behind me. I can't see it and don't try to see it. I'm lying in the middle of the road.

My bike is never seen again. That's not the strangest part. I say this with confusion. Forget it, I'm in pain, let's finish the wreck, then discuss the missing bike later. If I forget, remind me.

Time to split, let's go. "Lee!"

Need to get up, get up and get gone, before Carol or Mr. or Mrs. Acevedo walks out here and sees this mess I made.

I can't bend my left arm at the elbow, not at all, stuck at 90 degrees.

Okay, okay, not *too* fast, don't rush, *methodical*, breathe. Rise *slowly*, then go help Lee up. I start the stand process, lift my right and left legs, keep my left hip on the asphalt. I raise my left and right feet together, a foot off the ground.

My Red Wing boot-clad left foot swings down freely at an unfamiliar, 90 degree angle to its leg. Lying on my side, feet & legs lifted a foot off the asphalt and parallel to each other, the sole of my right foot faces Carol's driveway, my left sole faces the asphalt.

"NO!"

The left foot pivots freely, forming a grotesque right angle to my leg. An angle I see and feel. I am 99% certain the foot is severed 99% from the leg, at best hanging by skin.

Today, I shall bleed to death and die on Witherly Lane, in Carol's ivory arms. Stop it, don't panic.

I lie back down, try to realign the severed foot to its leg, lay back in my original position, fetal. I need to confirm the worst. I'll hike up the left pant leg, to assess damage, and look for blood. I figure, if the ankle *is nearly* severed there should be a *lot* of blood. If that's the case, I'm a goner. No, wait, I'll tie a tourniquet, use my belt! Head raised and with right hand, I reach down the left leg, as far as I can, to the knee and pull the left pant leg. Pull it in increments, inch by inch hike it up etc. etc. etc. I repeat the procedure until the super-bell pant leg won't hike up anymore.

I'm afraid to look, but I must.

I can see my white, knee-high tube sock with two yellow stripes at the top (70s basketball socks). They're white, not red. No blood, good! And good is good, right!?!

I'm exhausted from the injury evaluation, there's nothing left to do. I cannot move, I'm stuck.

"I have no place to go!"

I sigh and cradle my head back into the bend of my injured left arm.

Lying in the middle of Witherly Lane I close my eyes. The street is warm and hard, too hard. I hope help arrives. I have no one to blame but myself.

*   *   *   *   *

. . . Hello, my name is Jens, is Carol home? She is. Yes, I'll wait, thank you.

Yes Mrs. Acevedo, I go to Mission San Jose . . .

Rocky and Bull

I pass out on Witherly Lane. I don't remember paramedics or ambulances. Two days later in a Kaiser Hospital bed, in Palma Ceia, Hayward, with a color TV on the wall, I woke up.

The orthopedic surgeon introduces himself, "hi, my name is Rocky. You broke your tibia and fibula, just above the ankle. It's bad. I reset the leg bones and wrapped them in this plaster cast. I used to work for the Oakland Raiders football team. I was the team's bone surgeon. I worked on so and so and so and so. I'm good at what I do." Middle-aged, charismatic, rugged good looks, sharp mustache and medium length afro, athletic build, confident and black. Rocky continues, "You almost lost your leg . . . you're *very* lucky." "Thank you."

Rocky shows me two X-rays, one before the bone set and one after. The *before* X-ray is startling.

Two inches above the ankle, the tibia and fibula are broken clean apart. At the breaks, the tibia and fibula are out of alignment two inches! The upper tibia is in line with the lower fibula. "You're lucky, I've set these types of breaks before. You're damn lucky kid." I don't feel lucky but Rocky's words comfort nevertheless.

Rocky holds up the *after* X-ray, after Rocky realigned the bones, a bony bulge at each breakpoint. "You've been unconscious since the day before yesterday, you've been through a lot, get some rest and when you stand, don't put any weight on the break." "Okay" and thanked him again. "Another surgeon set your arm-break. He'll explain when he gets here. We'll replace this

leg cast in six months, with a shorter one. "Okay, thank you doctor." Rocky leaves, I never see him
again.

You're the best Rocky!

Mom is there too. Not much talking. She's upset and sad, calm but anxious.

The classic hardrock, white-plaster leg cast encases the entire leg, from an inch below my
briefs, down to and including my foot. Only wriggling toes stick out.

Later, a second orthopedic surgeon arrives; he set my arm break. Confident, barrel-chested, and
white, he's rude and abusive to the pretty nurse. Today they call it sexual harassment. I don't recall
his name. "Your left radius bone snapped two inches below the elbow, and required surgery to
repair the break." With a mirror the doctor shows me the hideous, bright pink, five-inch long scar
over my elbow in-line with the arm. It curves like a snake.

"We opened the arm and from the elbow end, installed a metal lag-bolt through the center of the
bone. The tightened bolt holds the two sides of the break together tight, until the bone heals. We'll
remove the cast in 3 months. See you soon, get some rest, cheer up, you're lucky."

"Thank you doctor."

I'm taking serious pain medication, narcotics. I receive two pain shots per day, one in the
morning, the other before bed. The hospital food is very good, I look forward to it and eat every
morsel. I have few visitors. Nicole never comes. Better to know that stuff now, rather than later,
before a relationship gets serious; like I know what "that stuff" means. I'm glad neither of us got
hurt. We only knew each other for two weeks. Nicole was on a fence I never saw. Her harbored
doubts were obviously confirmed. Jens is out of commission, perfect time to walk away from a

budding, but potentially disastrous relationship. Nip it in the bud. She must have considered, "I could have been riding with him." A perspective to respect.

The next day Mom comes by. "Hi Mom." Mom says, "Pappa is sick, he has cancer, cancer of the liver. He's taken several tests and the results say the cancer has spread through his body." Mom continues, "the radiation treatments he received did not work as we had hoped."

"Your Father has been admitted to the terminally-ill ward." "What does terminally ill mean?" "It means Pappa is dying . . . and he's not coming home."

I say nothing.

A pair of crutches lean against the corner of my hospital room, near the bed. If I take a codeine/acetaminophen pill every four hours and lay there, don't move, the leg pain is bearable. I watch TV, read fishing magazines etc. etc. etc. To use the restroom, I swing myself out of bed, lean on the wood crutches, do my #1 business and get back in bed. When I stand, blood flows through the leg and a killer throbbing pain lasts an hour in bed. Damn. That's the worst of it. When I get vertical, two or three times a day, blood circulates, pain radiates, and tears drip off my chin.

Next day I visit Pappa. Doug Cannon from the Hayward Quaker Friends Meeting arrives in my room after dinner. Doug's wife, Birdie, is the director of child nutrition for the Union City School District. Mrs. Cannon gave me the magazine cover design gig, two years before. Mr. Cannon produces a wheelchair and I sit in it. He rolls me through the cold hospital hallways, down stainless steel elevators and out, in November twilight.

The parking lot pole-lights are lit and I spot the Cannon's new, light-blue VW bus. New Volkswagen buses look like old VW buses, their design barely changing, year after year. We drive quietly, not far.

Pappa's hospital looks like mine, but smaller, only one-story. We park and get out of the new German antique. Mr. Cannon pushes my wheelchair onward under more parking lot lights. Doug behind pushing, me in front moving closer; like the front car of the Grizzly Roller Coaster at Great America with Gary Forest, but without Gary, just me. I grip the arms tight, I'm scared.

Doug Cannon is a good guy, a loving family man, and supportive to his friends. I should look him up. 35, spry, strong, white, thinning hairline blonde in color, gold wire framed glasses. Pappa's hospital room. End of the line.

Mom is there, smiling, not smiling. A few of Pappa's friendly co-workers from Cal-State Hayward are there, doing goodbyes, they're just leaving. Pappa is awake, but incoherent. He doesn't see me or anyone else; he's out of it. Like Kevin Finley the day we drank a quart of Vodka. Pappa occasionally blurts gibberish. Two ladies from his work are there, office administrators, Pappa's known them for 12 years. The two ladies start bickering about something ridiculous and Pappa snaps out of his morphine fog and says, "Oh Marilyn, pipe down." Both of you pipe down." Jack's humorous response causes hysterics and lets everybody know, if for only a moment, Jack is still here. Pappa's reproof delivers comfort. It's explained to me, though a patient on morphine is seemingly out of it, they understand what's going on around them. I smile for one second.

I spent 20 minutes with Pappa, and left the way I came. At least Jack is spared the mess his son made.

I live at Kaiser Hospital for seven days, minus the forty minutes to visit Pappa.

I say goodbye to the hospital staff, and go home. Back to Jackson Street.

The Whole Bag

I hear Lee is okay. He visits a week later. Lee says, "Jens, after the wreck, I couldn't walk for three days, then I started limping around. But no broken bones." Good news, and good is good right?

Yes, right, thanks for the tactful reminder: I told you at the beginning of the previous chapter, that since the day Lee and I wrecked, until today, there's a significant question that's never crossed my mind. A question so basic, that anyone with half a brain would have asked it. It's embarrassing to admit, that for four plus *decades*, I've never wondered:

What happened to my Honda CB360? Where is my bike? Or more to the point, *I want it back.*

Worked and saved all summer, bought it from Mr. Raeder across the street, the motorcycle *Davey* fixed. I don't understand why I never inquired about it, I *never thought* to inquire. Not until I wrote this. That's not right. A 42 year *touch* of amnesia? That's crazy.

If you know what happened to my Honda, call me.

I haven't gone #2 in ten days. I'm not concerned, because that's uncharted territory. On crutches, I'm able to get in and out of the bathroom, or get to the kitchen, or past the kitchen and dining area, and step down to the living room where the TV is. Mom still works 4-8 hours a day at Emporium Capwells and Pappa is terminally ill. Home alone.

Definition of constipation: terrible, a concrete rock lodged, where concrete has no earthly business being. A painful logjam! No end in sight!

In the restroom there's no preparation for what's next. I'm aware it's been ten days since my last bowel movement, but am ignorant of the consequences (no shocker there). I'm confused by the whole constipation thing. I hate typing the word, "constipation." Like the experience, the word is too long, too many syllables.

Pain on the john, intense pain. Pounding the bathroom wall now, yelling. No end in sight, shouting continues, constipation continues, pounding continues etc. etc. etc.

"Jens you alright!??!" Who the hell is that? Again, "Jens you okay?! Alex Zolanski is in the house. I straighten up and say, "Yeah Alex, I'm alright, thanks!" "Okay, let me know if you need anything." "Will do, thanks Jimmy!" Damn, he hears me yelling from across the street, two houses down. I guess the lungs are in good shape. First and worst con-stee-pay-shon (knock on wood). Tears f(ol)low. I reach for pain killers, take the prescribed dose, plus one. I survived a horrific accident, only to die on the john?!?

Alex Zolanski's hero status is intact. What a loving and caring guy.

November 9th, 1978 I'm lying in bed, in my room, home alone when I hear someone enter the front door, light-steps down the hall, who is it? Don't know, don't care. Tap tap on the door, "come in."

Olney Starr opens the door and takes one step inside, her countenance is sad, uncharacteristic, she's been crying. I knew. "Hon, I'm so sorry, but he's gone. `` We're all real sorry hon." I look at her, "Okay" nod. I begin to shake. Olney's head slowly retracts and disappears; she gently pulls my door closed. My core muscles contort and twist hard left, my face pushes against the textured bedroom wall, nose flattens, I smell sheetrock. I repeatedly convulse and weep. My eyes sting and I taste salt. My chest is tight. Alone with sad news.

The ensuing days are busy. My sisters are uptight. I don't know how they feel. I see them, but their inner thoughts and feelings are invisible. I don't know how my mother and sisters deal with

Pappa's premature death. We never discuss it. Just take it hard. No one shares feelings. Good, I don't want to hear it anyway.

We have a service for Pappa in town, in the Centerville area where morticians hang out.

Jackson Street shows up.

Pappa is loved and respected by our neighbors and beyond. Jimmy Lansing, four years older than me, stands up and speaks; "Our street, our neighborhood, is . . . a family . . . and Jack is part of that family."

Pappa would be 98 today. I see guys that age, every week in the local obituaries.

An insanely popular new potato chip came out in 1974; Doritos Nacho Cheese. They taste too good. A friend drops off a bag. Not a small bag, a big party-size bag. I eat the whole bag in one sitting! I never pigged out like that before, to that extreme. Chip plow! Something's wrong, out of whack. Halfway through the bag of chips-for-10, I remember thinking, "Stop, I had enough 10 minutes ago. C'mon' dude, save the rest for later." Another voice said, "screw it, eat the damn things, they taste too good! And good is good, right?"

I have a steady stream of visitors for the next four years. 17 and no Dad? The party is on, for real. My contemporaries, Jackson Street's finest, bless their hearts, suffer from a horrendous lack of industry - Darin Vanderberg notwithstanding - and drug addictions. They're eager to offer their condolences, love and support, the only way they know how: hitch their wagons to my hellride.

Kevin Finley, Guy, Curtis and Danny Wellbaum, Marlo Topper, and others, encourage me to get out of the house. "I don't know how you stay in all day, I'd go crazy" etc. etc. etc. The leg still kills when vertical. I'm taking a steady supply of codeine/acetaminophen, one every four hours, the prescribed dose.

The far wall in my bedroom is lined with three, six-foot long hardwood shelves that Pappa made; he stained them with his favorite stain, Watco Danish Oil, medium walnut color. I still use it. Pappa uses a cloth rag to apply Watco Oil to finish many of his wood projects. My entire model collection is displayed on those three shelves. My life's work. My favorite, Rommel's Rod, was a parting gift I'd received from Mr. Turentine when I left Ruus Elementary in Palma Ceia, Hayward.

Rommel's skeleton sits in the backseat; you can tell it's him by the Nazi General cap he wears; up front his driver's bony fingers grip the steering wheel, both hands. The 1976, Mission San Jose High, Annual Model Contest Winner: the red 1940 Ford pick-up is there. The models are parked bumper to bumper and fill the shelves.

On a crutch, I hop to my closet and withdraw Silver, pump it two times, and load the action with a single 5mm lead pellet. I set the full, yellow plastic pellet box on the bed, next to me.

Prone in bed, I lower the silver barrel slow, set my iron sights on an old model, 12' away. With 20/15 vision I aim at the front wheel hub . . . PSHT!

Bam! Rommel's Rod is slammed backwards against the wall, the front wheel is knocked 90-degrees, yet stubbornly clings to its axle. Good glue job. Pump, pump, pump. "Time to meet your maker again, you brilliant Nazi bastard!" Pow! Blam! That shot right on the money knocks General Rommel's capped skull clean off, only the torso remains. Rommel's driver still clutches the steering wheel. What defiance! I can see why Pappa wanted to kill Nazi's. A 5-millimeter pellet in relation to the model's 1/24th scale, hits Rommel's door like a cannonball, taking out the door and the headless General. This is fun. Sick and sad, but fun.

Pappa, the main deterrent of my bad behavior, is gone forever. I am heartbroke, insecure, angry etc. etc. etc. Pappa's untimely death shakes my family violently; Jackson Street is hurting too.

I venture out finally, crutch my way down Jackson Street, to Danny's house. I haven't seen Nicole. Over, old news.

A friend of Nicole's, and younger brother of a friend of mine, Kurt, drives up Jackson Street to score weed. We talk. He's friendly and candid. Unsolicited he says, "Nicole's not the same . . . since your accident. She's quiet." He's honest and his assessment is unexaggerated, I can tell.

I'm glad Nicole is messed up. That's messed up.

Fortunately, our relationship is objective, free from the ties that bind.

Should I call? No.

Later, I see Nicole for the first time since the crash, at Charley's Market in the parking lot. She's driving a brand new, root beer brown, 1979 Chevy Scottsdale, stepside truck. She's by herself. She looks exactly the same, through the open passenger window Nicole say's, "I worked and saved, and bought this new truck, paid cash, no payments." "That's great Nicole, the truck is very nice, congratulations." I am proud of her.

Weeks later, in front of the Wellbaum's, Danny says, "Jens, it's Nicole." I know it's her because I recognize the truck. A Chevy Scottsdale truck slowly drives down Jackson Street, pulls up in front of the preschool and parks, between the Zolanskis and the Toppers. Nicole's new boyfriend is driving her truck. Nicole sits in the middle of the bench seat, close to my replacement, a white guy, two years older than me, cleancut, gainfully employed, here to score weed.

Three weeks after Pappa dies, Kaiser shoots new X-rays of my injuries, to monitor healing progress. The leg breaks Doctor Rocky set are doing well. The arm break Doctor Macho screwed together, has separated! The surgical lag-bolt threaded into the inner hollow space of the radius bone, stripped out! The bolt is too small. The break came apart, back to square one.

The re-do surgery is scheduled. I'm knocked out again, cut open again, Doczilla drills two small holes through the bone, a hole on either side of the break, threads surgical wire through the holes and cinches the break back together again.

Three months are needed for the arm bone to heal. Three weeks of healing time are lost and the new scar is uglier, but the wire works and I'm glad Doc Macho caught the botch.

It's not a screw up if you can fix it.

When I'm laid to rest with my Fathers, three items will remain: ash, a lag bolt and a piece of wire.

Pappa got me started young, building models. He believed they'd help me learn to follow step-by-step instruction. When I start one, I want to finish it. A pattern developed; I'd work too many hours on the model, get tired, make a couple mistakes, and get frustrated. Haste makes waste. A dozen times I heard my parents say, "Jens take a break, you're tired." I never believed it, or understood it. Ambition, stubborn or foolish? Sure.

All the plastic car and truck models I've glued together over the years, from fourth to 12th grade, are no longer displayed proudly on Pappa's three shelves in my bedroom on Jackson Street in the Mission San Jose area of Fremont. Only model debri, riddled with 5mm holes.

It's time to get out, get outside. I grab my crutches, and pivot through the front door onto the porch. I lumber forward, out, blinded by the light of January, a broken vampire, prison pallor. I'd lost weight, down to a shrimpy 160 pounds with severe muscle atrophy; in the broken limbs especially. My left shoulder and arm are noticeably diminutive, the left leg, now a half inch shorter than the right, 7/16" to be exact, I don't want to sell myself short (pun intended). In front of the mirror my left hip drops down noticeably. I don't know it yet, hidden by the cast, the left leg is grotesquely the same diameter from top to bottom, knee to foot, like a telephone pole.

Throwing arm strength is stubbornly intact.

To challenge myself, for kicks, I start walking with the crutches without letting either foot touch the ground. My last option to impress the world, which has suddenly become very small.

My new geo-boundaries are: west; the Toppers, Wellbaums and Cortezes, east; the Finley's, north; the Lansings and south; the back porch. Unless I'm driven, these are my new parameters. A drastic takeaway from the North and South American Continents, to . . . pop six codeine/acetaminophen. I feel better, empty bottle etc. etc. etc.

Pappa 1978

One Question

The 15 weeks before the arm cast is removed, are a blur, a blackhole. Existence within the house-triad: bedroom to toilet to TV to kitchen. Okay nerd, a quadrilateral. Pot burns daily in my room. If I light up before Danny Wellbaum comes over, and Inger is home, Danny whispers to me, "Jens, you're crazy, I can smell it in the living room, through the vent." My dog Joey becomes collateral damage. In the bedroom, a cramped circle of friends smoke a joint, round and round and round. Joey forms part of the circle, lying on the bed next to me, asleep, stoned, groggy.

Poor doggy.

After Pappa died, Joey becomes a neighborhood character (not me, Joey) taking multiple daily struts on Jackson Street and beyond, to clear his head (okay me), making it as far as Tim Cucuk's and Ron Mudder's house on Mckay Street. Friends keep me abreast of Joey's whereabouts. While certainly not the first dog to cruise, Joey's definitely the neighborhood's first stoner-dog; he's smaller, not a full-size dog, 21 pounds. Joey lays down in the middle of the street and naps, for 15 minutes or more! The fact Joey survives is a miracle. Eventually I learned that one's bad choices always affects others, hurts others through a ripple effect of consequence, in simple or complex ways. Even pets, especially pets. Joey's antics provide comic relief for my stoner friends and I, but at his expense and peril.

Neighbors encounter one of two Joeys everyday on the street, either a spirited head n chest-up, Johnny Travolta style strut, Stayin' Alive, Stayin' Alive, or, out cold lying in the middle of the street. Cars and motorcycles slow and swerve to avoid the lifeless, despondent heap of disheveled, curly black and white hair. Jack is gone, nobody wants to be the person to kill Joey. Damnitt!

Deep in the black hole I have a dream, or vision. Simple, but striking. An ordinary real-life scene, no drama. Colors and lighting are correct and real, absolutely real.

It's morning at home, I'm unaware it's a dream. Volume levels are natural, not distorted, frightening or euphoric. No skyscrapers free-falls, or supermodel back rubs.

The dream is boring and ordinary, except for one detail: Pappa is alive.

       *   *   *   *

I wake early, first-light brightens the bedroom curtain from black to light green. I notice my two full-length white plaster casts, covered with expressive, heartfelt, artistic sentiments from family, friends and stoners. I smell plaster - the arm cast, bent 90 degrees at the elbow, covers my dwindling bicep and only fingers protrude - and wipe the sleep from my eyes. Today is yesterday's again, again; Pappaless melancholy. No future besides limping to the next joint. I prop up, exit my room, turn left and crutch down the hall to the kitchen. Light spills into the hall and living room through the kitchen doorway.

I hear light clatter from the kitchen, someone cooking or washing dishes. Mom works afternoons & nights at Emporium Capwells and sleeps in till eight or nine most mornings.

She's up early today.

I still prefer to wake early, for classic cold cereal and cold milk, and am usually the first one up; looking for Captain Crunch like the hungry five year old in San Francisco, 12 years ago.

I round the corner and enter the kitchen . . . dumbstruck, Pappa, you're alive. And cooking breakfast? I think, oh . . . good, good, *good*! Alright! Everything's *okaay*. Ahh, it has all been just a *bad dream*. Only the worst nightmare, just a nightmare. Whew!

I don't care for Pappa's breakfast. He cooks some weird stuff, like fried potato pancakes made from leftover mashed potatoes, or chocolate oatmeal. No joke, once in a blue-moon Pappa makes chocolate oatmeal. Or for an afternoon snack, broken graham crackers in a glass of milk. No thank you.

No matter, I'm very happy to see him and that the whole, terminally ill, dead from cancer thing, has just been a terrible misunderstanding. I ask in an elevated, clear tenor voice, "Pappa, where have you been?!?"

He is quarter-turned away, facing the yellow electric stovetop. Pappa turns and faces me, smiling and healthy with a spatula in his right hand, smiling with real teeth, strong and white. I see, hear and smell potato pancakes sizzling in the cast-iron skillet, shhhhhh. Pappa says, "Jens, I've been *all over*." Pappa hangs the words: *all over*, out there for a second, for emphasis.

*   *   *   *

I wake up, oddly I feel good, and get dressed. My heart is beating. Up to my feet, crutch down the hall in one-legged bell-bottoms, one sock, one boot and a white T-shirt, pass the kitchen where Pappa and I spoke, look in, smile. Strange, I feel very good . . . like Christmas morning. Not Christmas good, but normal good. I feel secure, confident . . . normal . . . like before Pappa died.

I didn't know how good I felt before Pappa died, until he did.

Out the front door, onto the porch, step down the two concrete steps one at a time to the walkway and stop . . . I look around.

It's serene. My mind is at peace, mild goosebumps, I'm whole. Humpty Dumpty *is* back together again. I look right, toward the Tyrell fence, Pappa's Vespa is parked, on its center stand and covered, the bottlebrush tree on the fence line is in full bloom. Left toward the garage window, the large yellow and black Harley Davidson decal, Pappa got from his friend David Wakefield, is centered on the pane, looks cool.

That's when I knew how bad my life is and will continue as such. On the porch, for 10 seconds, I felt perfect, *exactly* like before, then, the scene's colors bled out, back to black. So black, there's a blue tinge; time-lapse photography from an apocalyptic movie: first, pastoral nature scenes, green trees, a babbling brook, a fish jumps, innocent forest creatures hop about etc. etc. etc. Then a nuke drops and instantly, everything burns, withers and dies. The blue stream vanishes, replaced by a scorched cracked earth. Flora and fauna reduced to ash in 3 seconds. Color to black, life to death.

The Q&A dream with Pappa (miraculously alive) and the resulting euphoria, stands valiantly against death and the gates of Jackson Street's new hell, and girds me for a minute.

The vision provides an answer to a question I didn't know I had, and upon waking, for a few *precious* moments, I am fathered again; the last ray of sunshine. A silver lining between Pappa and no Pappa. Too much, too much.

I spoke to Pappa, asked him a direct question, "Where have you been?" I asked him that, maybe because I wasn't raised on heaven and hell; I know nothing of it. It was an honest question, only 53, Pappa went somewhere, and I got *a* chance to ask him, where? I'm glad I did. Not every grieving son has the opportunity to ask their dead dad where he went. Or maybe they do but don't mention it. Jack's answer: "I've been all over."

What does, "I've been all over" mean? Four words. "I've", that's easy. "I've" refers to himself, to Pappa, makes sense so far, "Been," past tense, already happened, a reference to an action transpired. Pappa's only been gone from us for two months, so whatever "been" was, was done in two months, okay good. "All," the word *all* is tougher to determine. All means all, means all, not here or there, it's "*all* over." You have to put the two words together to even ponder the meaning. Pappa said, "all over." To say to someone in common vernacular, "I've been all over," could mean different things depending on context.

A concerned parent confronting their teenage child who's two hours late for dinner, may ask him or her, "where have you been??" If the child responds, "I've been all over," the parents may determine the response, too vague, disrespectful, unsatisfactory, and ask for specifics. If I ask a friend, "Which part of the lake did you fish"? "I've been all over" would mean a few popular spots most likely. So the declaration, "I've been all over" without a reference point or boundary to confine "all over" inside of, is tough to define. All over what? The *other side*? Time travel? Speculation.

If a person has faith-based convictions concerning a departed soul's whereabouts, heaven or hell for example. One could say, he or she's been all over heaven, or all over hell. That's more specific and satisfactory.

I was raised in a family, not adhering to one traditional religion; Christianity, Hinduism, Islam, Buddhism, or Confucianism. Jack was raised in the Church of Christ under his mother's watchful eye and musical ear. As a teenager, Inger was confirmed in the State Lutheran Church of Sweden. Whether Jack and or Inger abandoned the faith of their childhoods or kept it intact is unclear, however, our parents' philosophy regarding the spiritual lives of their children was for us to decide for ourselves a spiritual direction (if any) to embrace; to choose our own path, make our own decision.

In 1978 at 17, I don't have any spiritual convictions or direction, nor do I ponder eternity. I only know what I see and hear, taste and feel, what I like and dislike, love and hate (hate is a strong word and rarely invoked). In the dream, Pappa beams throughout the encounter, so for me, in the land of the living, the dream's message is positive, good for three minutes. But good is good, right?

No more Pappa dreams, no more questions asked. I got one, that's it, but glad for it.

The dream's meaning is obscure, but in spirit and appearance Jack looks happy and strong. I only know the great way I felt after waking up, life's delicate order restored, at peace again.

Fathers take *care* of yourselves. Don't be selfish, sell the motorcycle. Be generous, sacrificial, have your kids *ASAP*, don't procrastinate! Be selfish later, *after* they grow up. After the children grow wings and leave the nest, then be your own kid.

Garage AD

On crutches I venture out, start to get around. I need more space than a 10' x 10' room. I convert Pappa's studio to my own devil's den. It's cool; well lit, a working wall-phone, and plenty of tools. I got some weights, a bar, a bench; a used, high-power Kenwood stereo receiver, a cassette deck, and four giant speakers shelved 9' off the floor on opposing walls. The audio package delivers apt wattage, and is well suited for chafing neighbor's hides, seven days a week: Tyrells, Starrs, Lansings, Schultzes, Zolanskis, Raeders.

Mrs. Schultz chafes *my* hide after insulting mom. Personal stuff. I call towering supercop Ray Schultz on it, face to face. Ray says, "Jens, about her comment, I agree with you. You're right, there's no call for that and I'll talk to her about it." Nod, "okay," nod. 'But regarding her accusation that you're selling pot out of the garage? I've seen it myself, watched you conduct business through binoculars." Oh no, busted. Sad, because I remember the instance Ray was talking about. I was no dealer, though I was surrounded by them.

Conversation ends abruptly, the outcome a wash, tilt the garage door down to a 45-degree angle, establish privacy. The garage isn't for the faint of heart. If you come, you come to party hard, rock hard or work out, usually all three; or shoot the breeze, but please, keep it interesting.

One leg, one arm, no wheels. Man, this year was supposed to be the best. A reentry to civilized high school. Not happening. No junior prom, no senior prom, no high school dance. No Friday night football games (they're Friday right?). No basketball games in the gym? In four years, not one.

And I love basketball!

The extent of my world travels in 17 years? North: Muir Woods National Monument, south: Solvang, California, east: Reno, Nevada, west: Ocean Beach, San Francisco.

Music scenes and social spheres, the sights and sounds of the San Francisco Bay Area, reduced to . . . a garage. In my *new* condition, it works. Lee Hill, Danny, Guy and now Curtis Wellbaum, Tim Cucuk and Martin Bostok are daily garage fixtures. Kevin Finley too. Kevin doesn't seem quite as cynical, I think he has a girlfriend. Gary Forest lives at the Youth Ranch in Livermore and is doing his senior year at the Livermore continuation school. Jackson Street guys are working or dealing, doing harder drugs; snorting crank (meth) and cocaine, dropping acid and eating psychedelic mushrooms, black beauties, purple micro-dot, whites, smoking hash, thai-stick, sinsemilla, cigarettes. I see Gary on the weekends, once in a while.

Jackson's true blue comes alongside during my hour of need. I spend more time at Tivas and Bucky's house if that's possible. Hanging out front with Tivas and her friends in the Cortez driveway, sitting on a car, leaning against the telephone pole. Simple and fun.

Customers and dependents, young, strong and lost, patronize Jackson Street's hot-zone, morning, noon and night. Many are consoled here.

My new situation forces me to slow down, develop friendship skills or at least witness them. I discover, I don't have to chase the world. If I stand still for five minutes, it comes to me. I learn what a friend is. Maybe not the healthiest influences, but loyal compadres nevertheless.

The gals on Jackson Street are awesome too. Nice to me before *and* after the accident and Pappa's passing. Charlene and Paula Lansing get it done at Mission, graduate with their classes. They've always been sweet to me. The Zolanski's door is always open, the Starr's too, though

Kenny Starr could do without my obnoxious rock n roll sledgehammer pounding his eardrums. The volume knob has a 10 on it for good reason, me.

The Fremont Unified School District doesn't give up on me either. To the contrary, a home tutor comes to the house once a week. She administers assignments and works hard getting me up to date. She's a very nice lady, Mom's age and my champion. I wish I could remember her name and send her a thank you card. Perhaps I can locate her through District records.

There's no sugar-coating it, I'm *way* behind in high school credits. I neglected school work for too long, all along. My champion keeps me floating, however, bringing me very close, within striking distance to graduate, to walk with my Class of 79'. With my tutor's help and inspiration, I make up four years of deferred high school education, almost.

Since the accident, every time I get high, my neck feels like it's about to snap. When stoned I become physically still, convinced that any sudden movement will sever my spinal cord and paralyze me. The sensation is real, I don't think it, I feel it. Somethings gotta give.

Gary Forest is seeing a chiropractic student at the Life Chiropractic College in Hayward. Gary says the chiropractic students practice their new skills on the hurting public, for free.

My neck freaks me out, so I take Gary's advice and go to Life Chiropractic on B Street in Hayward, near Fourth Street. There are grand old houses in the area, some duplexes too. I'm examined by a young, black chiro student; around 30 years old, he's confident and friendly. He does adjustments on Gary and after a few spinal tips and quips, I trust him. He takes an X-ray of my spine to establish a baseline for treatment. He says, "you have scoliosis, curvature of the spine. See, the lower back is an S shape." He cracks my back in two places but when he tries to crack my neck, I resist. Fearing paralysis, I tighten my neck and prevent the intern from proceeding. On the third visit, he distracts me with a funny story while gently turning my head left and right, like a massage or stretch, then twists hard, *crack, crack!* Woah, that feels goo . . . *crack, crack, crack the other way!* Oh, I, ahh, hmmm, feel better. Much better. After a few more visits, I adjust my own neck, bringing urgent relief throughout the day.

One of my guitar heroes, Ronny Montrose, starts a new band called Gamma. Ronny's highly successful first band, Montrose, fell apart when lead singer Sammy Hagar went solo. I bought Gamma's debut cassette.

I like Ronny's resilience, not kept down, rather, he reinvents himself and rises again.

As I prepare to listen to Gamma for the first time, Curtis Wellbaum moseys into the garage. If the big garage door is open, even a little, visitors arrive within 15 minutes, I'm never alone.

With comical facial expression and exaggerated tone Curtis says, "wanna get high?" He holds up a small clear, zip-lock baggie of oozy green sinsemilla buds for my review. He opens the baggie, "smell this." I sniff the buds. "Woo hoo, yeah. You want to hear the new Gamma?" Curtis says, "oh, oh, oh, let me see, let me *see!*" I show him the tape and his countenance brightens. He knows Ronny's history too. Curtis rolls a perfect joint from one bud, cigarette perfect. The only person who rolls better than Curtis is his brother Danny. Marlo Topper rolls a very good joint too, but Curtis' are uniform, tight and smoke beautifully.

He lights up. We pass it back and forth, stoned after two hits, "oh maa haan." Giggling Curtis says, "lets see the tape, let mee seeee the taaape!" "Here"; both of us were laughing and excited. All the tracks are new, cutting edge music in our favorite genre - we don't say, *genre* then, nobody does.

Since the accident, Curtis and I have gotten to know each other more. Curtis is much different than his two older brothers, Guy and Danny. Not physically combative, less handsome, physically weaker. Bigger nose, fun-loving, artistic, charming and wily. Bluntly, Curtis has a big mouth, he's audacious and outrageous, without the ability to back it up. There are similarities however, to his brothers, Curtis has a great sense of humor and enthusiasm. He can really cut it up, get us in stitches, and keep us there. He has a serious side too, Curtis is the business man of the family, the wheeler and *dealer* etc. etc. etc.

Curtis puts on Gama, we're giddy

I tolerate freedom of expression from friends. I always have. Example: I was looking forward to listening to Ronny's new band for the first time, by myself; check out his new direction, soak it in in my favorite musical way, alone. I tolerate friends who irritate me, let small stuff go. A small price to pay for someone to know, a friend. They, in turn, tolerate *my* issues. That's part of what I meant earlier, about learning how to be a friend. It's messy, but worth it.

Curtis pushes play, the two tape reels behind the clear plastic cassette body instantly turn. The first track is called <u>Solar Heat</u>; nothing happens right away, just speaker crackle . . . low and hush from the two west speakers, "shheww" . . . east speakers, "shheww." Repeat build slightly, repeat build a little more. Ronny's rhythm guitar comes in quietly, "uh, uh, uhhh" up, 1 2 3, organ up and down a scale responds, doo doo doo doo doo doo doo guitar again, "uh, uh, uhhh, down 1 2 3, organ repeat builds, . . . Ronny up, uh, uh, uhh, organ . . . Ronny down, uh, uh, uhh, then snare drum, chhh, chhh, chhh, Ronny, uh, uh, uhh.

On beat, Ronny's intro lead guitar wail, deeer duhhhhhh, a fast ascending descending scale, repeat scale, now descending scale response transition to sustained high notes in between repeat descending scales, Ronny takes off on his lead solo. Hot! At song's end, Ronny's high note is stuck, like he's having a heart attack or screaming. The note hangs on, where's it going? A segway to the next track; <u>Ready for Some Action</u>. An amazing, blazing guitar riff opens this next tune. Everything upfront, play now, pay later, a VISA song!

Curtis and I are *beside* ourselves. Heads pumping, air guitars plugged in, impressive air-stage antics, wow what an experience! I'm glad Curtis and I hear the new music together, rather than separately. Makes it better; memorable enough to wind up here

Throughout the day, Jackson Street moseys over for a listen. Nobody's first listen compares to mine and Curt's.

Curtis

1979!

Beyond music, pot, transforming Pappa's garage into a rock n roll workout oasis, and neck redeeming chiropractic adjustments, not much happens in the four months after my accident and Pappa's passing. I have no idea of my sister's comings or goings, their friends, dreams or pain. I isolate, insulate and self-medicate.

The arm cast was removed mid-February. The initial surgery fail delayed cast removal three weeks. I regain partial range of motion at the elbow. Rehabilitation is not encouraged, enforced or graded. You're 17, you'll heal. They were half right, I have 90% range of motion in my left elbow today, but only 65% in my left knee. The limited ranges were avoidable, with basic physical therapy; a shame. Old enough to blame myself, young enough to point fingers, I like the tension.

Kevin Finley walks his own path now, a wrong turn in my humble opinion. Kevin leads his merry band of intelli-toughs: Billy Nelson, Randy Coe and others. Randy Coe lives in the same Gomes neighborhood near Lake Elizabeth, where John Velasco and Frank Oleander live. Randy Coe's mother and father are both deaf and mute, but Randy hears and speaks fine. Randy Coe is funny, tough and very smart.

Free of the arm cast, my mobility improves. Atrophied, I swim inside my shirts, size medium.

For kicks (pun intended) long-legged Kevin Finley starts kicking the top of door-ways; he's so limber. I kick the doorknob pretty well. He and his amigos drink, smoke and carry on. They have their own thing going on. After a good enough buzz they often punch or kick each other point blank, to see if they can "take it." I avoid this behavior at all costs and give them a wide berth.

I stay in contact with Lee Hill, Danny Wellbaum, Gary Forest, and Darin Vanderberg once in a while. New partners in crime are Curtis Wellbaum, Tim Cucuk, Martin Bostok (the twin) and a new face, Steve Harrold. I met Steve through Martin and Tim. He lives on Jackson Street, four houses down from Danny and Guy. Steve has a cool younger brother Greg. Steve and Greg fight all the time in front of everyone. It's hilarious. Observing Greg and Steve and the Wellbaum brothers too, I begin to understand the major differences between having a brother and not having a brother. A brother is an incalculable benefit.

I spend an inordinate amount of time in the garage. All day people drop by, off and on, to visit. I never know who will stop by or when. It's fun. We lift weights, smoke a little pot, drink, kick the heavy bag, and punch a speed bag. The blur of that speed bag and the rat a tat tat, is a blast. We listen to great music, the best of the best. Kids from all over Fremont come too, not just the Jackson faithful. The miniscule ambition I do have isn't business driven or getting ahead, I already feel ahead. Mostly a little physical conditioning, major partying and non-stop music. This attracts people.

I enjoyed another first with Curtis; *authentic* Mexican food; Taco Bell was it to this point. A tiny flat-top house on Fremont Boulevard, between Blacow Road and Washington Boulevard, across the street from Jack in the Box, is La Casita Mexican Restaurant. It's the best Mexican food. Thank you Curtis.

Constant pot smoking causes constant munchies and Curtis says, "let's go to La Casita!" I don't remember how we got there. Neither of us have a ride and I'm not going to crutch two and a half miles. We must have bummed a ride. More on my Mexican food premiere in a few minutes.

After four long months in the long leg cast, fettered to Jackson Street, I devised the great escape.

Pappa's 1972 red Vespa Rally is parked on the side of the house under a torn gray cover. Idle for six months, flat tires, dead battery. I remove the cover, unlock the front end and roll it into the garage. The battery is dead, so I add water and charge it. After 100 fruitless kick starts, I remove the spark plug, it's fouled, I replace it. After 50 kicks, it reluctantly starts up, very rough and unsteady, belching smoke. I run it until I get a smooth idle, then shut it off. I hand pump the tires, they hold air.

After four months I can put my 170 pounds on the broken leg, pain free. However, because of the long cast, I cannot bend my left knee to sit on Pappa's scooter.

I take a 1"x2" piece of hardwood and cut it to 16" length, sand it smooth, round the corners, at one end drill two 5/16" holes, four inches apart, trace the holes from the wood to the front shield of the Vespa on the left side a foot above the floor board and drill holes in the scooter's front shield. I bolt and locknut the piece of wood, level, to the shield and cantilever the piece of wood to the left of the shield, creating a leg cast support, to get me out of my way.

The scooter's rear brake-foot pedal is on the right floorboard, no problem. The front brake is a right side hand-lever, no problem. The 4-speed gear-shifter is a left side twist-handle, klik-klik-klik-klik, neutral between first and second, no problemo. And the clutch, a hand lever on the left side. Perfect. Better than perfect . . . done.

Free [way legal] again!

Curtis and I may have gone to La Casita that way. We're seated inside, Curtis requests fresh tortillas and butter. The cost? A dollar. We lap them up and a couple baskets of tortilla chips too.

The red salsa at La Casita is delicious and addictive. I've yet to break this habit, chips and salsa, and the red sauce at La Casita is still my favorite, although today you have to ask for it. Their chicken soup is to die for.

This is a good time for a Lee Hill update. Luckily, Lee only suffered a minor (but painful) setback from our accident in October. Unable to walk for three days, a limp for two weeks and Lee's as good as new. I'm glad he recovered quickly because the accident is in no way Lee's fault. To borrow a title from a favorite song, Nobody's Fault but Mine. To cheer me up, Lee says, "Jens, your limp is rock n' roll." I want to believe it, but do not, still I appreciate the effort. Incredibly, Lee never says in my hearing, or behind my back that the accident was my fault. This is what sets Lee apart from other people. Not only does he *not* defend his ego that way, he's *protective* of his friends. We were goofing around, punching or slapping, not seriously, just fooling, like all my friends do. And Lee says, "Jens, friends don't fight each other." Yes Lee, you are absolutely correct.

I don't remember whether Lee was riding the Honda 175, or the Honda 450, but I do remember what happened on Olive Avenue in March of 79'. Lee's riding east on Olive Avenue, in between Palm Avenue and Starr Street, and is cut-off by a lady in a car, crossing Olive Avenue on Scofield Drive. Her reckless turn forces Lee off the road and he crash lands on some juniper bushes lining the sidewalk, on that strip between the street and the sidewalk. While landing on bushes is preferred over landing on concrete or asphalt, maybe not this time. Lee lands on his bumb and a stiff juniper branch has its way with Lee. YEOOWWWWW!!! THAT'S SMARTS!!

I visit Lee at Washington Hospital in Fremont. He's in bed, flat on his back, a special donut cushion under his hiny. Lee fills me in on the accident graphics, an embarrassed smile on his face. It occurs to me now who Lee looks like.

Last week, I watched the original Walking Tall from 1973. Lee Hill is a spitting image of the movie's lead actor, Joe Don Baker, who depicts Sheriff Buford Pusser. Minus Sheriff Pusser's Elvis-type sideburns and the height difference, the resemblance is uncanny.

"It was her fault Jens," and whispers, "I'm getting a settlement; keep it to yourself: five thousand dollars." Five thousand dollars! Might as well be a million, a fantastic sum. "I'm going to buy a new bike, a new [1979] Honda XL-500."

The 1979 Honda XL 500 is an urban myth; the ultimate machine, a red, single-cylinder 500cc four-stroke (quiet and reliable for long-distance) dirt bike . . . street legal. The closest thing to it, the Yamaha TT500, is also a single cylinder street legal bike, but way too low-geared and loud, and its kickstarter can break your leg if you kick it wrong.

The 1979 Honda XL 500 is equipped with an electric start.

Davey's older brother, Douglas, has a Yamaha TT 500. You remember Davey, the motorcycle-repair genius with long ginger hair in a ponytail, who in 15 minutes for five bucks, got my CB360 running like new. Brother Douglas is older, slightly balding, with coarse, short ginger-hair. Douglas is taller and broader shouldered, Doogy the Red, a wild man, but cool and smart. Not smart to upset Doogy though, he sees red on occasion; his temper, if initiated, can be violent and uncontrollable which I don't do. Dennis maintains, by and large. The TT500 can be hard to start. The extreme compression can break your ankle if you don't fully commit to the kick.

In addition to the electric start button, the Honda XL500's kick start is valved in such a way as not to hurt the kickee.

For 16 year old Lee, a young man yearning for constant adventure, owning the XL500 is as - how to metephate the profound immensity? - Christopher Colombus *receiving the Pledge*, from King Ferdinand *II* and Queen Isabella *I, to find the new world.*

New Worlds beckon and Lee Hill's ship has finally come in.

Monetary restraints and black sheep stigmas vanish. Low self-esteem is cured; released from society's underbelly, a Cinderel-lee story. Only *one* man in town drives the mythical Honda XL 500. There is only *one rider fit* for the XL500 Stallion: A-Lee-xander the Great.

Lee is poised for Fremontian greatness, the likes not seen since Kit Carson led Pathfinder John C. Fremont to destiny (three times).

The Honda XL 500 unlocks Lee Hill's ambition, great things are coming; Lee's inner circle understands this.

I also know, deep down know, my life is ruined. The nagging, ceaseless desire to walk and run tortures me; the slow runner I am, misses being slow, terribly. You want what you can't have, but what you did have? Times 100. Left in memory only: a decent physical specimen, not athletic, but strong. Before, I thought I could do or be anything, before. I even said that to Kevin Finley once, walking home from school (what an Arrogantosaurus). Not now.

Pot used to be fun, now? A coping mechanism, alcohol too. I love to drink.

Steve Harrold is intelligent and energetic (primary mode of transportation: skateboard), highly likable and in your face if he likes you or not. He warns us, "alcohol is the worst thing you can put in your body, it damages every internal organ." Steve's dad isn't around, his parents are divorced (unusual but increasingly more common). I admire young Steve, he speaks with authority, his facts are in order,and he likes to party.

When I'm alone at the house, and it's quiet all around, I grab Pappa's 22 gauge rifle from the War. Pappa's rifle is accurate. I have a clear orange, hard plastic box, with a sliding top, it holds 100 each-22 caliber rounds. The orange box is half full. If nobody's around, I take the rifle into the backyard and shoot. I do it twice, then figure, I better quit while I'm ahead. *No jail, no jail, no jail.* I'm shooting up Rommel's Rod again, but worse.

I walk down the sidewalk with a drink in one hand, and a lit cigarette in the other, in front of Jim Tyrell, Kenny Starr, Mr. Zolanski, Mr. Lansing, Mr. Schultz, Mr. Raeder, and Mr. whoever. I don't even see them. No one says a thing to me. Five years later, having a candid conversation with Mr. Tyrell, he reminds me of those days; he says, "you were in bad shape Jens. You'd walk down the street with a drink in your hand." His eyes sparkle electric blue, mine, steel gray.

A new repeat customer arrives on Jackson, a nice guy, Dave. Mild mannered, well spoken, from a well-off family, an egg-head, a humorous sad sack intellectual. We all enjoy Dave's company, tease him, but he takes it. He likes getting high with us on a regular basis, sometimes at the garage, sometimes out front of Danny's house. Five years older, the guy's so unassuming, funny, intelligent but not whack.

And he drives a . . . drumroll please . . . blue Honda 360! Identical to my old one, which is exciting.

The Vespa suffices, but I want more. Dopey Dave seizes up his 360. Runs it out of oil and seizes up his twin engine 360! He tries the electric start, nothing, I push on the kick starter, won't budge, pistons frozen solid. Dave's at the garage. I light up a joint and hand it to him and say, "leave it here Dave." "Cool Jens, thanks"... how much do you want for it? He sold it for two joints.

In three days I rebuilt the transmission and replaced the cracked piston rings. In the trunk of a friend's car, we drove the cylinders (one piece) to the back of the Honda Shop. I speak to the first mechanic I see and hire him on the spot to deglaze the cylinder walls. Cycle Center is located on Fremont Boulevard in Centerville. The shop owner lives in the flat-top between the Cortez's and the Cardoso's on Jackson Street. Their head mechanic lives across the street from the Wellbaums and across Marion Avenue from the Toppers, on the corner. He's tall, 10 years older, white, a big blonde permanent hairdo, overly talkative, a flamboyant swashbuckler, and standoffish to me. A real partier and a big time cocaine head.

Then and there, the motorcycle mechanic deglazes the cylinder walls for $25 bucks. I'd seen him before, partying at the head mechanics house on Jackson Street and he recognized me.

Back to the garage.

I torque the cylinder head and install the cam, - for cam chain installation, I carefully follow a Haynes Manual to establish *correct timing* between the crank and camshaft. I'm not thoughtful of the grease on my hands and the manual pages get smeared with it. Lee came by to check on #2s progress, and chastised me for the soiled manual. A Leeism states: "a good mechanic keeps his repair manuals clean." I'll be mindful of that in the future if I plan to be any kind of mechanic at all. - button up the engine and install it to the frame. I remove the clutch-cable cover and install the drive chain to the engine sprocket, then adjust the drive-chain tension at the rear wheel, and re-install the aluminum clutch-cable cover.

I'm excited, but wonder, can I pull this off? This is my first internal engine work: a rebuilt transmission and top-end. The transmission is especially complex and I'm proud of the job. Tempered by life's trials, my enthusiasm is not unbridled like before, but I'm excited nevertheless.

It runs good, not great like #1, but a steady idle and strong.

I could ride #2 to New York City tomorrow, but that thought never crosses my mind. Like a Native American brave, I don't wander beyond 20 miles from the tepee. I'm comfortable at home, in the garage, on Jackson Street and hope to return and finish high school, graduate with Mark Munster and the rest of my estranged classmates. I'm looking forward to it.

#1 had 4K miles on it, #2 has 25K. I fit up #2 exactly as #1: Barnett racing clutch, performance clutch springs, adhere the Barnett decal perfectly on the black chain-guard, stick another Santa Cruz decal on the right side of the gas tank along the bottom edge, install an air-fork kit on the front end.

The front end pulls up with ease.

Finally I swap out the stock exhaust for a used, two-in-one exhaust header, from Cycle Salvage, from the man with different color eyes. The bike has a nice rumble.

Like an idiot, I let wheelie king, Tony Francois, sweet talk me into taking #2 for a ride. Tony rides a wheelie like no other. 45 minutes later, Tony and #2 return; with eyes wide and mouth stuck open Tony says, "I flipped it on Denise Street!"

The handlebars are bent. Damn Tony! Tony, two years older and feared due to his mental instability and alcohol fueled rages, reenacts the accident to us in dramatic, comical and exciting detail. I cannot, however, separate the thrills of Tony's spellbinding story, from my disappointment of the restored-yesterday, damaged-today bike. Tony buys a 12 pack of Henry Weinhard's Private Reserve (batch # I don't recall), and produces a joint. The slow process of forgiveness begins.

From Lee's friendship and others, my mechanical skills improve. I replaced the Tony-bent stock handlebar with a used Honda CL dirt-bike type handlebar (Cycle Salvage). That's an interesting swap because electric cables are routed through the bars, on the left and right sides. To Tony's credit, he walks me through the painstaking procedure, which he can do blindfolded.

The bike looks aggressive, better than #1, to the untrained eye.

#2

Curtis the Pest

In March 1979 the Topper house was at its blurry zenith, at least until the parents got home from work. We're latchkey kids, before I heard the term. Al Butko and Valerie Topper are still together. Valerie's son is two years old, a cute toe head with Gary Forest glasses. His glasses have a lanyard so he doesn't lose them. Half the time Marlo is there. Marlo and I still battle it out on the driveway, but jumping around with a leg cast doesn't really work, so I stay closer to the basket. Mark still drives down the right side, drives to the hoop for his signature lay-up. He doesn't get past me, I stay with him, but he's stubborn. Mark is good at that shot. When I say, good at that shot, I mean he'll beat you with it. Marlo Topper *drives* to the basket.

Curtis Wellbaum is there a lot, Gary Forest too when he's not at the Ranch. Kevin Finley is here daily. Kevin still likes to have fun, but now has a ruthless knack to ridicule and or fight anyone, anytime. He can take it too. That part gets old and sadly we're not as close, sadly, we drift apart.

Mom makes an uncharacteristic, unkind remark about a younger single-mother and her kids up the street. They're new to the neighborhood, I've seen Maureen a couple times and her four children. The two older sons, Franky and Michael are young teens, pubie newbies. Franky's (the oldest) voice has already changed. Chrissy and Derrick are the two younger kids, six and four years old. Mom said, "her kids (speaking of Chrissy and Derrick) play in the middle of the street." I remember Inger saying that within my earshot. I do see them play in the middle of the street once. So what? I don't care. They live in John Audi's old house, on the corner of Troyer Avenue and Jackson Street. The Audi's moved away.

I sit in the Topper's living room, on the dark yellow fabric couch, stoned and comfortable,

Curtis too. #2 is parked out front. Curtis pipes up and says, "hey Jens, I'm seeing a tall cutie up the

street, Maureen's niece, Debbie. "Oh yeah? Cool." "Debbie has an older sister, she's pretty with

long blonde hair, you *need to meet her.*" "What?" "Listen Jens, I've got a new girlfriend, Debbie,

and her older sister is really cute too." Reliability is not an attribute Curtis is known for, the

opposite being true, but I like Curtis. He has the potential to surprise you.

My last leg cast is finally removed. Six-weeks prior, the long leg cast was sawed off and

replaced with a shorter one, from below the knee to the foot; only the wiggling dirty toes and

toenails could be seen. I'd grown accustomed to the cast. They were covered with art and funny,

heartfelt sentiments. The best drawing was a purple tree Danny Wellbaum drew. A large Oak tree,

in purple. Realistic and artsy, he sketched it effortlessly in one minute. I limp along without

crutches, and improve little. I'm no longer reliant on whomever "shows up" at the garage, I'm

independent again. I dismiss much of the silly banter I entertained previously. Curtis' latest

revelation, "there's a cute blonde up the street you need to meet," falls into the useless banter

category.

Curtis persists though, and a pattern develops: every Friday Curtis repeats the same thing, "Jens,

I'm telling you, go to Maureen's and meet Debbie's sister." The next Friday, "Jens, listen to me,

just go up there, you'll *seee* what I'm *saaaying!*" Next Friday, oh brother, here we go again; "Jens,

trust me, *go* to Maureen's house and *meet* Debbie's *sister*, now. She's really *nice.*"

We interrupt this story for <u>Breaking News</u> - On Jackson Street, a new sound is heard, a good

sound. "What is that?" A new shape and color is seen. "Who and what was that?" It's Lee, he's got

his new bike and he's on the back wheel! Lee Hill has a new XL 500! This is the biggest news flash in the County. Lee rides a wheelie from Steve Harrold's house, past us at Danny's house, past the Starr's and my house, and *around the curve*.

Move over Tony Francois, there's a new wheelie king in town, and his name is Lee Hill!

No helmet and the biggest smile ever, pure animal joy. Lee rarely rides on two wheels anymore. Soon, my word, Lee is riding wheelies with passengers on the back. Wheelies up and down Jackson Street, over and over. Wheelies on Fremont Boulevard, wheelies on every street in Fremont, all of them! I'm just getting warmed up, wheelies on Mission Boulevard, 50 miles per hour! With passengers! "You're not getting me on that thing, no offense Lee." "None taken Jens."

Lee did what?!? Freeway!?! All the time? 65 mph?? That's insane! *Splitting lanes on 680, on the back wheel??!!??* With passengers?!? No more, no more, my heart can't take it. Stop!

No, I don't think I will.

Inside of a month Lee is riding wheelies up and down Jackson Street (and everywhere else) *standing on the seat*! Next pass, standing on the seat *on one leg*! Next pass, standing on the seat on one leg, right hand on the throttle, *left hand up, holding a peace sign*! That was the ultimate, one leg, one hand, peace sign. Lee *can* cook and Lee *can* ride.

No, Lee never flips it.

A free ticket to the circus;

Watch Lee ride thumper, cast your anxiety away.

Four weeks, over and over. Curtis, will, not, stop. March becomes April and Curtis has worn me out with sheer tenacity. "Okay Curtis, *okay*. I'll go meet Debbie's sister, just *shut up, okaay?*"

I'm on edge, Curtis beams. A rare day, no pot to smoke, straight and clear-eyed but crispy round the edges. I snap at Curtis, then force myself off Topper's couch, break through the inertia pinning me down.

I limp out, away from the padded casket, a permanent squint under the April sun. I pull out the key ring from my loose fitting jean pocket; fiddle-faddle and find the little unique silver metal key with the familiar Honda Wing insignia etched onto the rectangular head, insert it in #2's ignition and turn clockwise one click. The jeweled neutral light on the speedometer face glows bright green. I opt for electric start and depress the button with my right thumb, it fires up fast, the points recently timed by Pete Winger, Tim Cucuk's next door neighbor on Lockwood Avenue.

Pete Winger is a Davey disciple, an apt pupil, a very capable motorcycle mechanic. Pete rides an older Honda 350 with dirt bars, an SL front end (slightly longer than the original) with an air shock kit, a custom glossy gray tank, of course a Barnett racing clutch and racing clutch springs, and most important: bored out cylinders and a big piston kit. In truth, Dave's driving a Honda SL 400 twin. Wheelies are a breeze for him and occasionally he does them, methodically up and down Lockwood Avenue, in front of his house. His father is divorced, a great mechanic, cynical and wise, and helpful to us boys. The last time I spoke to Mr. Winger, he said to me, "Jens, just get a Harley, and cruise. Keep the front end down." Pete's dad stays aware of every kind of evil residing in Fremont; in the garage his police scanner is *always* on. Mr. Winger knew of my accident, before the paramedics arrived.

#2 settles into a smooth idle, no need to rev it.

Two Leeisms enter my head: "Your clutch lever only has *so many pulls* before the cable breaks," and the ever relevant, "why rev it at a stop? That's dumb." I agree Lee. Especially air-cooled engines, right?

I mount #2 from the left side, testing the bum leg. It holds. The bike leans left on its kickstand, so you mount strictly from the left. With mixed emotion, I point the front end up Jackson Street, toward Troyer Avenue, shift my weight and the bike to my dominant leg, pull in the clutch lever, left toe down, click into first gear, silky smooth throttle twist-clutch release and rumble away from the curb. Shift to second gear and keep it there, bughhhhhhhhhhh. On my left I pass the ABC-123 Pre-School, the Zolanskis, the Lansings, the Schultzes and the Raeders. On the right I pass the Wellbaums, the Cortezes, the Cardosos, the Starrs, our house, the Tyrells and the Finleys.

I feel dumb, what am I doing? What will happen? Curtis is an idiot. I'm an idiot for listening to him. But Curtis won't *shut up*.

Coast left onto Troyer Avenue and left again, front tire against curb stop 45 degrees to the curb, in front of the house. I can lean right onto the good leg, turn right and take off, no sweat. The light brown house has a brown and green lawn with bare dirt spots, the door is dark brown with a round, gold door knob. Like a sparrow the house colors are non-descript. This is the same house where the young mother lives whom Mom said, "her kids play in the middle of the street." What am I doing here? *Curtis!*

This is John Audi's old house. The yard where John played a tackle football game with seven friends as Kevin Finley and I watched, uninvited. That's why the front yard had bare dirt spots, from John and his friends playing tackle in the yard.

Curtis mentioned something else about Maureen's pretty nieces, something I can't remember. *What did* Curtis *say* about the sisters? . . . Ahh . . . right . . . yes, Curtis said, "They drive here on the weekends from San Jose, to help their Aunt clean her house, because she's a single mom. Help their Aunt? Wow, that's nice. San Jose? Man that's far.

A baby blue, 1967 Ford Custom (Galaxy) is parked out front. Stock, clean, straight, a V-8 automatic; a cloth seat cover on the front bench seat looks sharp, red plaid, it stands out in the clean interior, classic.

The 60's slipped away, long gone. The 70's flew by, nearly gone. The Vietnam War ended, that's good. But Elvis and Pappa died, that's bad; Pappa's gone. No matter how hard I try, I can't stop limping, dead giveaway.

The brown door opens.

A statuesque, blonde haired beauty, five foot eight, stands in the doorway.

She's dressed in clean blue jean overalls that fit nice.

She smiles at me! A happy, genuine smile.

Her eyes twinkle.

Blonde hair cascades down around the overall straps, everywhere.

She says, "hi."

Her voice pings in a clear and pleasant soprano tone.

Sweet lady.

I did not expect . . .

I get off #2 - *stand up straight* - limp onto the sidewalk and step onto Paul's football field, to the 16 yard line.

Vision returns full strength:

Fair face, porcelain,

A lamb.

Bright eyes, kind, gentle, patient,

Innocence.

Her white smile flashes,

Joy.

Blonde hair, thick, long, bright,

I need sunglasses.

Willing to help the needy,

Angel.

"Hello, my name is Jens." "Hi, I'm Vickie."

Me and Kevin

Made in the USA
Las Vegas, NV
21 March 2024

87523472R00233